Better Library
and Learning Space

Projects, trends and ideas

Better Library and Learning Space

Projects, trends and ideas

Edited by
Les Watson

facet publishing

© This compilation: Les Watson 2013
   The chapters: the contributors 2013

Published by Facet Publishing,
7 Ridgmount Street, London WC1E 7AE
www.facetpublishing.co.uk

Facet Publishing is wholly owned by CILIP: the Chartered Institute of Library
and Information Professionals.

British Library Cataloguing in Publication Data
A catalogue record for this book is available from the British Library.

ISBN 978-1-85604-763-0 (paperback)
ISBN 978-1-78330-311-3 (hardback)

First published 2013
First printed in hardback 2017

Text printed on FSC accredited material.

Typeset from editors' files by Facet Publishing Production in 10/14 pt Palatino
Linotype and Frutiger.
Printed and made in Great Britain by CPI Group (UK) Ltd, Croydon, CR0 4YY.

Contents

Case studies

Acknowledgements

I am grateful to all those who made this book possible especially the 24 authors of the various chapters for their willingness to be involved in the project and for their time and patience throughout the editing process. I am indebted to Jan Howden not just for her contributions to the book but also for her wise counsel in appraising and refining the many versions of the content and ideas in the book. I would also like to thank Graham Bulpitt for his constructive comments on many of the chapters as they were developed, Lyn Oates who helped to edit the material at an early stage in the project, and Helen Carley of Facet Publishing for suggesting the book in the first place.

Les Watson

Contributors

Colin Allan is an architect with Building Design Partnership. He has worked on a wide range of projects, including many within the education, workplace, culture and leisure sectors. This rich diversity has informed his thinking in how people and space can come together in new, exciting and challenging ways. Colin was the Architect Director and Design Team Leader on the seminal Saltire Centre, Glasgow Caledonian University, and the iconic, award-winning Glasgow Science Centre.

Colin is currently working on new community school concepts integrating teaching, learning and social environments with the Scottish Futures Trust.

Hugh Anderson is an architect and Chairman of haa design Ltd, an integrated consultancy and design practice based in Glasgow, Scotland. haa design has been responsible for innovative work in both office and education and Hugh is co-author (with Alexi Marmot Associates) of the seminal report *Spaces for Learning* for the Scottish Funding Council, and (with Les Watson) of the report *Social Learning Spaces – the design and management of open plan, technology-rich learning and teaching spaces* for Jisc (the Joint Information Systems Committee), among others. Hugh has collaborated on the design and analysis of library and social learning spaces for Glasgow University, St Andrews University, Université de Panthéon, City of Glasgow College, Kilmarnock College and Banff and Buchan College.

Professor David Baker was born in 1952. After a number of library posts at Nottingham, Leicester and Hull universities, he became Chief Librarian of the University of East Anglia, Norwich, in 1985. He was promoted to Director of Information Strategy and Services in 1995, and became Pro-Vice-Chancellor in 1997. He was Principal and Chief Executive of the University of St Mark and St John, Plymouth, from 2003 to 2009, and Deputy Chair of Jisc from 2007 to 2012. He has written widely in the field of library and information management with 16 monographs and over 100 articles to his credit.

Chris Batt OBE was Chief Executive of the Museums, Libraries and Archives Council (MLA) between 2003 and 2007. After leaving MLA he worked for several years as a consultant leading research projects for Jisc on audience analysis, a wiki-based guide to digitization and a study assessing the value of university engagement with communities in the creation and curation of digital resources. International projects and speaking engagements have included work in Australia, New Zealand, Singapore, Canada, the USA, Iceland and a dozen countries across Europe. In 1998 Chris was awarded the OBE for work in developing public information and communications technology (ICT) services. He is a Fellow of the Royal Society for the encouragement of Arts, Manufactures and Commerce (RSA) and is currently studying for a PhD at University College London on the modelling of public knowledge systems in the network society.

Rob Bruijnzeels, a qualified librarian, has initiated various innovative projects, such as Libraries 2040 which has developed into a permanent laboratory and a creative learning environment for future libraries. In 2009 he organized The Architecture of Knowledge, a collaborative project with the Dutch Architecture Institute, in which future library architecture was explored. Rob is also the founder of the LibrarySchool (2011), a groundbreaking new training course, aimed at educating the librarian of the future. Nowadays he devotes most of his time to the Ministry of Imagination, developing concrete and innovative concepts for future library work.

Graham Bulpitt is well known for developing the Learning Centre model. The first example was established at Sheffield Hallam University in 1996 to act as a catalyst for new approaches to learning and teaching. Learning centres have now been established in a wide variety of settings, in the UK and elsewhere. In 2003, Graham was appointed Director of Information Services at Kingston University UK, where he was responsible for library, computing and multimedia provision. Recently retired from this post, he continues to work on European consultancy projects and is a Trustee of the Bishopsgate Institute in the City of London.

Valerie Clugston FRSA graduated from Glasgow School of Art in 1999 having gained a first class honours degree and the prestigious Newbery medal. She worked on the interior design projects for the Saltire Centre and Glasgow City Council with design partner Scott Mason, with whom she later established Nomad Research Design Consultation Ltd. Her work explores the use of people-centred design within education, healthcare and public spaces. She began teaching at Glasgow School of Art in 2003 and has remained a part-time tutor teaching at undergraduate and postgraduate levels. In 2012 she was nominated as a Fellow of the RSA in recognition of the work that she and the team at Nomad have contributed to the higher education sector.

Professor Sheila Corrall is Chair of the Library and Information Science Program at the University of Pittsburgh, USA, where she teaches courses on academic libraries and research methods. She was previously head of the Information School at the University of Sheffield, UK, and director of library and information services at three UK universities. Her research interests focus on the strategic management of information resources, collection development in the digital world, and the evolving roles of information professionals, especially in e-research and data management. She was elected President of CILIP: the Chartered Institute of Library and Information Professionals in 2002 and was awarded a CILIP Honorary Fellowship in 2012.

Jo Dane works as an education consultant in the Melbourne Studio of global architectural practice, Woods Bagot. She is a designer, educator and researcher with a passion for educational transformation enabled through research-based design practice. She has been researching education theory and learning environments for 12 years, and has a particular interest in developing new space typologies for effective learning in higher education. Jo works with universities to develop campus and learning environments for the future, using her understanding of effective teaching and learning behaviours to inform the planning and design process.

Dr Kyle Dickson directs the AT&T Learning Studio at Abilene Christian University. Since 2005 he has led strategic projects in mobile learning, course blogging, digital storytelling and collaborative space redesign. In addition, he regularly teaches undergraduate and graduate courses on British literature, drama, film and satire.

Professor Bob Fox is Deputy Director, Learning and Teaching Unit at the University of New South Wales, Sydney, Australia. His research interests focus on technological practice and change; blended and mobile learning; and innovative virtual and physical learning environments. He was Associate Professor and Deputy Director, Centre for Information Technology in Education, Faculty of Education at the University of Hong Kong for 12 years, where he has been Assistant Dean (Learning Environments), Faculty of Education, for the last two and a half years. He holds a concurrent appointment as Honorary Professor of the Faculty of Education.

Professor Stephen Heppell is CEO of Heppell.net, professor and chair in new media environments at the Centre for Excellence in Media Practice at Bournemouth University and a visiting professor at Universidad Camilo José Cela, Madrid. He draws on a unique €250 million portfolio of large-scale, effective research projects, over 30 years. His eclectic research focus ranges from the design of schools and school fitments, through the implementation of ICT in learning, to addressing the new pedagogic needs of everyone from elite Olympic coaches to pre-school children.

Jan Howden is the Interim University Librarian at the University of the West of Scotland. Her early career saw some great years providing library services in the health sector – for a few years with the only desktop computer in the hospital. She later worked for many years at Glasgow Caledonian University in various subject and customer-facing roles; including with Les Watson on the Learning Café (2001), an integrated service desk for most student-facing university services at the Base (2004), and the expansion and amalgamation of these ideas in the Saltire Centre (2006). Jan has been part of professional groups in Scotland such as the Scottish Confederation of University and Research Libraries (SCURL) and was also chair of the Society of College, National and University Libraries (SCONUL) Working Group for Information Literacy.

Ray Lester graduated in chemistry and took a PhD in chemical pathology. He worked for the multinational company Unilever as an information scientist and systems analyst, then as a librarian at the University of Bradford, University College London, Queen Elizabeth College and the London Business School, where he eventually became Director of Information Systems in charge of its library, computing and networking systems. He then moved back into science for the last six years of his working life, taking a similar job at the Natural History Museum. He retired in 2002, subsequently becoming Editor-in-Chief for *The New Walford Guide to Reference Resources*.

Phil Long is Professor of Innovation and Educational Technology in the School of Information Technology and Electrical Engineering (ITEE) and founding director of the Center for Educational Innovation & Technology (CEIT) at the University of Queensland, dedicated to research on learning environments that have the potential to innovate teaching, learning and creativity. His current research interests focus on emerging technologies, the cognitive interactions with them, and the spaces, physical and virtual, wherein they occur. His professional activities include leadership roles in numerous professional societies and journals associated with learning analytics and emerging technologies.

Professor Mike Neary is Dean of Teaching and Learning at the University of Lincoln. Before taking up this appointment in 2007 he taught political sociology at the University of Warwick. Prior to becoming an academic Mike was involved with community education and training in south London.

Peter E. Sidorko has held the position of University Librarian at the University of Hong Kong (HKU) since January 2011 after having been Deputy Librarian since 2001. He is the immediate past President of the Hong Kong Library Association, having served a two-year term from 2011 to 2012. Prior to his experience in Hong Kong, he spent almost 20 years working in various capacities in university libraries in Australia including the University of Newcastle, the University of New South Wales and the University of Sydney.

Matthew Simon is a career educator, library administrator and planner of library and educational facilities. Over his career, he has managed libraries at Columbia University, Queens College in the City University of New York, the University of Nevada Las Vegas (UNLV) and Delaware State University, serving those schools as project manager of major library building projects.

For the Queens College Rosenthal Library, he won the Albert S. Bard Award for Excellence in Urban Design. The UNLV Lied Library was voted the outstanding example of public architecture in Nevada by a jury of distinguished architects. As a consultant, he has planned over 100 libraries, performance centres and educational buildings. Author of over four dozen articles, papers and book chapters, he resides in Houston, Texas, with his wife, Elizabeth. Contact him (he will answer questions) at simonandsimon@ earthlink.net.

Jef Staes, learning and innovation architect, is a thought leader in learning and innovation. Based in Belgium, Jef has an international reputation as a speaker and author. He has given hundreds of keynote speeches and published a number of bestselling books on innovation and change management including *My Organisation is a Jungle* and *I was a Sheep* using powerful metaphors to explore the barriers to cultural change. His refreshing and insightful stories bring new perspectives to management and organizational learning, which have inspired many. He is a visiting lecturer at several management schools in Belgium and the Netherlands.

Joyce Sternheim is a library consultant, who specializes in future visions and innovative projects for public libraries. She has written several vision documents for the Dutch Library Association and was involved in the founding of the LibrarySchool. In 2011 she was awarded the Dutch Public Library Innovation Prize for her project StoryCoach (Verhalencoach), a new concept in which people are encouraged to discover which books, movies and music really affect them. Joyce is affiliated to the Ministry of Imagination, an innovative workplace for future library work.

Roland Sussex OAM is Emeritus Professor of Applied Language Studies at the University of Queensland, and a Research Fellow in the Centre for Educational Innovation and Technology. He is also Chair of the Library Board of Queensland, which is responsible for the State Library in Brisbane and for supporting 339 other libraries across Queensland. He has a special research interest in languages and social informatics, and the ways in which digital and social cultures interact. He has been involved in radio broadcasting on language for the Australian Broadcasting Corporation for 15 years.

Peter Tregloan is a Professorial Fellow at the Centre for Educational

Innovation and Technology at the University of Queensland and a Principal Fellow and Associate Professor in Chemistry at the University of Melbourne. He has been active in the development of a range of innovative virtual and physical learning environments that have challenged and extended established approaches for teaching large chemistry classes. In 2008, he was awarded an Australian Learning and Teaching Council national citation in recognition of this work. Current projects include the study of new learning spaces, programmes to promote active learning, the role of visualization in science and learning analytics.

Les Watson, well known for his work on the Saltire Centre, is now a freelance educational consultant on library, learning and IT issues. He has worked in education for 40 years as a teacher, lecturer, dean and pro-vice-chancellor and has managed libraries and information services in several organizations. He has considerable experience of library developments, creating, in addition to the Saltire Centre (2006), REAL@Caledonian (2001), tlc@bedford for Royal Holloway, University of London, (2008), and the Fountains refurbishment for York St John University (2011). He was lead consultant for the web resource Technology Rich Spaces for Learning in 2007 and has produced reports for Jisc and the EU on aspects of learning, teaching and information technology (IT). He is a fellow of the RSA and Visiting Professor in Learning Environment Development at the University of Lincoln, UK. He can be contacted from his website www.leswatson.net.

Paul White is an industrial designer with over 30 years in the commercial furniture industry. Paul is passionate about the value of elegant, energizing and enduring design. He heads CIE – pronounced 'sea' and suggesting unknown depths, mystery, uncertainty, beauty, adventure, ever-changingness, infinity, danger, exploration, unknown frontiers and enjoyment. CIE is a research and development think tank for product development for the library and education sectors. He is also founder and Director of Design at Instinct Furniture, a respected brand that operates throughout Australasia, fielding a comprehensive range of innovative library and learning furniture.

Sam Williams is the Space Planning and Strategy Manager at the University of Lincoln. After graduating from the University of Oxford with a Master of Arts in Biological Sciences (Lady Margaret Hall, 2003), Sam taught English in China before joining the University in 2004. Sam was part of the

University's chartered architectural practice, UL Architects, until taking on his current role in 2008. Sam also has a Postgraduate Diploma in Management Studies from the University of Lincoln, where he is leading the implementation of the principles of learning landscapes across the estate.

Introduction – about this book

Les Watson

Scope

This is a book for anyone interested in libraries and their learning space – what exists, why it continues to be important and what really matters when planning it. The focus is on learning space in libraries that is used for learning outside the classrooms of educational organization and by personal learners in public libraries, generally referred to as informal learning space. In addition to some ideas on built space (the what), consideration is given to ideas and concepts that underpin current library learning spaces and that will inform future ones (the why and the how). 'New old space' – space that fails to experiment with new ideas and ways of working – is a common phenomenon in all types of building and libraries are no exception to this. McDonald (2006) identifies an intangible 'oomph' (or I prefer 'wow') factor as one of the important criteria in the quality of new library space. Creating a space that works from the day it opens is obviously important but adding that 'wow' to create new spaces that inspire the library community its readers, learners and staff is more challenging. Tomorrow's library and learning spaces are waiting to be invented so focusing on the future and emphasizing what libraries and learning spaces could be, what matters when we are thinking about and planning these new spaces, how spaces might be used, and how they can attract, support and inspire those who use them is fundamentally important.

The way a space is designed and configured can enable (or disable) a wide range of activities and the services it can provide – space and service are inseparable, and it can be argued that the provision of space is a service in its own right. As service provision is dependent on the amount, type and organization of the spaces in a library then service delivery approaches and the portfolio of services and support provided are inevitably linked to space development. While library services are not the focus of this book, several authors touch on service issues.

Libraries have always also been places of learning. Ideas about learning, our understanding of learning processes and the impact of technology on learning have all changed considerably in recent years and require us to rethink how we organize and manage libraries and their learning spaces. And the impact of technology is not limited to how it affects learning but also extends into the very core of library operations enabling both space and service reorganization. The how and why mentioned above are covered in Parts 2 and 3 of this book, which contain guidance on library and learning space development and a series of essays about future potential for the library.

The projects and ideas included in this book come from a variety of sources and although many originate in the higher education sector they have lessons for all libraries in schools, colleges, universities, the public sector and private organizations. The book will be of interest to a wide range of readers including library and information services managers, librarians in public, school, academic and specialist libraries, library school students and academic staff, architects, facilities and estates professionals, learning support and development staff, interior designers, and anyone supplying goods and services to the library sector or with a general interest in libraries and their future development.

Structure

The three parts of the book contain contributions from 24 authors (plus myself) from a diversity of backgrounds ensuring a rich range of writing styles, perspectives and ideas. The flow through the book is from the past to the present and future inviting sequential reading, but each chapter is also largely self-contained so they can be read in the preferred sequence of the reader.

Part 1 describes features of library space in the 20th and early 21st centuries around the world, through a small number of selected intentionally brief case studies.

The first chapter in this part is by Jan Howden and me. It looks at some recent new library builds in the UK that illustrate current trends but also shows how it is possible to use 'old' space for 21st-century purposes by focusing on the activity, creativity and learning of the members of the library. We include the Saltire Centre as one of our case studies, having been instrumental in its development, but also because the ideas in the Saltire Centre still form an important part of our thinking about new library and learning space and the development of a service-rich library environment.

Matthew Simon writing in Chapter 2 takes a historical perspective and provides a US view that focuses on the library as community and the reciprocal, potentially transformative relationship between the library its staff, members and the buildings. In contrast to other authors in this part he emphasizes the challenge of refurbished space encompassing aspects of the Carnegie libraries from the early part of the 19th century as well as the more recent 'commons' movement, which has been largely led by libraries in the USA. He also explores the successful library as an accidental or purposeful creation.

In Chapter 3 Hugh Anderson covers recent developments in libraries in China, identifying a focus on the external form of buildings rather than the internal environment. The cultural differences between China and the west are clear in Hugh's case studies but there is also great diversity in them. Buildings on a grand scale that are there to make a statement are contrasted with ones that reflect deep human values and Chinese culture. What these facilities mean for learning and teaching is difficult to judge but the cases show that there is experimentation here and great promise for new ideas.

In Chapter 4 Bob Fox and Peter E. Sidorko from the special Chinese territory of Hong Kong describe cases that would not be out of place anywhere in the western world while at the same time retaining and nurturing aspects of eastern culture. These case studies contain the familiar 'hi-tech' open plan approach to the library and its learning spaces featuring multiple use spaces, the commons concept, and more recently 'boutique' library spaces, with a fit to eastern approaches to study and learning.

In Chapter 5, on developments in Europe, Joyce Sternheim and Rob Bruijnzeels highlight the importance of the library to knowledge-based economies and its role as a source of inspiration to its members. They emphasize the importance of community and the connection between the library space and those who use it, concluding that the role of the 21st-century library space goes beyond traditional library operations to taking more responsibility for the personal growth and development of the people who use the library than has traditionally been the case.

Writing about developments in Australia in Chapter 6, Roland Sussex, Peter Tregloan and Phil Long have an alternative view of space emphasizing external space and the role of distance in shaping Australian library provision. They write from a Queensland perspective but describe libraries that are indicative of developments across Australia that focus on dealing with extremes of climate and of distance, and promote a sense of community through the spaces they create and the services that they offer.

These chapters and their case studies paint a global picture of library space identifying common directions and ideas, as well as highlighting country and regional diversity.

Part 2 of the book is about the why and how of library learning space. It includes discussion of commonly acknowledged contextual factors, introduces some ideas of relevance to space development, and focuses on possibility. It covers some questions for libraries – will technology kill the library?, what are the new and current ideas in library space development?, and how can we be creative in our approach to the design of new spaces? Chapter 7 suggests an approach to thinking about the relationship between the library and technology – the library itself as a technology – and asks what the next stage of this technology could be. What the library could be is also part of the discussion in Chapter 8, which looks at information and digital literacy, technological fluency and learning. It describes aspects of learning that suggest that all libraries will need to rethink the form and configuration of their spaces if they are to thrive in a learning society. Chapter 9 covers ideas about space, such as its variety and the need for balance and flow. The experiential nature of space and its emotional impact are also covered here. The concluding chapter to this part, Chapter 10, describes some approaches and ideas that emphasize a creative approach to space planning and development.

Part 3 of the book has 15 chapters providing a broad perspective on future possibilities. The 14 short essays are written by a diverse range of authors, including librarians, learning specialists, academics, architects, an interior designer, a furniture designer and a management specialist. Chapter 25 contains my concluding remarks on the ideas in the book. The brief for the chapter authors was to describe the library of the future from their individual perspectives. Many authors expressed concern that they did not know enough about libraries to write of their future. However, they were asked to contribute to this book precisely because they don't know; those close to and deeply involved in the work of the library often have answers to questions about the future of libraries that are bounded by the realities of day-to-day library operations – it is, in my view, more likely that the fresh ideas for future library and learning space will come from unexpected places. Understanding the broadest range of perspectives is at least helpful and possibly invaluable when faced with unknown possibilities. As mentioned above, the journey implicit in the pages of this book is from the past to the present to the future, and it takes us from the known to the unknown, where there is no monopoly on possibility and all ideas are welcome.

The changing environment

In his short work *Making Sense of Strategy*, Tony Manning (2002) outlines a four-stage process for developing strategy that also works for thinking about any new project such as a library refurbishment or new build. The first stage in Manning's process is 'Anticipation', which he describes as 'being alert to change'. We cannot ignore our changing environment when planning new library and learning space. But my sense in the projects that I have been involved in is that there is always much more that we don't know than we do know and it is difficult to be sure what will have future impact. This produces a feeling of 'information anxiety' (Wurman, 1991) that is common for anyone embarking on a project aiming to develop something new, and results in a tendency to be risk averse and focus on dealing with what we know.

Some of the most common 'knowns' affecting the types of spaces and their configuration that we might want to create are technology related. For example the increasing availability of digital information, rapidly increasing networked interconnectedness, greater mobile access to information and the rate of increase in the amount of information (of all types) that is being produced are all likely to impact what our libraries and learning spaces should be like and in some cases make us question whether they should even exist.

Similarly, ideas around human behaviour, sociality and learning in the information age are well known and need to be considered when we design our new spaces. Discussion of these and other factors can be found in Part 2 of this book and are touched on by several authors in Part 3. Rapid change in these and other factors is a fact and often a worry for those involved in building projects, which from start to completion can take many years during which significant change can occur, potentially making some aspects of a new space redundant from day 1. So being alert to change is important, not just at the start of the project but also throughout it, and this alertness has to be accompanied with the flexibility to accommodate change within the project as it is being implemented, creating a real tension between the aspiration for currency and the constraints of project management.

Dealing with the 'knowns' is relatively easy – it is the unknowns and the unexpected that present the biggest challenge to space developers, and that is why Part 3 of the book also explores some ideas and trends from outside the usual remit of the library professional, which can inform project direction. Providing this broader view supports Tony Manning's crucial second thread of strategic development – 'insight' – which he describes as 'seeing the opportunities to offer something different and new'. It is through seeing these opportunities that we create that 'wow' factor.

The resource factor

Many of the factors mentioned above come down to choice – for example how much book stock to retain post project or how flexible should the space be. But the current era of financial constraint following the crash of 2007 appears to offer no choice and so can become the major influence in a current or planned project. With the expectation of reduced funding it is natural to think that projects need to be reduced in scope and aspiration. But this need not be so – project resourcing is important but so is squeezing more from the resources available, and this is always possible. New approaches to service provision, for example, can enable more efficient use of resources, making longer opening hours or the introduction of new services with potential for reduction of running costs long term possible. Imagination (another thread in Tony Manning's strategy framework) and ideas, discussed in Part 2 of the book, combined with a willingness to experiment can produce real savings, better use of space and improved service. A strong case for investment can be made in any climate providing it will clearly produce a better facility for the future. In his book *Aftershock*, Robert Reich (2010) describes an imaginative approach as part of his ideas to get the economy back to strong growth, including increased investment in 'public goods' such as libraries. It should be remembered also that austerity is not universal, as the case studies from China in Chapter 3 show. High levels of investment in libraries and learning facilities in one country should raise alarm bells in others wishing to share in the growing economies of knowledge and learning – the case for investment in libraries is strong even in austere times.

It's not just libraries

Whether due to austerity, technology or human behaviour it is clear that libraries are not the only organizations under threat. As bloggers replace newspapers, Amazon puts high street shops out of business, e-books threaten the publishing industry, and ipods decimate the music industry so libraries fear the growth of Google. It seems inevitable that the old order of atoms will be replaced by the new order of bits. In the retail world that means more online shopping and fewer (or no) shops. The simplistic view that the 'internet is to blame' is not the whole truth, however. Amid the turmoil in the high street there are some continuing success stories based on new models of service – shops that use a click and collect service for example are doing better than ever before and Apple stores have grown out of a mainly online business to become some of the most successful shops in town. A recent article in the *Guardian* newspaper asks 'How about Apple as a retail company?' (Gassée, 2013). It notes:

> The success of the Apple Store is stellar, a word that's almost too weak: The Apple Stores welcomed three times more visitors than all of the Disney parks, and generated more than $20bn in revenue last year – that works out to an astonishing $6000 per square foot, twice as much as the No 2 shop (Tiffany and Co). . . . Apple's 400 stores aren't a business, they only exist to create an experience that will lead to more sales, enhanced customer satisfaction, and, as a consequence, increased margins.

Maybe there is something here for the library – what experiences can we create that will help to build the 21st-century library business?

These examples illustrate that space still has a place and imaginative models that successfully integrate the physical and the virtual are the ones most likely to work for the future – some libraries, and learning systems, already do this but there is still much more to do.

The need for this book

Despite the factors mentioned above new library learning spaces continue to be developed. How, and whether, these new spaces make any difference whatsoever to effective learning is not clear. Their development rests on a shift that recognizes the importance of informal learning in education and in society more widely. New library learning space has the potential to excite and inspire those who use it and to become their place of choice for a wide range of learning activities from private study to group-based project work. The factors that enable the development of a successful space are not just 'soft' and 'intangible' but also often combine in unexpected ways to produce their overall impact. It is difficult to capture the excitement and inspiration associated with learning space itself in words and pictures. In many of the case studies authors have used the external architecture of the building rather than internal space to capture this feeling partly because internal space that mostly shows bright modern furniture and high quality tables and chairs is now the norm, and the only way to really appreciate the uplifting effect that great learning space can have is to experience it. The role of this book is not just to show examples of new library learning space but also to explore the factors that produce it and peer into the future to see what it might be like.

In the 1940s James Webb Young's brief book *A Technique for Producing Ideas* was first published (Webb Young, 2003). He describes a very simple method for coming up with new ideas that applies to any field of endeavour. Not only is it simple – it appeals to human intuition. In summary, having professional knowledge, engaging with ideas from other areas of knowledge, and providing space for these domains of knowledge to mingle and incubate, by pushing them to the back of your mind and thinking about other things, usually results in a flow of ideas – some good some bad. I have deliberately included a wide range of voices and perspectives in this book, some library specific and others more general, which will hopefully stimulate, through association and imagination, and generate new knowledge and ideas in the reader. Laying sound foundations for the creative process is time consuming, involving extensive interactions with others and their ideas in addition to developing your own. Waiting until you start a project is often too late – once initiated the speed at which a building project progresses leaves little or no space for creativity. The development of a successful new library and learning space is more art than science and relies heavily on imagination and creativity – you can never start to prepare too early.

References

Gassée, J.-L. (2013) Could iWatch be the Next Apple TV?, *Guardian*, 18 February.

Manning, T. (2002) *Making Sense of Strategy*, McGraw-Hill.

McDonald, A. (2006) The Ten Commandments Revisited: the qualities of good library space, *LIBER Quarterly, North America*, **16**, June, http://liber.library.uu.nl/index.php/lq/article/view/URN%3ANBN%3ANL%3AUI%3A10-1-113444/8010 (accessed 30 June 2013).

Reich, R. B. (2010) *Aftershock – the next economy and America's future*, Knopf.

Webb Young, J. (2003) *A Technique for Producing Ideas*, McGraw-Hill.

Wurman, R. S. (1991) *Information Anxiety*, Pan.

PART 1

Projects and trends

PART 1

Introduction

Les Watson

In this part of the book a number of libraries from each of six regions of the world are described in short case studies by 11 authors. The purpose of these case studies is to give some insight into important aspects of the libraries and spaces as viewed by each author. This approach contrasts with providing a systematic description of each case study using a list of common factors, such as that found in the excellent online database of UK projects compiled by Jisc infoNet (2013). Some of the authors concentrate on interior space, others spend more time describing exterior architecture, and yet others take an approach that considers 'soft' attributes such as educational rationale or societal impact. The variety of approach adopted shows us that library space is not an isolated component of the library but is a result of both architecture and interior design and is integrated with service, function and purpose. It also reminds us that each library is a response to specific factors seen in the context of its setting. For most case studies we have used a keyword or phrase to attempt to convey an important characteristic of each library in order to focus attention on its 'main' purpose.

There is a brief summary of the clear trends in these case studies at the end of Part 1, which shows that new libraries and their learning spaces across the globe have some common directions although they have developed their own identities.

Reference

Jisc infoNet (2013) *Learning Spaces Infokit*, www.jiscinfonet.ac.uk/infokits/learning-spaces/ (accessed 13 August 2013).

CHAPTER 1

UK projects and trends

Les Watson and Jan Howden

Introduction

There is no doubt that the environment for libraries, and particularly for library development, in the UK has become really tough since the economic crash of 2008. Over the past 15 years there has been a traumatic shift from a period of boom to one of bust in the financial environment, which has affected resource availability. This period of fiscal constraint is a key factor influencing the continuation of library as place, and sits in a broader global context of major technological, informational, societal and behavioural change discussed in Part 2 of this book, and questions the need for physical library spaces. Judging from press and television reports in recent years, it seems that funding is the biggest single most important factor faced by UK libraries – particularly small local public libraries. Public libraries show around a 13% reduction in income between 2008/09 and 2011/12 (LISU, 2013). These same press and television reports also indicate that libraries have changed little over the past 50 years, which is confirmed by those protesting against library closures or service restrictions; these protestors build their primary arguments opposing these changes around the library as book repository and place of reading (Horn, 2008). It is easy to see how government and local authorities might dismiss such protests in an age when more information than ever before is available through more channels than ever before to more people than ever before. 'Between the birth of the world and 2003, there were five exabytes of information created. We [now] create five exabytes every two days' (King, 2013). And thanks to a mixed economy of paper and e-books, more people are reading than ever before (Sweeney, 2011). An important consequence for libraries of this massive increase in information resources on the internet is that it creates more opportunities for informal personal learning than ever before – there is an unmet need for learning facilitation and support, potentially giving libraries an important future.

Despite the tough financial climate there have been many new library developments in the UK, particularly in the university sector, in recent years including refurbished and repurposed space as well as completely new buildings. Some of the buildings described in the case studies below were built in the pre-austerity years of the 21st century when funding was more easily available; others were embarked upon at a time of financial plenty but completed only recently. These UK case studies illustrate a range of ideas that are current in library space development in the UK in academic and public libraries, and the directions that library space development and use is taking in the UK at present. The building in each case study is a response to its locality, organizational need and the resources available, and each exists in the context of the broad global factors that are mentioned above. To quote Stewart Brand (1995), each is a 'prediction about the future' as, although new spaces have to be fit for purpose on their first day of opening, they must also be fit for an unknown future. Being fit for the future is the biggest challenge facing any new development especially, as Brand also writes, as 'predictions [about the future] are always wrong!' So – there are no right answers here, just some examples of work in progress to make us think and better understand what is happening to library and learning space in the UK.

Case studies

Ayr Campus Library – Scottish Agricultural College and University of the West of Scotland

Keyword: integration

Ayr Campus Library (www.uws.ac.uk/about-uws/campuses/ayr/) is a shared library between the Scottish Agricultural College (SAC) and the University of the West of Scotland (UWE). It is housed in a new £81 million building, which opened in August 2011.

The campus is a large horizontal black box set in a riverside landscape with the library occupying 1326m² or 8% of the building. Many of the group rooms in the building have woodland and river views and other windows look out over internal courtyards with white façades. These features, combined with the glass roofs in the three-storey sections of the building, give the interior of the whole campus a light transparent feel, making the most of natural light and landscape.

The entrance to the library (Image 1.1) is at a key point in the overall campus space. From the campus reception a bridge crosses the main refectory and café areas providing a view of all three floors of the library through the glass walls, and also of the computer labs, meeting rooms and other classrooms, making the library feel an integral part of the overall campus facilities. This transparency and resulting vicarious observation of others opens up the library and signals the range of environments provided on campus. The base for the shared service team in front of the main entrance is also clearly visible and welcoming. The library security gates light up the entrance inviting the visitor to enter.

Low-level furniture in the entrance area is used for casual individual breaks in

Image 1.1 *Entrance to the Ayr Campus Library with a window onto the group learning floor above (copyright University of the West of Scotland)*

study, to review the recent library purchases and journals available there, or as a place to meet various academic support services for drop-in questions. The area has a relaxed feel, enhanced by warm wood tones and colours. There is little evidence of this being a shared library other than a display of SAC and UWE t-shirts and other branded items. On this entrance floor there is also a small, learning-commons-style group of 15 computers. The stairs to other floors are discrete and well positioned, giving maximum open flexible space on each floor. The middle floor entrance to the building reduces vertical traffic through the building by requiring users to choose their destination on entry to the building.

Other floors

The upper 'group study' floor is a busy open area for 40 people, which can also be used as a presentation space for around 20–30 people. There are five glass-fronted group study rooms surrounding the open floor with a capacity for 64 people in total. These rooms are furnished with moveable tables and smartboards and plasma screens.

The lower floor is the 'quiet study' space and has large open tables equipped with power, making laptop computer use popular in this area. The collection of 50,000 volumes is distributed across the upper and lower floors in traditional blocks of high-level shelving, which is light and accessible.

There is limited but high quality signage in the building supplemented with a small number of information plasma screens. The 'light touch' signage adds to the calm atmosphere as unnecessary information does not flood the space.

The building successfully integrates labs, studios, computer labs and social learning areas within the library. The overall feel is of a well ordered easily understood space that integrates two discrete student populations successfully. ■

The Forum – University of Exeter

Keyword: identity

The previous library at the University of Exeter was a tired 1980s building that would have required demolition and rebuilding if it were to house additional services. Adjacent to the library the University also had a well used but outdated row of student shops. This was a difficult, uninviting site with the library separated from the other facilities by a set of steep outdoor concrete steps. The challenge for the University was to find a way to develop the whole site and create a central focus for the campus. Initially two projects were considered – a library refurbishment and the Forum project to develop an integrated home for services for students.

These two projects became one. The resulting £48 million project has created a stunning curved glass mall joining together the library and the Great Hall of the university. The Forum (www.exeter.ac.uk/forum) has a complete range of services for students, including a student information desk, IT help, careers zone, group study rooms, a 400-seat lecture theatre, technology-rich exploration labs and a large retail outlet and café laid out along a covered street that provides social space and an exhibition space – and integrates all of this with, but not in, the library. The result is an exciting, vibrant place, which provides a real heart to the campus combining key services for students with academic and study facilities. The co-location of these facilities has been designed in such a way that, although each functional area has differing requirements for factors such as noise levels, privacy and group size, they can all operate successfully. The library, in particular, has benefitted enormously from this project being part of that vibrant heart of the community and yet retaining those characteristics of the academic library that Exeter students value highly.

The library

The University of Exeter has managed to preserve the identity of the library alongside modern space that has significant additional functionality and services that are closely located but do not interfere with the group, quiet and silent study spaces the library provides. All floors of the library have been given a modern, bright feel and the project has extended the library to provide more space for books and study, including formal and informal study space. The interface between the refurbished library and the Forum services mall is a buffer zone with study spaces on the ground and first floors of the building that both unite and separate the quieter library world from the vibrant busy Forum space (Image 1.2).

Image 1.2 *View through the Forum showing library 'buffer zone' on the right (courtesy of Jisc infoNet)*

This idea of integration with separation works well in providing a central heart to the campus, which includes but does not intrude on the identity of the library. Also on Floor 1 of the library at the interface with the Forum there are group study and meeting rooms, which are open to the Forum but can also, by closing off a set of doors in the corridor, become part of the library when such rooms are in high demand – for example at pre-examination, project completion or assignment hand-in times. Further extension of the influence of the library into the broader project is the creation of external piazza space. This stunning external space achieves the two major goals of the Forum project, providing a sense of arrival at the campus and also, and equally importantly from the library perspective, extending the social learning space to the exterior of the building. The Forum provides excellent access to the widest range of services while preserving the identity of the library for the academic community. ◼

The Hive – University of Worcester and Worcestershire County Council

Keyword: inclusion

Between a railway viaduct and the sombre 1990s Crowngate shopping centre in the UK city of Worcester stands a bright shiny 21st-century building. It is the Hive (www.thehiveworcester.org), a building that houses a university and public library, archive and archaeology service and local council enquiry service. The building, which cost £60 million, is resplendent in shining glass and golden external cladding. It is a partnership between the University of Worcester and Worcestershire County Council – the first such partnership in Europe.

Most areas of the building that are accessible to the public are open plan and simply but elegantly finished with white walls, plain white shelving and glass display cases. The use of wooden cladding on the stairs and ceilings gives the space a clean Scandinavian feel enhanced by the commissioned artwork, providing interest and visual stimulus (Image 1.3).

Three of the five floors, levels 1 to 3, are arranged around a central stairwell. Level 0, the floor for 'young people, social study, games and film and music', covers a smaller footprint than the main upper floors and is open to the other parts of the building via the stairs. Level 4 contains special collections and journals and is a quiet study area housed in self-contained space not open to the other floors of the building. This monastic space is accessed by an enclosed stairway or by using the lift. Separation between noisy activities and the traditional 'quiet' library has been successfully achieved with this design. The 'sound gradient' of the building, noisy (active)

Image 1.3 *The Atrium (copyright The Hive, Worcester)*

from the bottom of the building to quiet on the top floor works well for the clearly designated quiet space on Level 4 but less well for floors 2 and 3, which along with floors 0 and 1 share the open stairwell.

The social study space on Level 0 has informal seating, group workspaces and gaming stations. The area feels both spacious, because of the floor to ceiling exterior windows along one side, and intimate at the same time.

Level 1, although open plan, has been designed with some separate discrete areas. For example the café and the extensive children's library are 'rooms' with open entrances from the main floor space. If there is a theme for this floor it is activity. It is the arrival point for all users, location for the Worcester Hub (a one-stop shop for access to all council services), and houses the main self-service book issue and return points and library enquiry services. This is a busy purposeful space.

Level 2 houses part of the collection and has a range of formal study space. This floor gives public access to the Worcestershire archaeology service, meeting rooms and a business centre. To one side of this floor a walkway tells the audio story of the history of the city using a number of overhead sound domes activated by movement, and nearby tables have touch sensitive surface technology for exploration of a range of related material. Most of the collection along with a variety of formal and informal study spaces is found on Level 3, where a glass façade provides great views across the city.

The partnership

The Hive is the result of a unique partnership between the University and Worcestershire County Council. Some of the services provided have separation of responsibility simply co-habiting the building, but for the library service there is integration. A striking feature of the way in which this building works is that library services are provided from minimal desks (pods) on each floor from which small numbers of library staff provide users with help and advice, giving an expert service that has a delightful informal feel. Walking around the Hive and seeing the mix of public and university users and the diversity of services and facilities on offer it is clear that the building is open to all, excludes no one, and is well used and liked. ▪

Leeds Central Library

Keywords – user as producer

Leeds Central (www.leeds.gov.uk/leisure/Pages/Central-library.aspx) is the main library within a network of 40 smaller public libraries situated in the central business district of Leeds beside other municipal buildings, including the attached Henry Moore Sculpture Gallery. Nearby is Little London, an area of multiple deprivation. The library building is late Victorian with an Arts and Crafts interior. Some aspects of the architecture – such as the life size stone mythical dogs and other creatures that feature at the end of each banister, the high-vaulted oak-panelled ceilings, or the completely tiled and stained-glass windowed rooms – are breathtaking, but most of the many rooms are best described as basic.

However, the sheer number of rooms in the building proves ideal for the natural zoning of activities. And zoning is needed – people are everywhere in this building. Quieter individual activities are focused at the top of the building, with specific centres of activity sited on the middle floor and general public service areas on the ground floor. This building works hard. Some of the major successes include Studio 12, a place where those in the 18–30 age group engage in creative projects using state-of-the-art technology with access to a level of support that enables them to gain professional qualifications in the development of multimedia products. The Studio 12 atmosphere is active and alive with people working together in groups and teams.

In the local and family history room couples actively engage in working with computers and maps while others work alone. Behind this activity is a large, global network of users of the service – the digitized web-based collection of local photographs receives over 40 million hits a year. The power of the web brings far-flung people from Leeds closer to their city.

A range of IT-based information sessions is offered on demand, from knitting to CV writing, meeting identified needs determined through conversations with library staff, which establish learning needs and suggest ways of meeting them rather than fitting people to a menu of defined courses.

A strategic decision was taken some time ago to prioritize changing team roles over spending on new furniture or any interior makeover, prioritizing service over space development. The team was trained in a range of areas from basic computing skills, to teaching skills for the lifelong-learning sector to support the strategy.

This is an amazing old building with old furniture that is comfortable and welcoming, and new furniture suitable for working with computers. On the entrance level, and now shared with the museum, is a recently renovated Victorian majolica-tiled café (Image 1.4). The profits from this beautiful, busy space – which is always absolutely full of people meeting and working on laptops – are used to supplement non-funded community learning activities.

Image 1.4 *Victorian Arts and Crafts interior in Leeds Central Library, showing the café (copyright Leeds City Council)*

The data collected in regular surveys of all services indicates that take-up of services in the library closely matches the social and ethnic makeup of the area, an indicator of the success of the project in being socially inclusive. This is a space that focuses primarily on evolving and changing its service portfolio to remain relevant – and developing its space to support this. ▨

The Saltire Centre – Glasgow Caledonian University

Keywords – learning, orality and sociality

The £23 million Saltire Centre (www.gcu.ac.uk/theuniversity/universityfacilities/thesaltirecentre/) has been a reference point for the discussion around libraries and learning in the UK since its opening in January 2006. The building focuses on providing extensive learning and library space and is also a campus hub with a one-stop shop for access to all student services. It is situated between, and connected to, the main teaching buildings of the University. This position on the campus symbolically unites the processes of learning and teaching. The building provides a large number and variety of learning spaces connected by direct indoor pedestrian access to faculty labs and teaching spaces.

The Saltire Centre has five floors and is entered by a bridge to Level 1, which arrives at a mezzanine level providing views over the Level 0 services mall. Level 1 is a busy space traversed by those using the library and others passing through to the teaching buildings – it is modelled on an airport departure lounge. A large touch screen enables people to interact with information about the University and the building, and a cluster of display screens models an airport departure board giving information about what is happening inside and outside the building. There is a small group study area, a seminar room, a print service and places for librarians to meet students. There is also open space that can be used for exhibitions.

Level 0, the services mall, is a large multi-functional space, primarily for 'social learning', set up with formal tables, informal sofas and other comfortable group seating (Image 1.5). A single point of access to many of the student services of the University is provided at the Base, the main service desk for the building. Much of the collection is housed on this floor in electronically controlled rolling stacks. There is also a café on this floor. Recently individual study carrels have been introduced, which are popular with laptop users who work quietly amid the buzz of conversation around them.

Access to other floors is by a central stairway, which spirals around the public lift. Each floor of the building is separated from the ground floor social learning space by a wall that runs from Level 0 to the top of the building, ensuring effective sound insulation on each floor.

The upper floors of the building provide a mixture of desk seating and informal furniture, much of which provides built-in power sockets. There is a sound gradient in the building from the active group work of the services mall to quiet study at the top of the building. Generous numbers of desktop computers are available on all floors. Each floor has a graphic 'identity' and colour theme, which aims to speak to users and set the tone for group or

Image 1.5 *Open Plan services mall in the Saltire Centre showing artwork by Toby Paterson, semi-private 'igloo' spaces and a variety of seating and workspace (copyright David Barbour and BDP)*

individual quiet study. The graphic content is humorous and evokes some of the subject themes for each floor. The recent addition of study carrels in places has increased the capacity by around 20% but has had little impact on the feeling of spaciousness. The Saltire is a very busy building with many areas often fully occupied, a feeling that is increased by the number of people moving through the building to access other facilities in adjacent buildings.

On higher levels of the building, with identities such as 'the home' or 'garden' defined by graphics and colour schemes, the spacing between desktops is also generous, and the space – although often fully occupied – is very quiet. On the quiet floor (Level 4) many individual study booths have recently been added and are often used by people with their own laptops. Since its opening the Saltire Centre has, not surprisingly, been modified to reflect student demand and staff opinion. As a result of its open plan nature and inherent flexibility it is a building for learning that has the potential to learn itself in the process of ageing. ▪

Trends

These UK case studies are of three types – new builds (Ayr, the Hive and the

Saltire Centre), a refurbishment (University of Exeter Library integrated with the Forum new build) and repurposed (Leeds Central Library).

Open plan space

In the new-build category the common approach has been to provide open plan space. Open plan brings the promise of ongoing reconfiguration as the building learns, through use and emerging trends, what is required of it as a space. Flexibility for the future is the key desirable feature of these spaces, exemplified by the services mall in the Saltire Centre and the large open floors of levels 1 to 3 in the Hive. Most importantly, in all cases, there has been careful consideration of how the areas connect but also avoid unnecessary traffic through the buildings with 'feature' stairs, or ill-conceived mezzanines or lightwells overwhelming open spaces simply for architectural effect. It is harder to be wrong about the future with open space that offers endless possibility, but open plan is not without its critics, who focus on the potential for noise and lack of privacy. However, careful selection and positioning of furniture and location of book stacks in all the examples we have used serve to contain noise and provide semi-private space (see Chapter 9).

Importantly, open plan also provides the opportunity to regularly 'redesign' the space by introducing new structures and items of furniture or rearranging existing furniture (relatively straightforward) and book stacks (more difficult and resource intensive), to create quiet and noisy zones, for example. Ayr, the Hive and the Saltire Centre all have endless possibility for reconfiguration and even the refurbishment at the University of Exeter Library, restricted by the existing architecture, still retains some possibility for change. At Leeds Central Library the Victorian building provides more restricted scope for change but has an accidental advantage of providing its own inherent zoning, similar to the example of the Carnegie libraries described in Chapter 2, which can serve the library well. Open plan is an important feature, which brings the prize of flexibility, but this has to be balanced by a zoning strategy; this is provided naturally in some older buildings.

Technology-rich space

Jisc's (2008) work on learning environments highlights the importance of learning spaces being technology rich. Each of these case studies features technology-rich space built on a wired and wireless infrastructure, which supports widespread use of computers and portable devices. All the case studies provide a variety of technology choices for those using the library. Machines are provided for specialist purposes such as the shared use of smartboards in open pod configurations; laptops are loaned in some cases and those bringing their own devices are welcomed. All these case studies provide a range of technology for individual and group use. Leeds, in particular, provides targeted technology with the specific purpose of social inclusion to enable all members of the library to experience the value of current music and video technology in a collaborative open learning environment. The trend for libraries wishing to explore aspects of cultural specificity or the new media-rich information environment (see Chapter 19) is to provide a diversity of technology options for specific purposes. Just as open plan provides flexibility of space, so the ways in which a space deploys technology is subject to continued change. Porter (2013) observed:

> Users will increasingly have integrated devices that they use for many different social and leisure pursuits as well as for their education and paid work. Smarter devices will be worn, and be voice, [eye] and even brain activated, giving the user the ability to access content and services from the networked, immersive environment of multimedia content in which they move.

In our case studies the emphasis continues to move from libraries providing device access to the provision of high quality network and data access. Open plan technology-rich spaces such as Ayr, the Hive and the Saltire Centre present minimal challenge to ubiquitous networking as compared with older buildings such as the Exeter and Leeds libraries.

Service-rich environments

Space and service are symbiotically linked and service change and improvement is always possible in any library, but a rebuild or refurbishment enables more extensive experimentation with the range of services provided and how these are provided. In common with all UK libraries, the case studies show improvement in the delivery of services through the use of self-issue and self-return facilities.

In the UK service improvement is focused on greater degrees of self-help where possible, removing barriers to service access and integration of services. For example, by providing a larger number of service points than usually needed the service desk on the ground floor of the Saltire Centre was designed to expand and contract in order to respond to demand for services. The central desk (a seated desk, for staff and users) has two satellite desks so that if queues develop additional staff have somewhere to work, and when these satellites are not being used library users occupy them. In order to reduce the barrier effect of the desk it also has low-level seating built in. However, despite these efforts to make the desk more of a shared facility between the user and staff, it is still a real barrier between the two. The aspiration to reduce the impact of service desks and bring a sense of partnership to service delivery (see Chapter 24 for examples) has been taken further at the Hive, where small informal pods are used at key points in the building. These small pods are also moveable, providing the possibility for 'pop-up' delivery points. The service strategies at the Saltire and the Hive, which are enabled by the space, encourage staff to switch from roaming duties to desk duties as required, providing an enhanced service for users that responds to needs in a timely way.

Service integration

Another feature of the case studies is integration. The Saltire Centre brings together a range of services for students within the library whereas the Exeter University Forum project brings together university services and facilities in one venue that adjoins the library, allowing it to retain a distinct identity. The Hive provides even greater integration, bringing together the University of Worcester library and Worcester County Council library and services into one space on Level 1 of the building. Service integration is an important attractor, which is essential to development of the library community (see Chapter 17).

Developing learning communities

Community development is not just concerned with service integration. All the libraries described here are active in developing and maintaining a community of users around their learning activities, including students and staff in the academic libraries described and lifelong learners in Leeds Central Library. The development of library learning space is essential to these activities. However, just as many websites deploy resources in the promotion of their services so that users identify with their site and services, so libraries also need to link their physical outlets to the virtual, exploiting the potential of combined online and physical environments to create and maintain their learning communities. For example, massively open online courses (MOOCs) and the flipped classroom will be more effective if local networks operate to enhance the experience. The more libraries can do to create technology-rich spaces with learner-focused service provision for all, that links seamlessly to their online provision, the greater role they can have as open learning environments enabling learning communities to develop. Steps are being made towards this in all the examples in this chapter, and indeed, in some cases, the library members are doing it themselves.

References

Brand, S. (1995) *How Buildings Learn – what happens to them after they are built*, Penguin.

Horn, C. (2008) Authors Fight for UK Libraries, *The Bookseller*, Issue 5348, 9 May.

JISC (2008) *Technology Enhanced Learning Environments*, www.jisc.ac.uk/whatwedo/programmes/elearning/tele/definitions.aspx (accessed 26 April 2013).

King, B. (2013) Too Much Content: a world of exponential information growth, *The Huffington Post Tech*, 20 May, www.huffingtonpost.com/brett-king/too-much-content-a-world-_b_809677.html (accessed 20 May 2013).

LISU (2013) *Trends in UK Library and Publishing Statistics: public library income tables*, www.lboro.ac.uk/microsites/infosci/lisu/lisu-statistics/income.pdf (accessed 30 June 2013).

Porter, S. (2013) *Future Technologies*, Inform, Joint Information Systems Committee.

Sweeney, M. (2011) UK Ebook Sales Rise 20% to £180m, *Guardian*, 3 May.

CHAPTER 2

US projects and trends

Matthew Simon

Introduction

I am intrigued by the transformative power of built space – in our case the library. How does the interface of library space and library patron, library space and library collection, library space and library staff, and library space and library space create something new and more valuable? I wonder how it is that a space that works well for one individual may totally frustrate another? I wonder how library spaces can be designed or improved to facilitate learning – in effect, 'learn' to be better learning spaces?

Great library learning spaces can be accidental. Conversely, good intentions by librarians, engineers and architects may not result in space that functions as intended. Can elements common to all great library learning spaces be identified that can guide librarians, planners, architects and engineers?

Successful libraries are transformational spaces

In the USA, dozens of libraries are considered great architecture but may not be great or even good libraries. They are often deemed great by critics because of the reputation of their designers, not because of the satisfaction of the occupants.

A grand exterior design is secondary to what takes place in its interior. Once inside, the visitor should experience a sense of having stepped away from the pressures, distractions and often toxic energies of the outside world. In that way a library resembles other transformational spaces such as churches, synagogues, mosques and temples.

Perhaps libraries do not create the other-worldliness of religious places with their vaulted ceilings, subdued lighting and evocative art. But they should create an awareness of a special place – a place where learning takes place, where contemplation and thought is encouraged, and where those who are curious can readily commune with the authors of the books and texts they encounter – even though separated through space and time.

The exterior of the building is only one variable in the creation of a great learning space. It has a specific task. The exterior must beckon the patron to enter. For example, the Carrière and Hastings design of the New York Public Library at 42nd Street and Fifth Avenue in New York City, with its iconic lions, Patience and Fortitude, framing the steps leading upward to the main entrance, has been photographed many millions of times (Dickson, 1986, 62). It is considered great architecture, even though it has little to do with what goes on within. Most people who lunch on those steps rarely, if ever, actually enter the library. But the genuine greatness of the Library arises not just from the majesty of its exterior. From its opening a century ago on the site of the old Croton Reservoir, generations have entered – some purposefully, others by accident – and become the students, writers and researchers who patiently waited for the delivery of requested texts to the pick-up station. And then used those materials as their own to read, learn, compile and organize, and ultimately create new material, which often became part of the library – sustaining the process and, in effect, building itself from within through the activities of those who use the library.

Library interiors should not be formula-driven; what satisfies one may not satisfy another

In the 1960s, environmental psychologists such as Sommers (1966) conducted important research on how individuals interact with one another in the built environment. Sommers' work charted how students use study tables in libraries. What they discovered was revolutionary – for example, that men and women perceive and use space differently. Women interact with the people and objects they share space with in ways distinct from men. They also discovered that in furnishings, one size definitely does not fit all. In my experience, the most notable example was at Hollins University, formerly a women-only liberal arts school in Virginia.

The preferred seating in the old Hollins Library was the sofa. It was comfortable for study, conversation or napping. It permitted the first occupant to control the space – inviting others to sit down or, if sprawled out length-wise, discouraging them from doing so. And, because they were usually situated against a wall or back-to-back with another sofa, permitted the occupant to be able to see who was around or approaching. It was a perfect solution for a specific population. Hollins had plenty of traditional library seating, such as tables and chairs and carrels, but the selection of the furnishings clearly reflected the preferences of Hollins students and faculty – an important consideration in any library development.

Wells College Library

Architect Walter Netsch's application of his field theory, which consisted of rotating simple squares into complex geometric elements radiating outward from central cores, led to visually striking libraries. In seeking to move beyond 'the boredom of the box', Netsch created imaginative and, in his terms, 'organically' integrated spaces in the same way that Buckminister Fuller employed interlocking triangles to design his geodesic domes. In at least one library design, Netsch used the double helix, as found in DNA chains, as the inspiration to create a helical path of open spaces where faculty and students could work side by side in a collaborative manner (University of Illinois, 2008).

Image 2.1 *The main study floor of Wells College Library showing the massive ceiling structure and subdued interior lighting (copyright Wells College Archives)*

His design for Wells College Library, also formerly a women-only school, was intended to reflect the sylvan character of the campus. Small individual nooks are hidden among the high stacks. The high wooden ceiling, aggressively divided by large, dark wooden beams, which hold the lighting, is supported by enormous thrusting wooden piers that loom high over patrons' heads. Natural lighting is subordinated to indirect lighting from the ceiling. Staff spaces are located on the perimeter of the building – physically isolated from the patrons.

The students and faculty I interviewed in focus groups about their use of the library, for the revision of the college master plan, were wary of being approached from behind. They did not like the outsized building supports. They did not like the multi-level public spaces that presented challenges to those with mobility problems. They did not like the low levels of illumination or the lack of ability to adjust the intensity to match their need (Image 2.1). They did not like the lack of seating options. Group studies were minimal. Most preferred to study in their dormitory rooms, the student dining facility or lounges. ▩

Successful library learning spaces are sometimes accidents but can be created

I do not suggest that libraries are not well served by architects. Architects translate our plans and ideas into designs and thence into real structures. Architects often make design suggestions that help solve long-standing problems. But, to achieve what is necessary in our buildings, we must enter into a full dialogue with them, guided by our imperative to create spaces that best serve the needs of those who will be using the building.

Philip Tompkins (1990, 81), a librarian, defined this role as developing a

> facility with an environment that will empower users to create a distinct
> learning culture with new roles for faculty, computer professionals, librarians
> and students . . . a facility that will continue via computer courseware,
> information software and print products the learning that is formally initiated in
> the lecture hall.

Tompkins wrote from the perspective of an academic librarian. But the challenge for all libraries is essentially the same: how do we create environments that enable people to learn? And what lessons can we glean from the experience of other librarians who have improved learning spaces?

I will explore, in brief case studies, how library learning spaces themselves reflect the experience of those who work or study in them. The creation of effective spaces is not limited to architects and library staff, but includes patrons who, as humans do, manipulate their environment to better serve their needs and purposes. And in so doing, good libraries become great, in a way that has little to do with the physical beauty or artistic merits of the building's architecture. My understanding of the potential for transformation of library spaces is guided by many others, in particular architectural critic Stewart Brand (1994).

The libraries I describe here have been in service for more than 20 years. As few of us ever participate in the design of a brand new building, my focus here is on renewing and improving the effectiveness of existing spaces. Only after a building has been in service do the idiosyncrasies of the design – the dimension of the spaces, their adjacencies, the environmental systems such as heating, air conditioning, air flow, acoustical conditioning – either fade into the background or become the source of irritation and complaints. It is only after a decade or more, when new technologies and pedagogies have taken hold and after we understand how learning takes place in our libraries, that we gain a sense of whether the environments we have built are, indeed, truly successful.

Case studies

Carnegie Public Libraries

Keyword: flexibility

Scottish–American industrialist Andrew Carnegie, through his extraordinary vision and great wealth, established the public library as a universal element of a successful progressive town or city. Carnegie's great gift was twofold. He is most remembered for providing the funding for the Carnegie libraries, but he should also be remembered for commissioning architects to provide designs that became the basis for the classic Carnegie Library structure. The Carnegie Library gift administrators did not specify how buildings looked from the street – only that they be centrally located in the community and have consistency in their basic plan.

How have hundreds of these buildings, most now more than a century old, endured much longer than the 'modern' library buildings that were built during the 1940s, through the 1980s? They were and remain models of learning spaces, 'learning' themselves through use. Their ability to be reconfigured or updated is predicated on simplicity of design and the use of a structural design that provides open spaces not clogged with support columns, which have the potential more than anything else to doom libraries to functional obsolescence.

Old Carnegie libraries continue to be used in the ways in which they were intended but have been renewed to reflect the changing needs of the communities they serve. After a century, some spaces and furnishings would be instantly recognizable by the great-grandparents of modern users. But, other spaces have often been transformed: the children's room might now have a functional stage and amphitheatre seating – risers that accommodate parents and children and can double as play space; furniture and shelving sized for children and tots; and rubber mats to protect knees and elbows from scrapes and bruises from inevitable falls and collisions.

Some libraries had added additional wings or rooms as the user population and collections expanded. Dual use of space emerged – the community room might also house the genealogical division. Computer installations provide access to websites for information seekers, those searching for work or ideas for their own do-it-yourself home improvement projects. Other spaces might organize books and other materials for distribution by bookmobile, or to fire houses or senior living centres.

The early 20th-century design featured walls that could be penetrated as needed and, somewhat unique for its time, had an open architecture with a few large rather than more small rooms. There was an awareness that the library could be adjusted, improved, updated, expanded and made more accessible to those with mobility problems. ▩

Parkway North High School Library, St Louis, MO

Keywords: look, listen

The later part of the 1960s and early 1970s was a period of rapid change in libraries in the USA. The open classroom phase in education was characterized by the elimination of walls, the common delimiters of space. Instead, the size and configuration of school and library spaces became much more fluid. Open classrooms were designed in colleges. Parkway North High School (PNHS) was designed and built, in 1970–1972, during the prime of this trend. Over the ensuing four decades, walls were erected in attempts to create some calm amid the chaos often found in large gatherings of adolescent girls and boys. PNHS staff realized that trying to create an experiment in open space to facilitate learning by self-motivated teenagers was not going to work in a facility with over 1200 students, many of whom were not self-motivated, moving around a 5.5 acre building.

The library was especially problematic. Open lofts provided too much privacy for teenage couples, and were too remote from the librarians to supervise. Because the library was centred on a major axis of the building it was constantly traversed by students and teachers moving from one class to another, creating endless diversions from study and learning. The lack of doorways made securing the book collections impossible; nearly 1000 volumes per year disappeared from the shelves. These initial difficulties compounded ten years after the building went into use, when Parkway School District moved the ninth graders (age 13–15) into the high school, increasing the school's student population to over 1600. To accommodate the new students, the two lofts were designated classrooms, new 42-inch-tall shelving was erected, creating the library's first perimeter, and additional space was designated for magazines and audiovisual resources.

Near the beginning of the third decade of use, the entire library space was defined with exterior walls, a secure computer lab, more than 100 personal computers on library tables, smart boards, a video-conferencing room and offices for staff. Today, the library can simultaneously support three classes in the library proper and two classes in the computer laboratory. These spaces are available to students for homework, research, independent learning or other less academic pursuits, as their schedule or self-motivation permits.

PNHS is not a model for emulation by other organizations. Its original design was based on what at the time was widely considered cutting-edge educational research, which, once removed from the educational research journals and symposia, was undercut by the realities of the emotional maturity of students, and the need to provide some isolation to library users and protection for expensive library resources and equipment.

As day-to-day usage, users and technology changes, a body of anecdotal evidence and carefully noted behaviour accumulates. In the case of Parkway North, the library space started out, envisaged primarily as a student learning space, then was configured into traditional library and instructional spaces. The current iteration is an amalgam that through design and construction reflects the current needs and preferences of students, teachers and staff. PNHS Library was improved by erecting walls that demarked the Library's space, created different zones to accommodate group or individual study, and enhanced sightlines so library staff could oversee students. Librarians and teachers should heed what they observe and hear. Blind belief in the prescience of educational theorists or architects can thwart the best efforts of those who use our libraries. ▩

Sinclair Community College, Dayton, OH

Keyword: needs

Sinclair is a very large, urban institution that offers a variety of programs leading to a two-year (Associate's Degree) or toward matriculation in a traditional four-year college or university. All the students are commuters; most work and many are parents.

The library is located in a subterranean space, without access to natural lighting. Surprisingly even though its location is adjacent and below a large, attractive food court, the use of the library was very limited before it was redeveloped. Constructed in the 1970s, the textured, grey concrete walls were dark and fortress-like. The furnishings and carpeting, bright orange and red, were uncomfortable and inflexible. Enormous stack ranges, holding books and journals that had not been used in years, created zones where students felt isolated and unsafe.

The challenge presented to the planners, architects and designers was complex:

- Visually and architecturally link the library to the food court to encourage students and instructors to enter the library.
- Identify campus services needed by the students, so they could take care of their needs (for example access to tutors, counsellors and computing facilities) without having to move long distances through the campus.
- Enliven the space through intelligent, sustainable design to bring the 'outside inside' by permitting penetration of the large, interior garden, which defined the interior space, with paths and seating and by changing the palette used to provide a much more attractive and more sedate colour scheme.
- Upgrade the lighting to provide a more complete spectrum of light.
- Use prisms to channel the sunlight into the interior.

Considerable attention was paid to creating spaces where students could study individually or in teams or groups, and where students could easily use their iPads, personal digital assistants (PDAs), laptops and other devices. The footprint of the shelving was significantly reduced by eliminating duplicative or obsolete collections, and providing online access to indices and periodical databases. Three years after opening, the usage of the library has exploded and it has become a vibrant learning and social environment, where students feel secure. The Sinclair Community College Library had not been updated since its opening in the 1970s, and was avoided by students and faculty. It was

Image 2.2 *The Sinclair Community College Library (courtesy Alan Scherr Associates)*

transformed into a vibrant, popular learning centre by highlighting its interior garden, proximity to the food court and providing a variety of seating and study opportunities (Image 2.2). ■

Delaware State University – William C. Jason Library

Keyword: leverage

The William C. Jason Library is a six-storey structure dating to the mid-1980s. Over time, because preventive maintenance had not been kept up to date, roof leaks developed. The interior had mould and mildew problems. Interiors were never repainted or recarpeted. Lighting fixtures broke and – because essential electrical components were no longer manufactured – remained dark. The Library became unpopular with students and faculty, who found other places on campus or, worse, at other colleges to study, conduct research or socialize. The challenge presented to the librarian was to develop the Jason Library into an attractive and popular academic college centre, a place where students and faculty felt comfortable and where campus recruiters could bring prospective students and their families to demonstrate that learning is central to the institutional mission. They were able to secure $1.2 million to achieve this goal.

The librarians, aware that the funds that had been raised would not suffice, partnered with the university's athletic departments to create a student athlete academic centre. This would be located in the Library and considered shared space, featuring over four dozen computers on oversized carrels that could comfortably accommodate up to three users, a 12-seat instructional space, with a smart screen white board, offices for the assistant directors for Athletics for Academic Excellence, offices for tutors, and a centrally located server room to support the hardware and any personal devices the students chose to connect into the system. Seating was selected that could provide adjustable and comfortable accommodation of patrons of different sizes and/or physical condition – including American football players whose weight exceeded 150kg.

Five 'smart classrooms' of varying sizes were designed. These were intentionally given multiple purposes and left open for student use when classes or programs were not in session. Among the multiple purposes was the Rosetta Stone® Language Laboratory, where students or faculty could use learning software to develop fluency in dozens of languages, an instructional space tied with the new Delaware Online Education Library, which provides continuing education for teachers and administrators throughout the state, and two more traditional classrooms. Also added was compact, moveable storage for the University's archives, rare books and library-owned art collections.

Other enhancements included a new exterior lobby serving the library and the University's Art Exhibition space, an electronic security system, placement of a historic Steinway concert grand piano in the central atrium for regular performances by students and faculty, a new enhanced public services desk, restrooms, and an expanded and protected electrical services. A bistro was also designed, which could be operated after hours (during art exhibits or performances) or to support the extended access hours during the weeks leading up to examination. ■

The Alden Library at Ohio University

Keywords: client needs, vision
The Alden Library design reflects the belief, widely held in the 1970s and 1980s, that the space requirements of academic libraries would continue to grow. The university it serves is located in Athens, Ohio, a town physically remote from the large metropolitan campuses scattered across the state in Cincinnati, Columbus, Cleveland and Youngstown. At the time it was designed and constructed, the discussions that led to rapid inter-institutional

resource sharing were at an early stage. The Ohio College Library Center (now OCLC), which pioneered the creation of shared catalogues, was a small operation when the library was designed. Interlibrary lending was dependent on the US Postal System. University library self-sufficiency was a requirement. Hence, the design was based on the anticipation of ever larger, more comprehensive collections rather than on the specific environmental needs of students and faculty.

By the late 1990s, many companies were offering and developing products that hinted that digital access would link libraries and enhance efforts to share collections across institutions, states, countries and the world. Increasingly affordable laptops linked to local and wide area networks freed the users of library information from doing their work at the personal computers found in libraries and offices.

The administration of the Alden Library, faced by steadily declining use of the library and aware of the success of new learning centres in other universities, decided to explore ways to better serve their university community. Student needs were, of course, central to the planning, but there was also a recognition that faculty are a primary motivator for student use of the library. Over the years many Ohio University faculty rarely or never visited the library and used its resources. The assignments they gave to their students were often based on textbooks or packages of readings that students purchased from the university bookstore.

The facilities plan and subsequent design was not only based on the needs and preferences of students, librarians and staff. It also focused on what would re-introduce faculty to the Alden Library, encourage the library's use by faculty, and provide an incentive to direct their students to the library. The project architect, the DesignGroup, worked closely with all the groups involved to understand the problems the library faced, and the vision of the librarians. The firm's website (DesignGroup, n.d.) provides a glimpse of the design's objectives:

> The new Faculty Commons combines the Ohio University, Center for Teaching and Learning [CTL], Inter-Library Loan, Graphics Services and Copy Services. As a place for faculty to gather, collaborate and improve teaching in the library, the Commons will provide a lounge for faculty interaction with a display of faculty research, a multi-media lab for demonstration of new software as it relates to teaching, a teaching and learning classroom as well as open and closed collaboration spaces, and CTL staff office and conference space.

Image 2.3 *The Alden Library at Ohio University (courtesy Ohio University Library)*

But the librarians have another objective – one that does not appear on websites or in easily accessible documentation. Their work reflects a continuing evolution of their service model that is focused not so much on the traditional reference and collection management but integrates librarians, different staff, related services, print and media collections, and electronic resources. As they have planned the continuing renovation of the Alden Library, they are expanding the second floor prototypical learning commons throughout the building.

The learning commons is visibly a success. On the day of my first visit, early in the morning, it was busy. Students worked at the library computers or used their own personal devices. Many studied in pairs or groups. Staff were engaged helping the students and others locate an elusive source and making suggestions for further reading. But there was ample provision for students who preferred to study by themselves. The showcase classroom was occupied by a class and its instructor. The popularity is not simply based on a gifted design and word of mouth, however. Central to the Alden Library learning commons is publicity. The library administration wants the Alden Library to become a centre for learning for students and faculty. They want the Alden Library to be one of the factors that persuade prospective students and their families to apply for admission. I came across a wonderful video conceived by a student that describes the learning commons at Ohio University (Bonds, 2010). The video is charming and even more impressive are the many other videos that have been posted to YouTube, which describe the learning commons, the Library, its collections and its many services. The Alden Library at Ohio University offers a variety of easily moved furniture, and open, semi-private and enclosed spaces enable students and faculty to create their optimal learning environment (Image 2.3). ▇

Conclusions

Both new and renovated libraries in the USA are integrating learning spaces and traditional instructional spaces into their facilities. This is not so much an innovation in design but an extension of historic traditions of public, school, and college and university libraries. Though these facilities are firmly based on library tradition, they reflect a rapidly changing service paradigm that is based less on the traditional reference interview and more on a fluid, collaborative model that relies on student and faculty information literacy, digital information often not housed in the library, and group study and team teaching.

Public libraries, community colleges and school libraries are forming partnerships with one another to offer seamless access to quality learning spaces. These new learning spaces are an extension of the multi-purpose rooms that were an integral part of the original Carnegie Library funded designs.

Academic librarians of all types of institutions are working closely with their instructional counterparts to encourage students to use library resources as a requirement for term papers and assignments.

In summary, learning spaces in American libraries typically include the following features:

- highly flexible space to support a wide variety of activities
- storage areas for extra chairs, smart boards, computers and replacement parts
- modular furniture that can be readily reconfigured into conference rooms, traditional classrooms or computer laboratories, in addition to relaxed study and learning environments
- redundant telecommunications to provide access to local servers and the internet
- additional electrical support to provide power, for use or recharging of student-owned devices

- distance learning capabilities to permit linkage to other learning centres
- external and internal corridors that permit the use of learning spaces when the rest of the facility is closed
- acoustical conditioning to reduce the intrusion of conversations, lecturers, phone use, or sudden intrusive sound which distract learning
- lighting that provides a range of light intensity, and enhances colours and skin tones
- access to restroom facilities for the off-hours occupants of learning spaces
- access to service kitchens to provide refreshments for meetings, conferences, team projects or receptions
- hard-wired overlapping security with video surveillance, hard-wired to campus or town security, recording devices and panic buttons.

The information commons – a brief history

More than two decades have passed since information commons were first designed as the public service centrepieces of American libraries. Many articles and books have been published to guide those planning such facilities. However, the continuous evolution of the information commons has rendered many of their recommendations obsolete. Some key ideas remain but as the information commons becomes the learning commons more is expected.

The Commons

According to the Oxford English Dictionary (2013), a commons is 'provisions shared in common; rations'. Its usage in American libraries began about 1993 at a time when 'rationing' and 'sharing' of IT resources was essential to providing access for many students and staff. Within a decade, it was widely used to describe a specific interior space in American libraries that offered the use of library-owned computers. In 2013, the preferred form is now learning commons (Bennett, 2003, 5).

A resource at the centre

Arne Duncan, the Secretary of Education in the administration of US President Barack Obama, states 'the school is at the center' of childhood education (quoted in Rotella, 2010, 26). His statement is applicable to library learning commons. These are generally located in close proximity to the main entrances of library facilities and drive the public's perception of programmes of the library. They provide information about the holdings in all formats or resources that are available, online or in their original physical format, in the library or in other locations. They facilitate access to that information. Newer learning commons expand on the original terminal clusters to include different instructional spaces, media labs, food service areas, group studies and tutoring offices. Many are designed to provide 24-hour access.

More flexibility

Public spaces in traditional American libraries served generations of patrons with scant attention to much more than routine maintenance. New technologies and our understanding of how learning is encouraged now require continuous attention to the currency of equipment and reconfiguration of the space and furnishings. Users are encouraged to move furniture to suit their personal or group needs.

More capacity

Early information commons quickly showed that their success depended on much more than purchasing some computers and setting them up in a public area for anyone's use. These information commons relied exclusively on pre-existing electrical and telecommunications cabling grids. This became problematic as patrons brought more of their own devices to use or charge in the commons and used wi-fi networks to access the internet, overloading electrical circuitry. Bandwidth requirements also grew exponentially because of media streaming. To anticipate increasing demand and assure optimal connectivity, new networks are designed that feature scalability.

More support

Some library patrons have a high level of sophistication about computing. However, many visitors to learning commons benefit from and appreciate having ready access to knowledgeable and technology-savvy staff, who can answer questions or provide suggestions that guarantee a successful visit.

References

Bennett, S. (2003) *Libraries Designed for Learning*, Council on Library and Information Resources.

Bonds, C. (2010) *The Learning Commons at Ohio University*, www.youtube.com/watch?v=0D_M5JWt9ok (accessed 11 April 2012).

Brand, S. (1994) *How Buildings Learn: what happens after they're built*, Penguin.

DesignGroup (n.d.) *DesignGroup Firm Profile*, www.designgroup.us.com/downloads/DesignGroup_FirmProfile.pdf (accessed 1 April 2013).

Dickson, P. (1986) *The Library in America: a celebration in words and pictures*, Facts of File Publications.

Oxford Dictionaries (2013) Commons, http://oxforddictionaries.com/us/definition/american_english/commons (accessed 12 May 2013).

Rotella, C. (2010) Class Warrior: Arne Duncan's bid to shake up the schools, *New Yorker*, 1 February.

Sommers, R. (1966) The Ecology of Privacy, *Library Quarterly*, **36**, July, 234–48.

Tompkins, P. (1990) New Structures for Teaching Libraries, *Library Administration & Management*, **4**.

University of Illinois (2008) Field Theory, www.uic.edu/depts/oaa/walkingtour/4a.html (accessed 13 January 2013).

CHAPTER 3

China projects and trends

Hugh Anderson

Introduction

China's dramatic rise has manifested itself in urban growth and a growing collection of stunning modern buildings, increasingly designed by native Chinese architects. Several of these buildings belong to new or massively expanded university campuses each featuring its centrepiece 'library'. Other libraries have formed part of school or community campuses but, not generally being in standalone buildings, have been less dramatic although, ironically for the same reasons, it is these buildings that possibly show greater organizational thought.

Not unsurprisingly the emphasis of recent Chinese design has been on external form, where dramatic shapes and modern materials celebrate power, progress and an ability to match what is being done elsewhere in the world. Less thought has been paid to the subtleties of internal function. This review has revealed relatively traditional notions of what might constitute the library or 'learning centre'. To suggest that architectural emphasis is only on the dramatic would be to sell these many talented architects short, however. The subtlety and beauty of the limited number of buildings reviewed reveals an architectural potential that will no doubt continue to grow.

Chinese library design is therefore in its infancy compared with the west and reflects the priorities of the current regime. A centralized system based on bureaucratic control does not provide much opportunity for innovation. In particular the liberal attitudes to learning and teaching that underpin the newer and more experimental UK higher education libraries appear to be absent in China. The result is a focus on library operations in most of the libraries reviewed – in simple design terms a fairly regimented arrangement of book stacks and study tables.

Seen more positively it is essential to remember that the Chinese educational system is very different from that in the west and has been for thousands of years, so much so that the Chinese mentality is different, accepting – even welcoming – a degree of control and imposed order. It is therefore clearly inappropriate to judge Chinese educational practice by the criteria that have been adopted more recently in Europe, although China is increasingly adopting western styles of operation and is increasingly operating in a western world. Chinese heritage – being different from the experience we are familiar with in the west, with a continued reverence for education, exemplified by the order and calm of those projects, which contain many of the traditional features of educational buildings – has something very useful to remind us of in the west, in our change-obsessed modern world.

While open to architectural competition, most of the new Chinese university buildings are executed by the large regional architectural institutes, a follow-on from the traditional state-run architecture and engineering departments. Although technically at arm's length from the state and with close working relationships with the university architectural schools, these institutes are nevertheless subject to central funding processes and priorities, giving little opportunity for local client and design teams to debate the nature of the building brief. In addition, the procurement system appears to draw a distinct line between the building envelope and the internal fit-out, allowing for little interaction between these two and thereby little innovation. The situation is not necessarily so different from the increasingly centralized control of government-funded projects such as schools in the UK and the traditional attitudes of many architectural practices, which focus almost entirely on external form with little thought for the changing organizations that are going to occupy their buildings.

In reviewing the current status of Chinese library design, it is important, as suggested above, to appreciate the nature of the Chinese educational system, where centralized control, coupled with the overwhelming need to focus on the quantity of students being processed, gives little opportunity to focus on 'freedom of investigation' or 'self-discovery', which characterizes education in western countries and has underpinned the impetus of new library design. The educational emphasis on the 'what' rather than the 'how' is possibly an inevitable consequence of the huge competition called for in making it to the higher reaches of the educational system in the first place, and the instructional approaches and rote learning and examining that tends to go with this.

Lastly, for a country that is apparently so rich, it might come as a surprise (until one remembers the vast size of the country and the considerable gap that exists between rich and poor) that resources for the operation of schools and universities are massively limited compared with what we are used to in the west. Currently this exhibits itself in a dramatically reduced take-up of computer technology. It cannot be assumed therefore (as has become a starting point for the re-imagining of the western library) that 'information is everywhere', or that all students have computers, or access to the internet, or that library design is predicated on the computer revolution. While this might be expected to change in the near future, it cannot be said in the meantime that Chinese library design even has the opportunity to think about being based on an internet-based educational system.

The conditions therefore for fresh thinking in education and library design do not currently exist in China and the innovation that does exist must be appreciated against this restricted background. The following projects give a taste therefore of a system which is starting to look dramatic but is still at the beginning of an evolutionary process and may well evolve in a different direction from that commonly accepted in western education systems.

Shandong University of Science and Technology

Keyword: scale

While not the largest library project in China, at 35,000 square metres the Science and Technology library on Shandong's new campus is not to be underestimated. The campus is vast, laid out in heroic style with the library forming a focal point at one end of a giant mall. At this scale and at the rate of building that this project called for it appears that there was little opportunity to think of the subtleties of the learning process. The building of a requisite number of square metres has come first, with the task of making it operational being a later consideration. The layered terraces of Shandong University of Science and Technology Library may give opportunities for differentiated space as new social demands arise (Image 3.1).

As an exercise in Architecture (with a big 'A'), the project is representative of much of what is taking place in China just now, at a scale and with an emphasis on building, which is foreign to most designers and educationalists in the western world. The project is representative of those projects that can be

Image 3.1 *Shandong University of Science and Technology Library (copyright China Architecture and Design Research Group)*

criticized for taking little or no account of the ultimate user, for building in huge and inevitable obsolescence, as technology and learning inevitably change. Against this the project also demonstrates boldness in preparing for the titanic growth that is taking place in China in a way that planners and politicians in the west appear to be incapable of. The issue is possibly therefore not so much about whether what is being provided is appropriate for learning and studying as whether what is being provided has an intelligent approach to flexibility and half a chance of dealing with change when this eventually comes.

Judged against these broader criteria, the building with its vast size still poses a challenge. Without being able to comment on its environmental systems strategy, its IT infrastructure, the constraints or otherwise of its fire strategy, it is clear that the building will involve large-scale circulation routes, an institutionalized form of management, deep internal space, and little natural light and ventilation (despite its tiered terraces facing down the University mall). Although not clear from its current plans, it seems inevitable that large swathes of space will be taken up by bookstacks and internal study spaces, all in an arrangement, which is likely to be difficult to convert to the complex, integrated range of social, study and support spaces that are the hallmark of current western library planning.

Accepting the premise for state-organized, large-scale educational programmes, however, the building has space, clarity and a simple hierarchy of organization that gives it the potential for a more localized response to technology and learner needs in due course. In addition its terraces give opportunities for a differentiated quality of space, as new social demands arise, and is an enlightened response to a particular brief. The complex is undoubtedly inspirational and will definitely survive as user numbers grow – a consideration that can be overlooked within deliberation-obsessed western practice. ■

Ordos Library

Keyword: opportunity

Ordos, characterized by its gargantuan central Genghis Khan Plaza and vast boulevards creating open vistas to the hills of Inner Mongolia, is a modern frontier city. It is located within a mineral rich region that until recently enjoyed an estimated annual economic growth of 40% and boasts the second highest per capita income in China, behind only the financial capital, Shanghai. The Ordos library complex is, like the Shandong University Library above, an ambitious project, by the China Architecture and Design Research Group (Image 3.2).

Image 3.2 *Ordos Library Complex, a free form architecturally driven arrangement, which has potentially unique opportunities for individual study and group working (copyright China Architecture and Design Research Group)*

Like the Shandong building, at 32,000 square metres the scale of the complex gives little opportunity to focus on the niceties of learning and studying, but its poetic, swirling arrangement does suggest a more humane approach. Many of the difficulties inherent in large buildings and buildings designed within a centrally managed Chinese regime might be similarly identified in this project, but, in its different architectural approach, it highlights a different set of problems and opportunities. These relate in the main to the approach taken to flexibility. The free form floor plan of the Ordos library is just as formally driven as the axial arrangement of Shandong. It is architecturally driven but generates a very different set of internal opportunities.

At first sight the complex is beautiful, full of architectural opportunity, but as almost every architectural turn is unique and a large amount of space is devoted to a sculpturally wonderful circulation route it is indeed complex, clearly posing an organizational challenge. On closer study, however, it reveals significant opportunities. While it suggests difficulty in accommodating internal reorganization over time and a major loss of usable space, seen from the point of view of the user and the trend towards a greater emphasis on individual work patterns, the need for a complex mixture of group working and individual working and a subtle overlap between socializing and working, the complexity of the Ordos plan starts to reveal something different – opportunities for local adaptation, which rational Shandong might find more difficult to accommodate. It might not be easy to carve up the building as sometimes becomes necessary, but there is ample opportunity for informal usage and for the large size of the complex to take on a human scale. It demonstrates a completely different approach to the problem of flexibility, but one that in the face of a people-orientated move towards library design might not be inappropriate. Those 'inefficient' circulation spaces in particular, which might not be very appropriate for accommodating traditional bookwork, hold opportunities for the internet-based social learning which will surely arrive in China before long. Similarly the library 'halls' are not dominated by book stacks even now, and may have the potential in the future (within a sufficiently sophisticated environmental control system) to accommodate a variety of semi-formal workspaces or even to be divided to accommodate specialized work spaces. Ironically, the Ordos response to creating image might not therefore prove too short sighted compared with modern library design. ■

Wuhan University of Science and Technology, Xiamen Campus

Keyword: balance

At nearly 40,000 square metres the Wuhan University building is one of the largest recently completed and once again illustrates the issues of a large building complex. It handles the problem of scale differently from Shandong and Ordos, such that it works well, within the current system of learning and studying, and still has the potential to change over time.

Organizationally the building consists of several substantially discrete elements, drawn together by a magnificent atrium, which is of a scale to match the building complex, but is intersected by bridges, cut through by ramps and staircases and divided by waterways and elegant clumps of bamboo (Image 3.3). In so doing its scale is reduced and an atmosphere of calm introduced echoing the contemplative tradition of China's ancient institutes of learning. In addition the arrangement subtly incorporates other Chinese traditions, the passing over of water (preferably bejewelled with tiny fish), the presence of plants, fresh air and natural sunlight (ironically all elements being rediscovered within western practice as beneficial to effective learning). The library complex does not incorporate (except in a very limited way) those cafés and eateries which add to the more lively atmosphere beloved of the informal western 'learning centres' – but then this is China.

From the entrance via the water and the sunlight, visitors can pass directly to a 400-person conference room and a suite of smaller seminar rooms or to a variety of individual library areas (of approximately 750 square metres each) relating to different disciplines with separate check-in and help desks. Nine of these 'mini libraries' are stacked within the 'fingers' characterizing the form of the building from the outside; three of them are combined with generously expanded balcony spaces within the central atrium, a pleasant and useful adjunct that one can see taking on more informal uses

Image 3.3
Xiamen Campus Library, showing how the building consists of several substantially discrete elements drawn together by a magnificent atrium (copyright Hua Hui Architects)

over time. Within the different library areas themselves there is a relatively conventional mixture of book stacks and study tables, of a size and configuration that might easily vary over time or even take on very different internal arrangements, one with another.

In general the complex provides a successful balance between large and small, a simple access pattern combined with visual complexity and interest, centralized support functions combined with localized opportunities for differences in learning approach. It is a massive facility appropriate to mass demand, with a traditional and reverential approach to the act of studying and learning and an inherent flexibility that might underpin its usability in the future. ▪

Sichuan Fine Arts Institute Library, Haxi Campus

Keyword: humanity

At 14,300 square metres the Sichuan library is modest compared with its university contemporaries, but still allows for some 1200 seats and 1 million books. It is a substantial building, designed within a vernacular tradition, with several vernacular references, and is sensitively located on the edge of open countryside. Its form is deceptively simple, monumental but not imposing, allowing it to combine with local domestic buildings at the same time as providing a rich internal variety of library and circulation spaces, all flooded with natural light. The current arrangement of workspace is relatively conventional but has the clear potential to change over time, in line with its more relaxed scale and arts orientation.

Organized as a long thin tube (with appropriate references to a traditional Chinese-style horizontal scroll) its focus is on its longitudinal circulation and climbing staircases leading to a glazed gable end, providing light and magnificent views to the countryside beyond. It is essentially a humane building with a sensitive use of modern and traditional materials 'dense, hard and solemn on the outside', 'soft, intimate and light on the inside'. Thus its interpretation of the challenge of a modern library is solidly traditional, focusing on the atmosphere considered appropriate for 'contemplative learning'. Sichuan Fine Arts Institute Library is a relatively conventional library at present but with the clear potential to change over time (Image 3.4).

With its simplicity of organization the building is likely to survive the vagaries of fashion but in its focus on architectural purity its quiet atmosphere is similarly at risk of being spoiled by the inevitable onslaught of computers, trailing cables (are those solid stone floors that combine ever so beautifully with the fair-faced concrete?), group working and modern students, more

Image 3.4 *Sichuan Fine Arts Institute Library (copyright Tang Hua Architects)*

hung-up on fashion and Facebook than quiet contemplation. There are lifts within the building but how does one get to them in the first place? At present the horizontal circulation taken alongside or through the middle of the work areas provides a pleasant balance between calm and liveliness, but what will it take to preserve this civilized balance? In the west one might fear the introduction of partition walls and 'keep quiet' signs. In China a more respectful attitude to learning and the personal space of others may just help to avoid such a reactionary breakdown.

Insofar as libraries want to continue to be special spaces with a distinct character, which make them places to seek out and use for a more elevated purpose, the Sichuan Fine Arts building will undoubtedly endure. A sufficient infrastructure of wire ways, ways in which ventilation and noise and smells can be controlled, will assist this. ▩

Li Yuan Library

Keyword: special

The Li Yuan Library lies at the opposite extreme of the mass production 'learning machines' that characterize China's burgeoning cities and universities. It is minute by comparison, immaculately crafted – more of a 'reading room', a space specifically designed for quiet contemplation – than anything attempting to meet modern learning in a technological era.

The library or 'reading room' is not just set within a village context but is a deliberate five-minute walk away from the village centre, making the act of going there deliberate and psychologically focused. The project was commissioned by a charitable trust and crafted by a small team including one of the commissioning donors. In contrast with China's spectacular university projects, which leave the operation (and sometimes funding) of the library itself to a totally different team from that which created the building, the Li Yuan project shows the difference of a learning and working space designed from the inside out.

It is a modest project yet rich in internal variety in the formal and informal ways in which children (and adults) might want to use it. It is holistic in the fullest sense of the word from the form of its construction, to its creation of a unique internal environment and its accommodation of books, seating, circulation and support spaces. It does not suggest how technology might be sensitively accommodated over time but then its brief appears specifically not to have called for this.

Once again if one particular challenge of the library, as a place that will

Image 3.5 *Li Yuan Library, a haven of quiet and calm – library as 'special place' (copyright Li Xiaodong Atelier)*

endure over time, is that it should be a 'special place', one that induces a desire to want to be there, then the beauty of this little gem makes the point at every turn (Image 3.5). One has the sense that just being there would infuse one with the wonder of being alive, enthuse one with a desire to explore and understand. No need in this building ever for there to be a proliferation of signs telling one how to behave.

In listing the ways in which its special atmosphere is created it is difficult to know where to start – the quality of its natural light filtered through sticks is so symbolic of the local act of living and existing; order within the disorder; books and knowledge made an integral part of using the building. The building may not be reproducible on a large scale, but it is a reminder that at the psychological heart of any library there should be the space or spaces, place or places which enthuse one with the wonder and mystery of being alive. ■

Trends

In a book that focuses on internal library space and 'informal learning' the case studies in this chapter present a radically different view of the world. There is a focus here on the building and its exterior as an architectural statement though Li Yuan Library, with its smaller scale, shows this trend is not universal. In a rapidly developing country this focus on grand scale inspirational exteriors is understandable.

A view of the library as a traditional library is clear in these case studies and the learning or information commons concept seems largely absent in the form that we understand it in the west. This is not a criticism, as is noted above; it would be inappropriate to judge these facilities on western criteria. A traditional view of learning, as instruction, and the role of the library, as repository, includes a focus on reflection, contemplation and individual study rather than group activity. Buildings of the scale described here, which provide for the individual, can undoubtedly morph over time to accommodate the activity of group work if this becomes the norm, making these facilities fit for the future. And this flexibility, which comes from technically supported, large-scale internal space, a feature in common with western library projects, provides the basis of durability and ensures that they will remain fit for the future. This potential for future change includes the possibilities for responses to both locality and the particular needs of the local community that are essential to success.

CHAPTER 4

Hong Kong projects and trends

Bob Fox and Peter E. Sidorko

Introduction

In Hong Kong we live in exciting times with many opportunities and challenges for reform and advancement in education – major curriculum reform, change in student demographics, and the ubiquitous use of mobile and cloud-based technologies.

Few students come to university without powerful mobile technologies, whether laptops, tablets or hand-size devices such as smartphones. Likewise, few students do not make extensive use of the free wi-fi across Hong Kong (Tsang et al., 2008) and the ever more powerful wi-fi facilities within universities and now in a growing number of schools (Chu et al., 2012). In studies into m-learning and the use of cloud-based technologies on university campuses in Hong Kong (e.g. Song and Fox, 2008; Lam, Lam and McNaught, 2010; Fox, 2011), students' study habits have been found to be changing with the adoption of new and increasingly mobile personal technologies and the need for new learning environments and new educational services.

The 25–30% growth in education places in Hong Kong universities in 2012 has led to the need for rapid expansion of both physical and virtual services and facilities. In planning for this expansion, universities have been asking what new kinds of library learning places are needed that will suit students today and in the future. Do we need to duplicate and expand existing student services and places, designed before the introduction of new technologies and new practices or should we fundamentally rethink our physical environment, taking into account students' changing study habits, changing curriculum requirements and emerging technological and pedagogical practices?

This chapter explores the challenges of doing things differently in Hong Kong university libraries, providing students and teaching staff with new library places that offer new ways of working and services and facilities designed to meet the needs of education today and for the future.

Background to the changing needs in Hong Kong educational libraries

September 2012 was the start of a new academic year in universities in Hong Kong unlike any other. All major universities adopted a new outcomes-based curriculum, which adds an extra year to the undergraduate degree programme. This has resulted in large-scale curriculum reform in all disciplines, creating the opportunity to consider what should be included in an undergraduate degree in the 21st century. All eight University Grants Committee (UGC) funded universities have re-examined their graduate capability statements to take into account what is seen as today's curriculum requirements to meet the challenges of the knowledge-based economy of Hong Kong. At the University of Hong Kong (HKU), for example, all degrees are expected to combine their outcomes-based curriculum with broad educational aims to develop students' capabilities beyond subject specific knowledge to include: 'tackling novel situations and ill-defined problems'; 'critical self-reflection, greater understanding of others', and enhanced 'communication and collaboration' skills (University of Hong Kong New 4-Year Undergraduate Curriculum, n.d.). In addition, universities are expecting students to graduate as information and digitally literate citizens. In September 2012 there were 3500 additional student enrolments in each of the major universities, placing huge pressures on centralized and distributed services and facilities for students (Fox and Lam, 2012).

In summary, these changes to the curriculum, changing study habits of our students, major increases in student numbers, ubiquitous use of smart, mobile and cloud-based technologies and the consequent need to create additional learning spaces have placed pressures on Hong Kong libraries to rethink their roles, services and facilities to meet these new challenges. The following case studies describe these changes in Hong Kong libraries.

Case studies

The City University of Hong Kong Library

The City University of Hong Kong Library (CityU Library) was the first of Hong Kong's eight UGC-funded libraries to undertake a major renovation in response to changing student needs for diverse study spaces, the growing use of digital resources and the declining era of print. The initial phase completed in 2007, was innovative at the time, and today remains something of a benchmark for the other institutes of higher learning in Hong Kong. One of the key features of the renovation is its use of east and west furniture and design motifs described below, which eloquently capture Hong Kong's role as the bridge between east and west.

The CityU Library facilities focus on three key areas of space utilization: technology, individual and group study spaces, and interactive learning. Perhaps most significant and interesting among these are the spaces allocated for interactive learning. One of these spaces, designated the Humanities Academy, is reminiscent of the fast disappearing courtyards so common among Beijing's hutongs. It is a distinctive feature that, while being contemporary, suggests a culturally traditional and studious environment. The central 'courtyard' provides an 'open room' concept where library users may gather and work collaboratively on open furniture. The area is also capable of hosting library events, talks and seminars with a capacity of over 60. The perimeter of the courtyard is lined on three sides with ten group study rooms including the Korean and Persian Rooms (restricted to academics), which are equipped with a range of technologies including high definition TVs, Blu-Ray players and DVD recorders. In an era where library renovations in the form of learning commons or information commons are increasingly generic, the CityU Library provides a contemporary feel with a sense of tradition, achieved through its use of furniture and layout, which leaves the user all too aware that they are in an Asian library.

Other features of the interactive learning spaces are the Mini Theatre and the multi-purpose lobby. The Mini Theatre (Le ciel de l'esprit) is an inspirational space intended for film and music appreciation for groups of up to 15. This free standing theatre is built in the shape of an egg in order 'to symbolize the hatching of knowledge from a state of turbidity, according to ancient Chinese writings' (City University of Hong Kong Library, 2011).

The Library's multi-purpose lobby provides an excellent example in the application of flexibility in the use of space. Too often, library renovations focus on the here and now and pay little attention to future needs. While it is impossible to predict what the future spatial requirements of academic libraries will be, architects, library space planners and library directors need to be mindful of this unpredictable future. Accordingly, spaces should be developed that are flexible and can be responsive to an ever-changing demand with minimal cost implications. The CityU Library's multi-purpose lobby is such a space. It functions primarily as an entrance lobby, and can be readily adapted to house exhibitions, seminars and other similar events with minimal disruption or cost. Additionally its flexibility means that it can be readily repurposed into the future, whatever that may hold. While the space is primarily used for functions and events, during revision and examination periods, the Library converts the lobby into a temporary study area when needed.

CityU Library has set a very high standard for innovative spatial design in academic libraries in Hong Kong. It is flexible, suited to a variety of learning styles, individual and collaborative, quiet and loud; it is also culturally sensitive, technologically rich and has many distinctive features that serve to inspire those who make use of it. Each different learning zone has its own special light, varied ceiling heights, furniture, design and parameter. ▪

The University of Hong Kong Main Library

The University of Hong Kong Library completed a significant renovation in September 2012, just before the arrival of the double cohort of students emanating from the introduction of the new four-year curriculum. This renovation, Level 3, was the culmination of some four years of planning, design and redesign. Over 3000 square metres of very traditional library space was transformed into a vibrant, bookless, multi-functional, flexible and hi-tech learning space. There are seven distinct zones on Level 3 and each has unique features and design that intuitively imply to students the type of activity or learning style that is best catered for in each of these areas, as described below.

The Technology Zone offers over 80 computers with a range of software applications in support of study and research. While the individual workstations cannot be readily reconfigured by students, these workstations are spacious and allow extra students to gather around with other pieces of hardware to work in groups of, ideally, two to three, but sometimes more at work spaces that are up to 50% larger than previous configurations. The surrounding perimeter of this zone is supplemented with flourishes of bright colours in diner-style booth seating arrangements and relaxing individual seats. These colours offset the dominating colour of the zone, varying shades of grey, representing the austerity of technology.

The Multi-Purpose Zone is a venue offering flexible space. Users can choose their preferred location for study as the tables and chairs are on wheels and are readily, and regularly, reconfigured. Interlocking kidney-shaped tables allow groups of around seven to work together easily. The entire space can also be reconfigured to cater for library events, such as exhibitions, conferences and book talks, through the use of mobile partitions that move along grooves in the ceiling to create one large venue accommodating 250 in a conference-style setting or into two rooms roughly dividing the space into half. With its state-of-the-art technology, the various pieces of equipment, such as sound and recording, electronic curtains, five projection screens and a digital podium, can easily be controlled through a central system using an iPad. IPads are also used to control audiovisual settings, lighting and temperature.

The Breakout Zone is a place for eating and relaxing where users can watch TV or read newspapers and magazines. Vending machines provide a selection of snacks and drinks. The seating is in the form of leather loungers in a variety of configurations and separated by low partitions that have glass whiteboards for brainstorming.

The Collaboration Zone provides an environment that fosters group discussion. In the centre are open clusters for group discussions built around refurbished columns, which feature all-in-one computers with touch-screen monitors mounted on moveable arms. Around the perimeter of the room, enjoying large windows looking outdoors, are 19 discussion rooms, each equipped with state-of-the-art technology, such as interactive whiteboards and TV panels, webcams and high-definition camcorders. Users can reserve these rooms for a maximum of two hours per day. The use of quick response (QR) codes enables easy and immediate, on-the-spot booking of these rooms as well as many of the study seats and computer workstations in the other zones.

The Study Zone is the extended hours zone of Level 3, opening 22.5 hours every day. It serves as an ideal place for private and reflective research as it provides a variety of single study places including some with three partition heights allowing varying degrees of privacy, moveable all-in-one study tables with seats outside the clusters of partitioned spaces, and a deep silent room. In the deep silent room the use of technology – including laptops, iPods and other musical devices – is forbidden, in response to users' demands for such a space. The dominant colour of the Study Zone is a cool and relaxing blue.

The University of Hong Kong Library chose not to name the renovated space as any 'commons' facility. Instead it stands out from the rest of the library's floors as all other floors bear the word 'floor', e.g. ground floor, first floor, etc., and the third floor bears the name Level 3. This signifies that this floor is different but at the same time it remains a steadfast, yet distinctive part of the library. ▓

The Chinese University of Hong Kong Library

In 2012 the Chinese University of Hong Kong Library completed a major renovation of the Library, including the addition of a 7000-square-metre extension, which has a 2000-square-metre learning commons, called the Learning Garden, located in the basement of the extension. The basement extension is unique. Far from giving the impression of a dark and claustrophobic basement, two large skylights located under pools that are part of the University Square allow an enormous amount of dappled light to shine through. Additionally the emphasis on white as the predominant colour adds to the bright ambience. This emphasis on brightness and reflected light through water gives the commons an open, almost garden-like feeling. Running the length of the Learning Garden is a long single table, which weaves and curves and undulates creating different zones at different points along its track. It gives the impression that it is the 'garden path'. As the table changes its height, width and shape, it provides students with the opportunity to discover new ways of studying and working collaboratively or individually. The Learning Garden is a 24/7 facility, which also incorporates other different types of learning spaces, including a collaborative zone, a stepped open forum, large and small bubble group study rooms, an IT zone and whiteboard walls, which students are encouraged to write on freely.

The Library renovations also created a research commons, a space specifically designed to accommodate the needs of postgraduate students and researchers. It provides flexible, technology-enriched spaces, information resources and expert help to support the scholarly research of students and staff. The renovation of the University Library took in the key concepts of openness, spaciousness and light. The key colour for surfaces such as the floors, walls and open stepped forums is white. Colour is added through either bright or pastel coloured furnishings. All the new spaces are technology rich and have been designed to be as flexible as possible, allowing for the spaces to adapt to the users' needs over time. ▓

The Architecture Library at the Chinese University of Hong Kong

This Library was originally established in 1994 to support the core curriculum of the architecture programme and it is the only academic Architecture Library in Hong Kong. At the centre of the new (September 2012) purpose-built School of Architecture building lies the Architecture Library, symbolizing the importance that the library has for the School. The Library has been designed as an extension of the learning and teaching spaces within the building for the School and is fully integrated and embedded into the life of the School. The building and its learning spaces including the Library are open to School of Architecture staff and students 24/7. With a heavily print-based collection, the Library has installed 24/7 radio-frequency identification (RFID) to enable the circulation and security of the print collection. The limited seating in the Library is intentional as students will use the Library as an extension of the other learning spaces, through the design of the building. Students are able to access all learning spaces in the building, including studios, workshops and laboratories, 24/7. The close relationship between the specialist faculty library and its faculty building is reinforced by 24/7 access for students to all learning spaces in the building. The small size and manageability of the client base and the spirit of ownership this engenders reinforces this close working relationship. Such openness is difficult to achieve in a larger academic library where the client base is necessarily diverse and restrictions on access are necessary for security and to protect property. ▨

The Hong Kong Public Library System

The Hong Kong Public Library System is a large and extensive network of 66 libraries plus ten mobile libraries. The main library of the Hong Kong Public Libraries System, the Hong Kong Central Library is the largest public library in Hong Kong. With 33,800 square metres spread over 12 floors and occupying a footprint of 9400 square metres the Library, opened in 2001, sets an imposing figure at its Causeway Bay location overlooking Victoria Harbour. The edifice itself may appear to be a mixture of styles, yet emanating from its exterior are a number of symbolic features including the

> arch-shaped entrance at the front elevation of the Hong Kong Central Library representing the Gate to Knowledge, while the graphics in the shape of triangle, square and circle denote different meanings. The circle stands for the sky, the square for the land and the triangle for accumulation of knowledge
>
> (Hong Kong Public Libraries Leisure and Cultural Services Department, 2012)

The Library hosts a range of facilities and services, including a children's library, an adult lending library, a special reading area, a young adult library, an exhibition area, the Arts Resource Centre, seminar rooms and a conference centre. First impression on entering the Library is the enormous atrium that provides an exceptionally airy and open feeling. Most floors are built around this large atrium, and one of the criticisms of the Library's architecture is the poor use of space resulting from this atrium. On the other hand, many users also find this space inspirational as such large open spaces inside buildings in Hong Kong are rare. The atrium is flagged with glass elevators on one side and escalators on the other, providing two visually striking means of travel between floors.

The size and diversity of services provided at the library reflect the use of space adopted in those service areas. For example the children's library is fitted out with colours, furniture and designs befitting that age group whereas the adult lending library reflects the tastes of an obviously more mature client group. ▦

Trends

Libraries in Hong Kong have made great strides in recent years in their provision of learning spaces. While these advances have been evident in all libraries, public, government, school and special across Hong Kong, they have been particularly pronounced in the academic libraries.

The demands placed on library spaces differ greatly depending on the client base being served by the library. The Hong Kong Central Library, as the largest public library in Hong Kong, caters for a more diverse user base than the libraries in any of the four other case studies. With Hong Kong citizens' propensity for reading, the Hong Kong Central Library is an extremely bustling facility catering for all elements of Hong Kong society. The relative homogeneity of Hong Kong students allows designers of academic libraries to create spaces that are conducive to the study and learning habits of the majority. By comparison, public libraries need to cater for all elements of society and have to be conscious of the needs of children, adolescents, high school students, university students, mature adults and the elderly. These different user groups have very diverse learning styles and require spaces that suit these styles. Additionally, public library users tend to use the public library for a more diverse range of information needs related to their studies, social lives, lifelong learning opportunities, general leisure reading, and cultural and creative activities.

The physical changes to learning spaces in academic libraries in Hong

Kong have been made in response to a number of technology factors, mentioned earlier, as well as changing user behaviours and study habits, curriculum redesign and changing information storage and access (Churchill, 2009). In response to greater student numbers academic libraries have also had to expand their spaces or ensure they are more efficient in accommodating larger numbers of users; provide spaces that are suited to new and varied learning styles; and design spaces that accommodate a range of technologies that enhance learning and provide seamless access to new information resources. A selection of learning space images from all eight of the Hong Kong government-funded university libraries can be found at the Joint University Librarians Advisory Committee (Joint University Librarians Advisory Committee, 2013).

Academic libraries have also had to adjust to changed expectations from their institutional communities. This can be exemplified by an increased demand for new general and specialist-style learning commons spaces. At the HKU, for example, as part of the major expansion of the campus, a 6000-square-metre learning commons was created to serve the needs of the entire university, and especially the three faculties that moved from the old campus to the new (The University of Hong Kong, 2011). This new Chi Wah learning commons provides additional services to those of the usual library managed spaces in academic libraries. In addition to new library services, there is an increased emphasis on multiple service support from student counselling, language support and many other services. The centre is managed by specialist staff who are not part of the library management. This hybrid facility will not be completed until 2013, though the majority of learning spaces have already been made available to students from across the campus. Both the library Level 3 facility and the hybrid learning commons on the new campus are extremely popular spaces for students' individual and group study. These facilities closely match changed demands for flexible, well equipped and comfortable places essential to the new curriculum. In other retro-fitted buildings on the old campus, new shared learning-commons-style places are being created. These are conveniently located, close to centrally scheduled classrooms and lecture theatres, comfortable and varied places for students to study. These new common, shared learning environments or precincts are located on the lower floors of more centralized faculty-based buildings, enabling much more efficient and pleasant spaces, which optimize student opportunities for study.

One other trend exemplified at HKU is a growing number of specialist or boutique faculty library facilities. The Faculty of Education's new library has been relocated to a new retro-fitted site where most of the library space is to be shared with the faculty providing potential for 24/7 multi-purpose use of the library space. The more traditional library area, designated for textbook and related resources, has been considerably reduced, and along with the library offices for staff, these areas can be locked and left, allowing the remaining open areas and break out rooms to be used by the faculty for conferences, events and teaching and learning spaces as required.

The area, located on the top floor of a building taken over by the Faculty of Education, has large bi-fold glass doors opening onto roof gardens, with mountain and harbour views. This facility heralds a new chapter in library and faculty relations and acts as one of the many indicators of how far academic libraries have evolved to provide the services and facilities demanded of them.

In comparison with the development of digital libraries academic libraries in Hong Kong have been relatively slow in repurposing their physical spaces. This has enabled our academic library staff to observe developments from around the world and to selectively implement those aspects that are deemed suitable to the Hong Kong environment. Similarly we have been able to observe developments around the world that have been less than successful and therefore learn from others' mistakes. Driving these changes has been a substantial investment in recent renovations that have arisen out of the need to accommodate additional students following the introduction of the four-year curriculum already discussed in this chapter. As a result a great deal of activity has been commissioned in just a few short years to expand spaces and accommodate new curriculum and alternative user needs by providing learning spaces. In this sense, the rapid changes have been necessarily revolutionary, having followed extended periods of inaction.

The future of academic libraries in Hong Kong is not clear. We have seen both evolutionary and fairly revolutionary changes in facilities and services, and attitudes towards libraries. There is realization that education now, more than ever, needs to prepare citizens with key competencies to face the challenges of the future. The wealth and prosperity of Hong Kong is based to a great extent on a knowledge-based economy, which demands capabilities beyond traditional academic expertise. No longer do we require students to graduate with subject matter expertise alone. Our graduates must have well grounded, broad capabilities. These capacities include tackling novel situations and dealing with ill-defined problems, working collaboratively in teams, communicating effectively through traditional avenues and new technologies, providing critical self-reflection and deep intercultural understanding of others as well as offering leadership and advocacy of the human condition. The University of Hong Kong's curriculum reform is a good example of this change, which is evidenced in the educational aims for undergraduate and postgraduate programmes (The University of Hong Kong, 2013). This shift in curriculum focus has demanded new facilities, services and practices from academic libraries. For example, different technology-rich spaces for students for group work, quiet study, or heated dialogue, discussion and debate.

A key term used in this chapter is flexibility in spaces. Academic librarians acknowledge that physical and virtual spaces will need to continue to change as the demands for these spaces change and as technology advances. In the last six years, academic libraries have accelerated the creation of new virtual and physical learning spaces to meet this continued pressure for change. What is certain is that libraries are seen as vital, vibrant and essential and are sure to continue to provide for the needs expected of them.

References

Chu, S. K. W., Tavares, N. J., Chu, D., Ho, S. Y., Chow, K., Siu, F. L. C. and Wong, M. (2012) *Developing Upper Primary Students' 21st Century Skill: inquiry learning through collaborative teaching and Web 2.0 technology*, Centre for Information Technology in Education, Faculty of Education, University of Hong Kong.

Churchill, D. (2009) *Literacy in the Web 2.0 World (New Literacies)*, www.slideshare.net/zvezdan/new-literacy-in-the-web-20-world (accessed 13 August 2013).

City University of Hong Kong Library (2011) *Mini Theatre (Le ciel de l'esprit)*, www.cityu.edu.hk/lib/about/facility/mt/index.htm (accessed 26 June 2013).

Fox, R. (2011) Technological Practice and Change in Education. In Kwan, R., McNaught, C., Tsang, P., Wang, F. L. and Li, K. C. (eds), Enhancing Learning through Technology. Education Unplugged: mobile Technologies and Web 2.0. *Communications in Computer and Information Sciences*, **177**, 1–7.

Fox, R. and Lam, P. (2012) Balancing Context, Pedagogy and Technology on Learning Space Designs: opportunities amidst infrastructural developments in Hong Kong. In Keppell, M., Souter, K. and Riddle, M. (eds), *Physical and Virtual Learning Spaces in Higher Education: concepts for the modern learning environment*, IGI Global, 72–86.

Hong Kong Public Libraries Leisure and Cultural Services Department (2012)

Introduction, www.hkpl.gov.hk/english/aboutus/aboutus_intro/aboutus_intro.html (accessed 20 August 2013).

Joint University Librarians Advisory Committee (2013) *Photo Gallery*, www.julac.org/?page_id=46 (accessed 26 June 2013).

Lam, P., Lam, J. and McNaught, C. (2010) How Usable are Ebooks in an Mlearning Environment?, *International Journal of Continuing Engineering Education and Life-long Learning*, **20** (1), 6–20.

Song, Y. and Fox, R. (2008) Affordances of PDAs: undergraduate student perceptions, *Journal of the Research Center for Educational Technology*, **4** (1), 19–38.

The University of Hong Kong (2011) *Learning Commons: innovative spaces for student-centred learning*, www4.hku.hk/cecampus/eng/enews/article.php?id=15 (accessed 26 June 2013).

The University of Hong Kong (2013) *New 4-Year Undergraduate Curriculum*, http://tl.hku.hk/reform/ (accessed 23 June 2013).

Tsang, P., White, B., Fox, R. and Kwok, C. K. (2008) *An Educational Guide to IEEE802.11 Wireless LAN Survey and Visualisation Experiments*, Pearson Prentice Hall.

University of Hong Kong (n.d.) *New 4-Year Undergraduate Curriculum*, http://tl.hku.hk/reform/ (accessed 13 August 2013).

CHAPTER 5

European projects and trends

Joyce Sternheim and Rob Bruijnzeels

Introduction: the library is the message

A remarkable amount of attention is being devoted to library design in Europe at present. Never before have libraries been designed with such dedication and quality. Although we are in the midst of an economic crisis, new, surprising and sometimes even iconic library buildings are being constructed in many places. These buildings can all be seen as attempts to redefine and redesign the library.

This redefinition is essential, as great changes in our society demand radically different approaches to library work. One force that has affected the core functions of libraries is the exponential development of information technologies, particularly the internet, which has become the place where people form their identity, maintain contacts and deploy initiatives. It is a platform where anyone can be an information producer, a writer, an expert, a musician or a film maker. Increasingly, knowledge is exchanged in the numerous communities that are built around themes and areas of interest. People share their experiences and add their own knowledge, making use of their social networks and internet sources to do so. The resultant information overload gives rise to a need for new values, interpretation and meaning. A new phase has begun: the 'conceptual age', as the author Daniel Pink (2006) describes it. It is an age in which right-brain qualities such as creativity, empathy, imagination, spirituality and the ability to make exciting connections will make all the difference.

Traditional library processes, such as collection development and cataloguing, no longer provide an adequate response to these developments. The library will increasingly have to take on a co-ordinating and inspiring role in the process of knowledge creation and exchange. In an era of co-creation, the knowledge and expertise of users will be indispensable to this role. Libraries have to adapt their processes in such a way as to facilitate participation and co-creation. The real challenge is to manifest these processes in the library building of the future. How can we create the best environment for inspiration, learning, knowledge-sharing and storytelling?

To find answers to this question, we discuss four new libraries in the Netherlands and Germany. Each of these buildings was conceived on the basis of a specific vision regarding the function and meaning of the library; the vision was then translated into an exciting design. What do we notice about these designs? What are their similarities and differences? And, more importantly, do they incorporate elements of the library of the future?

Case studies

BK City

Keywords: integrated library

The making of BK City – BK is an abbreviation of the Dutch word 'bouwkunde', which means architecture – is a fascinating story, which started with a dramatic event (see TU Delft, 2009). BK City is the new faculty building belonging to the department of Architecture of Delft Technical University in the Netherlands. On 13 May 2008, the old faculty building was completely destroyed by fire. It was a tragic incident; not only were archive materials and scale models destroyed, but the building had also had great emotional significance for the students. It was their clubhouse, the place where they gathered in order to learn. So urgent was the need to create a new place that a 'pressure cooker' plan was drawn up immediately after the fire.

The first step was to find new premises as soon as possible, premises where workshop-style education could flourish at its best. The prime criterion was that students should be able to follow each other's development, thereby creating a fruitful exchange of ideas and experiences. Another criterion was flexibility; the space had to be adaptable so it could expand or change functions. The solution would be temporary in character and, given the urgency and limited financial resources, it was not intended to make it spectacular.

Within ten days, the choice was made to use a former university building nearly a century old. The design team, known as the BK City Five, got to work on redesigning the 32,000 square metres of space in the old building. Another

Image 5.1 *Open plan space at BK City (copyright Rob Bruijnzeels)*

4000 square metres was added by building glasshouses in the exterior spaces. In order to cut through the building's labyrinthine structure, a street was laid straight through the building: the main street of BK City (Image 5.1).

Amazingly enough, the building was ready for use on 13 May 2009, exactly one year after the fire. It contains many different spaces, including lecture halls, conference rooms, studio spaces, flexible office space, workshop rooms and informal space, as well as a restaurant and an espresso bar. It has a total of 500 workplaces for employees and 1900 places for students and visitors. Wi-fi is available throughout the building, giving access to digital sources at every spot. The library is located at the very centre of BK City. It offers about 50,000 collection items and 100 individual study places. The library is not the central place of learning, but it serves as a place for quiet study.

BK City is so special because the whole building actually functions like a library. BK City presents an environment where inspiration, learning and creativity are perfectly integrated. Quiet (computer) workspaces are interspersed with lively activity areas where scale models are constructed. Because all the spaces are interconnected, as they are open plan, the entire thought, inspiration and design processes of the students are made visible, from consultation of sources, progressing to the conception and computer-aided drawing of new buildings, through to the eventual construction of scale models. Students are constantly in contact with their fellow students' ideas, knowledge and learning processes. This is what makes BK City so inspiring: virtually every area functions as a learning place and the results of the learning process are literally visible in the whole building. One would also wish this to be the case in the library of the future. ■

The Book Mountain

Keywords: fantasy becomes reality

In 2000, the then unknown architect Winy Maas (who cofounded the Dutch architecture and urban design practice MVRDV) designed the Brabant Library. This library was intended to supersede all the other public libraries in the Dutch province of Noord-Brabant. Maas detested the mediocrity of all these small branch libraries, with their ugly buildings and incomplete collections. The 230-metre-high tower of the Brabant Library could accommodate the ultimate collection: nearly five million books arranged on 17 kilometres of spiralling shelves. However, the Brabant Library was never meant to be built. It was one of seven imaginary libraries that had been conceived in connection with the project Libraries 2040 (Bruijnzeels and van Tiggelen, 2001). Nevertheless, Maas was still able to turn his idea of a spiral-shaped library into reality.

In October 2012 a new public library, the Book Mountain, was opened in the Dutch town of Spijkenisse (Image 5.2). Spijkenisse was not exactly famed for its attractiveness as a residential town. To revitalize the town, a town centre plan was drawn up; this envisaged the building of a theatre, a library and a number of new apartments. The library was intended to become an architectural beacon in Spijkenisse and an attractive meeting place for the town's inhabitants.

An architectural prize competition was initiated, and Maas emerged as the winner. His design consists of a rectangular, red brick base surmounted by a tall, glass superstructure. Inside the building is a ziggurat, a terraced pyramid of successively receding stories. This pyramid is covered from base to apex with bookshelves, giving the optical impression of a mountain of books. A 480-metre-long spiral route winds around this mountain towards the top. The inside of the mountain is used as working and exhibition space, incorporating a theatre and children's department.

Mountains are there to be conquered, and the Book Mountain is no exception. It lures you upward, to the summit, where you can enjoy a panoramic view of the town from the café. The ascent takes you past a variety of spaces where you can read or study. There is also an internet piazza with 24 PCs and free wi-fi internet access. The ubiquitously dominating feature of the

Image 5.2 *Inside the Book Mountain (copyright Rob Bruijnzeels)*

mountain, however, is its building blocks: the books. And there is something remarkable going on in the arrangement of the books. The lower four shelves of the bookcases contain the current collection, while the shelves above contain reference books with their spines ostentatiously facing the inside. High above those stand books that nobody asks for these days. These now inaccessible books function solely as material with which to cover the mountain.

The Spijkenisse library is an iconic building that makes a statement about the eternal value of the book. At the same time, it is also a comment on increasing digitization. Already, some of the books are purely there for decoration; in the future, others will probably join them.

As a building the Book Mountain is a wonderfully inspiring environment that invites users to linger. It makes us aware that perceptions of architecture and space constitute a factor that should not be underestimated in future library design. ■

Stuttgart City Library

Keywords: no compromises

The City Library of Stuttgart, Germany, designed by the Korean architect Eun Young Yi, has the appearance of a dull grey, concrete cube (Image 5.3). This

Image 5.3 *Stuttgart City Library Gallery (copyright Rob Bruijnzeels)*

made the building controversial even before its opening on 24 October 2011. A heated debate arose concerning the austere, introverted look of the new library, and it soon attracted unflattering nicknames such as 'the book prison'. As soon as the library was illuminated in the evening with blue spotlights, the criticism became somewhat more muted. Only when people enter the building does scepticism give way to admiration. For it is then that the immense spaciousness and brightness of the almost exclusively white interior reveals itself, with books and people providing the colour.

In the heart of the library lies a completely empty, cathedral-like space, the design of which is based on the geometric structure of the Pantheon in Rome. The windows and niches in the high walls not only provide a pleasing ingress of light, but also create contact with the surrounding spaces of the library. The only embellishment is a tiny, square pool with a fountain in the centre of the floor. It is a space that symbolizes contemplation and a sense of connection. It encourages you to reflect on the sources of knowledge and wisdom that surround you.

Another eye-catching feature is the imposing gallery hall that overlooks the empty space. It is a modern interpretation of the book galleries familiar to us in the old, traditional libraries. As you would expect, you can find a wealth of books in this five-storey space.

The 40-metre high building has 11 levels, two of them underground. The collection is distributed over eight levels, each of them based on a certain theme. Visitors can find their way around the collections with the aid of interactive touch screen and the 60 PCs for research.

Despite its bookish character, the building is equipped with state-of-the-art technology. Automatic scanners allow books to be returned around the clock. Returned media are transported back to the right level by small computer-controlled electric carts, which run on a system of rails. Visitors can use their library card to borrow a laptop in order to study at one of the many workplaces.

To us, the Stuttgart City Library is absolutely one of the world's most beautiful libraries. There is no doubt that the design can be regarded as extreme, for where else in the world would you find a library with a purposeless space? With the almost museum-like layout of the books, this library emphasizes the concept that the book as an information source will still be of value in the future.

The design is based on the conception of the library as a physical place where knowledge is exchanged: the library as a place of inspiration, inviting people to think, learn, develop themselves and acquire knowledge. On the other hand, this is manifested in a fairly passive way. It is up to visitors to go in search of meaning in this spectacular kingdom of books. The wonderful empty space in the heart of the building certainly invites one to do this. It turns the City Library into an exceptional place of collection and reflection. ▬

O.A.S.E.

Keyword: silence

The new O.A.S.E. Medical Library is part of the Heinrich Heine University and the University Clinic in Düsseldorf, Germany. The building, designed by HPP Architects, replaced the old library, which had been spread over three different buildings. The new building was intended to provide the perfect space for exchange, study and development. The initial letters of these concepts in German (Ort des Austauschs, des Studiums und der Entwicklung, meaning place of exchange, study and development) together form the word O.A.S.E.: oasis.

The slim, 38-metre-tall building projects above the other buildings of the university campus. Across the striking white façade runs a network of organic glass shapes. It is the architectural expression of a capillary system (Image 5.4).

The flowing structure of the façade is also continued in the interior. The open plan study and work zones in the eight-storey building have organic forms that merge into each other. They are situated around a green, cylindrical

Image 5.4 *O.A.S.E. exterior (copyright Rob Bruijnzeels)*

core that houses the stairs and the lift. In addition, there are 20 enclosed, rectangular group study rooms arranged along the façade walls. The library accommodates 476 individual study/reading places, 20 study rooms, an e-learning area with 30 computer workplaces and several social spaces. On the ground floor you can find a cafeteria and a forum.

Power points and network connections are available everywhere to enable unlimited use of laptops. Many areas also have interactive whiteboards or screens where groups of students who bring their own laptops can still learn and work together.

The most noticeable aspect of O.A.S.E. is its tranquil atmosphere. It gets steadily quieter in the building as you go from top to bottom. Absolute silence is required on most floors. Students work there in utmost concentration and look somewhat disturbed even when someone comes in. For that reason, a remarkable degree of attention has been devoted to acoustic insulation. All the rooms are as soundproof as possible.

The aims were to create motivating and comfortable individual and group learning spaces, a variety of opportunities for study and work, state-of-the-art technology and areas of recreation and communication. This mission has largely been accomplished. O.A.S.E. offers more modern and well designed learning spaces than any library we have seen so far. However, the social spaces are not as welcoming and engaging as they could be. Despite the use of lively colours and attractive, organically shaped furniture, these spaces do not really come to life. Without doubt, this is because there is virtually no place where students are allowed to eat or drink, as a result of the absence of a co-ordinated concept. The old building lacked study places and spaces for meeting and conversation. In the new building it seems as if these have simply been tacked on, with no thought given to the interaction between the various spaces and the desired overall effect. It goes to show that you cannot simply 'facilitate' meeting and interaction by creating an attractive environment, furnishing it with some comfortable chairs and providing decent coffee. You also need to add character to the place. Although the façade may refer to a capillary system, there is nothing in the interior to indicate that one is looking at the library of the medical faculty. It could just as well be that of the law faculty. By making an interior so nondescript, you create a feeling of apartness and hence quite the wrong atmosphere for exchanging knowledge and sharing experiences. ■

Trends

We do not claim to have a set of design criteria based on viewing these buildings, but we can list some aspects and features that are important to future library learning space design.

The first is the need for a strong conceptual approach. This is absent in O.A.S.E., with the result that the spaces, although attractively designed in themselves, do not form a cohesive whole. The outstanding characters of BK City, the Book Mountain and Stuttgart City Library are largely due to the highly conceptual approach that was chosen for them. In BK City, the metaphor of the city was used to create a bustling and varied environment. The Book Mountain presents the library as a mountain of knowledge that literally asks to be conquered. Stuttgart City Library has not explicitly opted for a metaphor, but does constantly suggest one. The hallowed atmosphere of the empty interior space, the austere architecture and the fact that the building towers above the other urban buildings strongly remind one of a cathedral – in this case, a cathedral of knowledge. As buildings, the Book Mountain and Stuttgart City Library have a strong 'wow' factor. With great bravado and self-assurance, they assert a place for the library as perhaps the last bastion of knowledge and wisdom. Both exert a great force of attraction on the public. They are inspiring places where one is keen to spend a number of hours. Furthermore, thanks to their exciting architecture, the buildings themselves are conversation starters. They prove that a powerful conceptual design is an inestimable factor in the successful development of new libraries.

O.A.S.E. also has striking architecture. Each of the individual spaces has been meticulously designed, with much attention to colour composition and acoustic insulation. It is a place where you can work with the utmost concentration, which is exactly what the students do. However, O.A.S.E. is not an attractive place for exchange and communication. The social spaces are not inviting. They are sparsely furnished, no artwork decorates the walls, and they have no books or magazines. One would expect that students would leave their mark in such a space, demonstrating what they are occupied with or the results of their interaction. Instead, one could see empty bulletin boards all around. It teaches us that interesting design work and custom-made furniture do not automatically produce lively and inspiring social spaces. There has to be something in such a space to stimulate people, make them curious and invite them to respond: art, an interesting question, a conversation piece or perhaps even something disruptive – anything that might help to stimulate conversation.

Using the collection to define the space is a second powerful idea. The Book Mountain and Stuttgart City Library are both collection-driven libraries. They turn the collection into a monument, thereby underscoring the archetype of the library as a collection. The Book Mountain displays the collection in a condensed form. The size of the mountain may be awe-inspiring and challenging, but at the same time it remains comprehensible – what you see is what you get. Stuttgart City Library also shows the collection to its full extent. Here we have a repository of knowledge that seems too large to comprehend. Fortunately, it also has the empty space where you can experience tranquillity, a space that invites you to contemplate all the knowledge, culture and information that surrounds you. However, no matter how imaginatively these libraries present their collection books and journals are still primarily a passive way of providing access to knowledge and information. As we wrote in our introduction, in the current era this is not an adequate response to the information overload and the need for deeper interpretation. The library will have to take a more active role in the process of knowledge creation and exchange. To do this we first have to grasp the essence of library work. What is essential and what needs to change? This requires us to think about the 'soul' of library work, about the original values and qualities, which are timeless.

In our view the primary role of libraries is to support the personal development of people. They facilitate the acquisition of knowledge by bringing people into contact with sources of information and (cultural) knowledge and providing them with the necessary skills to use these sources in an effective way. Current library operations still focus on the rather passive role of facilitator, but providing access to sources of information and knowledge does not automatically lead to a better understanding or to knowledge development. To survive and thrive libraries will have to support the development of the right-brain qualities that we mentioned in our introduction: the creativity, empathy, imagination and ability to make exciting connections, which take us from text to context, from details to the big picture, and from argument to story. How can this be done? In his book *The Atlas of New Librarianship,* David Lankes (2011) suggests a new mission for librarians: to improve society through facilitating knowledge creation in their communities. He redefines librarianship and library practice using the fundamental concept that knowledge is created though conversation. In his view, librarians should become facilitators of conversation; they should 'seek to enrich, capture, store, and disseminate the conversations of their communities'. The collection, including physical and digital media, can play a key role in the stimulation of conversations. It is a catalyst in the process of developing knowledge and giving meaning. It all starts with inspiration. By designing new and exciting ways of presenting the collection, libraries can trigger people's curiosity and interest. In essence, this already starts the first 'level of conversation': the inner dialogue that is engendered when you read a book, watch a film or take in information in some other way. After all, the new information coming in interacts with the knowledge, information and thoughts already inside your head. The library can then further enrich this inner dialogue by offering context; by showing everything that has been thought and written in relation to a subject. It gets even better, however, if the library stimulates its users to make their own connections in the collection, helping them to engage in further exploration and reflection. When they subsequently share the result with other users, even more new conversations are initiated. In Chapter 18 of this book we give an example of how this could work. We describe a project in which library visitors are challenged to discover new connections right across the collection and to share these with each other.

What we are really talking about are the new, more active processes of inspiration, creation and sharing that should be the main focus of future libraries:

- 'inspiration' – designing new and exciting ways to present the collection
- 'creation' – adding new and valuable significance to the collection
- 'sharing' – presenting and sharing acquired knowledge and insights with other users.

The old definition of the term 'collection' is no longer applicable here. A collection is no longer just an accumulation of physical and digital sources that the library offers. It is also about people, the knowledge they have at their disposal, and the conversations that are initiated when they share this knowledge with each other.

The big question is this: how can library design ensure that the knowledge and conversations of users become part of the collection? How do you record the new insights and newly acquired knowledge that they have gained via the collection and each other? In other words, how do you make knowledge reproducible? We do not know the definitive answer to this question, nor do we know how to create the right environment for the new processes of inspiration, creation and sharing. How can the library encourage people to share new insights and acquired knowledge? And how can we adapt the space to these new functions? There is no 'one size fits all' model for learning spaces in libraries. Apart from the fact that this would be terribly dull, it is simply not possible. Whether public libraries, special libraries or academic libraries, their design will always have to be adapted to their own users and the context of the surrounding community, so designs will have to be even more specific.

To find answers, we will definitely need a generous amount of right-brain qualities: the creativity, empathy and imagination we mentioned in our introduction. And we can only subsequently find out what works and what doesn't by experimentation. It is highly advisable, when doing this, to engage the help of experts from other disciplines: artists, philosophers, policymakers, public space designers, information designers and so on. They can help us to transcend the ingrained concepts of library work and develop truly new concepts – concepts that enable the library to evolve into a learning environment in which a continuous process of interaction takes place, between users and between the users and the collection. The library is then a nursery and podium where perspectives and insights are organized and shared, where one confronts one's own ideas and those of others. In Chapter 18, we demonstrate the surprising results that can be achieved when designers view library processes from the angle of their own vision.

To what extent have our four library case studies succeeded in creating the right environment for the new processes of inspiration, creation and sharing? The Book Mountain and Stuttgart City Library are remarkable for their architecture and for the unusual way in which the entire scope of their collection is displayed. This is awe-inspiring, without a doubt, but does not necessarily tempt one to embrace that knowledge or to share it with others. In our view inspiration is generated by seeing what other people have done with all that knowledge and information from the sources, and the new perspectives and associations that this has resulted in. When the sources are subsequently supplemented by this new knowledge and the new connections, a circular process of inspiration, creation and sharing comes into existence. The major challenge facing the Book Mountain and Stuttgart City Library is to manifest this circular process in the magnificent space that is available to them.

The same applies to O.A.S.E., but this also faces the additional task of creating a sense of community. As it stands, O.A.S.E. is a place where individuals collect; what it should be is a place where students know that they are bound together by a common goal: to study medicine and exchange insights on the subject. If it is not even apparent from the layout and décor of the space that this is a medical faculty, one cannot expect it to create a feeling of community that will encourage students to exchange ideas.

BK City is the only one of the four libraries that has succeeded in designing the ideal environment for the new processes of inspiration, creation and sharing. This is cheating a bit, because we are not talking about the actual library of BK City, but about the whole faculty building. To us, BK City is the representation of the ideal learning landscape. The integration of study, creation and exchange – so essential to the learning process – is tangible and visible throughout the building. The environment radiates the kind of vivaciousness and creativity that one would wish to find in any library. The fact that the results of the learning process are literally displayed in the building makes an enormous contribution to this. This would presumably be somewhat harder to achieve in a medical faculty library than in an architecture faculty, but it still provides food for thought. From now on, the question will not only be about how libraries can develop into lively and inspiring learning places; it will also be about how they can make the results of the learning processes visible in the building and collection.

BK City also teaches us that we have to approach the question of library space in a different way. The library of the future is a function that can manifest itself in different places and ways, regardless of the space that was once allocated to it. The library is no longer the place where the collection is located; instead, it is the sum total of the spaces in which the library's various services and facilities are offered. Place becomes space.

BK City was originally intended as temporary accommodation, but it became such a wonderful place that nobody wanted to leave it. It was therefore decided, in 2010, that BK City would be the faculty's permanent home. Should we take less time in library building development and adopt a more experimental approach that produces temporary solutions, enabling us to come up with more innovative designs – and throw away the ones that don't work?

References

Bruijnzeels, R. and van Tiggelen, N. (2001) *Bibliotheken 2040: de toekomst in uitvoering (Libraries 2040)*, Biblion.

Lankes, R. D. (2011) *The Atlas of New Librarianship*, MIT Press.

Pink, D. H. (2006) *A Whole New Mind*, Riverhead Books.

TU Delft (2009) *The Making of BK City*, Delft University of Technology.

CHAPTER 6

Australasian projects and trends

Roland Sussex, Peter Tregloan and Phil Long

Introduction: space and place, or working with the tyranny of distance

In 1966 the Australian historian Geoffrey Blainey published *The Tyranny of Distance: how distance shaped Australia's history*. This study has become well known for its explicit evocation of the large empty spaces of Terra Australis. Blainey's initial interest was in the cost imposed by distance on commodities and people, but the idea of linking distance and tyranny has had much wider resonance, in the ways in which Australians think of themselves and the space they inhabit.

Australia is largely empty – 23 million people occupy a land mass not much smaller than the continental USA. Australia is also highly urbanized. Overall it has a population density of 2.9 per square kilometre, the sixth lowest on the planet. This compares with the USA, which has 12 times that population density, and the UK with 93 times. But even this figure for Australia is deceptive. Over a third of Australia's population lives in just two cities – Sydney and Melbourne, so large tracts of Australia are very sparsely populated indeed. Consequently libraries have been forced to think of their coverage in much wider terms than the suburb or town where they are sited. The libraries in parts of Sydney cater for users in a library space similar to those of urban centres in Europe or the USA. In contrast, the library in Telfer, a mining town in the Pilbara region of Western Australia situated 1300 km from Perth, the capital of Western Australia, is one of the most isolated.

Until recently traditional models of library space were clearly expressed in the different kinds of libraries in Australia: the National Library of Australia in Canberra; the state and territory libraries in their capitals; the suburban libraries in the cities; and the country libraries. This model of library space was centripetal – libraries drew people to visit them – and directive, as if saying: 'Here I am, with my resources, you are welcome to come and use them as specified in the traditional conventions for library use.' Against this, however, has been a strong commitment to outreach in order to include readers who live too far away to allow easy access to a library or branch library. The Country Library Service in many states has been central to this outreach. Readers would send the central library in their state a profile of interests and favoured authors. Librarians would select several books matching the profile, and the books would be packed and sent to readers, without charge. The arrival of the weekly parcel of books in their brown paper wrapping – by post, rail, road, bus, truck, camel, plane and other means – has been an eagerly anticipated aspect of country life for a century. The readers paid only for the postal costs of returning the books to the library (Johnstone, 2012). A more recent model of outreach is found in mobile branch libraries, which operate in suburban and rural areas to bring library services to readers who find it hard to visit a library building in the larger centres.

A great deal of the thinking, policy making and operations of libraries in Australia has therefore been focused on neutralizing the down-side of distance. As travel times have shortened, the subjective idea of isolation has shifted. Qantas, the world's second oldest airline still in operation, was founded in 1920 and played a major role in communications in outback Australia. Telephony, radio, television and now digital networks have been avidly adopted for communication, education, culture and entertainment. Libraries in Australia were early adopters of digital technology in the 1990s with initiatives like the Information and Libraries Access Network, ILANET, which linked 2000 libraries in Australia using the x.25 protocol, and provided connections to 25 countries overseas. The key strategic importance of networks was captured in *Bushtrack to Superhighway: public access to electronic information* (Wright and Peasley, 1995). When you live in a space as large as Australia, such mechanisms are even more urgent than in heavily populated urban centres, or even rural centres, in Europe or Asia.

If libraries are to reach out to cover space, then their working models have to combine architectural with geographical space. Rather than operating in three dimensions with fixed spatial co-ordinates, our chapter addresses situations where the three dimensions are not limited to the boundaries of the physical buildings. Or to put it another way, the libraries that we describe are in certain respects both spatial and aspatial.

The traditional library was primarily centripetal: It offered a collection and services to which readers and users were drawn. The models we explore are also centrifugal, not just in terms of library space, but more particularly in terms of services and access to resources. Information technology does not only bring new access to people in remote communities; it can also substantially enrich the work of local libraries by removing many of the physical limitations of their collections and services.

In terms of space – as in buildings, ergonomics, people, equipment and functions – Australia's libraries have long been at or close to the front of the wave in inventing new spaces for libraries to fill and use (Biskup, 1994). What is especially distinctive about Australia, however, is the Blainey sense of geographical space as a real or potential tyranny. For this reason we have five case studies that embody five key features of space, which are distinctive of libraries in Australia. In one sense these cases represent the front end of the wave in Australian thinking and evolution of the library space for the 21st century; they are not necessarily representative. But in their focus and direction they certainly stand for key elements of the Australian library of the future.

Our principal example libraries are from Queensland, which is the library domain that we know best. Many other libraries in Australia are exemplars of one or more of the characteristics we highlight for discussion.

Case studies

Cooroy Library: climactic and environmental space

Keywords: ecology, environment
Newer libraries in Australia often give physical expression to their relation to the climate and environment. Queensland (population 4.6 million) is a very large space indeed, measuring 1.7 million square kilometres, seven times the size of the British Isles, or nearly three times the size of Texas. It is prototypically a place of sun, with seascapes to the east and north, and has large, hot, semi-arid inland stretches of country with little human habitation.

An example of an indicative library, which has a highly integrated environmental design, is the new library in Cooroy (stress on the second syllable), a country town of 2300 people situated 140 km to the north of Brisbane and part of the relatively affluent Sunshine Coast hinterland. Cooroy was originally a logging town, and the decline in the logging industry led to a major decline in the town and its social and economic life. The Library has

Image 6.1 *Looking down into the inner courtyard of the Library of Cooroy (courtesy Amie Boltjes and Luigi Staiano of Brewster Hjorth Architects)*

played a major part in reviving and focusing what is now a lively and vibrant rural community. The building has exceptional properties of environmental design and energy planning, and makes extensive use of diffused natural lighting (Image 6.1).

The Cooroy Library, which was opened in 2010, has exceptional design features that allow it to be part of its space without imposing an ecological cost. The building is cut into the ground, and part of the roof is covered with soil and grass, which helps to stabilize the temperature inside. The ventilation is designed so that cool air enters low on the walls and hot air exits near the roofline, saving about 30% in air-conditioning costs. A thermal solar-driven system on the roof heats the Library's water, and photovoltaic panels generate around 9000 kW hours per year of electricity. An underground labyrinth system with 1.2-metre-diameter pipes enables a saving of about 22,000 kW per year by providing free cool air for temperature control. A 20,000 litre water tank under the library collects rain water for use and irrigation.

The Library's light comes principally from diffused natural daylight, with verandas shading the windows from direct contact with the sun, so minimizing heat gain. At one end the library has a play area for children that is continuous with the roofed area of the library itself, and opens on to an outside playground.

There are meeting rooms for community and educational activities, and heritage rooms for work on local history and culture. The Library is connected to the fastest currently available digital network on the Sunshine Coast.

In its design, ergonomics, aesthetics and functionality this building is an imaginative and ecologically responsible statement of how to live and work in and with Queensland conditions. These conditions can be extreme, because Queensland can also be a place of droughts, cyclones and floods. Buildings and infrastructure have to be designed to be resilient to winds which can reach 250 kph in a Category 4 cyclone, and to floods which can rise rapidly and catastrophically; in the 2011 floods 75% of Queensland was declared a disaster zone.

But most of the time the environment is warm, amiable and bathed in a sunlight of special sharpness. The climate is such that people spend most of the year with their doors and windows open, and the flow of fresh air is central to vernacular architecture. This idea of open-to-the-air, and its metaphor 'open to all' or 'All yours', the motto of the State Library of Queensland (SLQ) in Brisbane, is well expressed in the imposing spaces of its Knowledge Walk. This area is roofed but not enclosed, and the space is open in every sense to the physical and social world outside (Image 6.2). ■

Image 6.2 *View from the Knowledge Walk at the State Library of Queensland in Brisbane (courtesy State Library of Queensland)*

Mt Gambier Library: centres for social gathering and interaction

Keywords: community, culture

Libraries are now increasingly planned in consultation with the communities that they serve. Well known international models include the libraries in Aarhus, Denmark (Hanspul, 2012), and Seattle, USA (The Seattle Public Library, 2013). The design and function of the Cooroy (above) and Mt Gambier (Mount Gambier Public Library, 2013) libraries were based on community needs determined through extensive and ongoing consultation. The result is libraries that are welcoming, open, attractive and responsive to community needs.

The Library's own self-description is friendly and supportive, with the recurring theme of 'our place'. The Mt Gambier Library (Image 6.3) won the 2012 Jim Crawford Award for Library Innovation (Local Government Association of South Australia, 2012).

It is common for Australian libraries to have not just children's corners, but well equipped children's sections, catering for all ages from toddlers upwards. These are supervised spaces with trained librarians in charge, and offer the children – and their older siblings and parents – a wide range of activities, play, early literacy and other learning and social opportunities. In suburban and provincial libraries parents often bring their children to the library after the evening meal, in their slippers and pyjamas, to borrow books, share stories and play before bedtime. In this way the early evening library visit brings together Mt Gambier's 'our place' with the 'third space' (Oldenburg, 1989, 1991): a place for people to come together, after home (the first space), and work or school (the second space). An impressive example of this is the library in Darien, Connecticut, a town of 20,000 where 88% of the eligible citizens are signed-up members of the library (www.darienlibrary.org/). In contrast – albeit over a much larger and less cohesive space – in 2012 less than half (44.9%) of Queenslanders were members of a public library (SGS Economics and Planning Pty Ltd, 2012, 17).

This community value of libraries is strongly demonstrated in the heavy use of their meeting rooms and auditoria. Some of these are for meetings of community organizations, some are for teaching and learning, some are for discussion and cultural groups. Libraries are not constrained by the kinds of walls that surround institutions like universities. Nor are they directly part of political organizations or parties, unlike local government. This means that they can be part of true democracy, a term which has been increasingly used of libraries and their roles over the past few years (see the Seattle library, above). Multiculturalism, for instance, is an issue that has become heavily politicized in Australia, as in the UK and USA. A library, on the other hand, is

Image 6.3 *The Library at Mount Gambier, South Australia – open in the evening; colourful, bright, welcoming – under a very large sky (courtesy City of Mount Gambier)*

not politically engaged, and so is freer to host conferences on these topics, and can function as an instrument of community discussion (RN Big Ideas, 2013). And events like the Brisbane Writers (sic) (2013) Festival, which are held at the State Library and attract around 30,000 attendees, show how a programme of events can map on to the physical spaces through shared metaphors of flexibility and interaction.

Australia's library models, then, are socially strongly engaged in the local community. Libraries are increasingly places of social cohesion and community gathering: free and welcoming spaces for community activities, groups, classes, cultural activities, learning and sharing. In a sense which was not true a generation ago, libraries now respond to communities, and reach out to the communities which they serve. This is a fundamental change of philosophy. ■

The Edge, State Library of Queensland (SLQ): technology crucibles and creative laboratories

---

Keywords: connected, creative

The social needs of a community depend partly on shared physical space. Where homes and patrons are disconnected from the information world of the internet the shared digitally connected physical spaces of libraries can also offer gateways to internet access and cyberspace: 'In Queensland 40% of the population would not have access to computers and the internet if it weren't for their public libraries' (SGS Economics and Planning Pty Ltd, 2012). After-school and early evening bookings for computer use in the libraries typically involve waves of school students doing homework and projects. There are numerous computer and internet training courses for users of all ages, with strong uptake among retirees and people whose education and working life did not include computer use. The connectivity theme has further implications. SLQ has free wi-fi, a fact known to every back-packer who visits Brisbane. It is common to hear many young (and some not so young) tourists checking in with family and friends by Skype on their laptops or mobile phones in Chinese, Korean, Japanese, Vietnamese, Indonesian-Malay, French, Spanish, Swedish, Tigrinya and many other languages, from the various open public areas of the library. One of their first spatial experiences of Brisbane is through the library, its facilities, resources and staff.

Technology therefore meets the library's civic commitment to the 'third space' in new and transformative ways. The original conceptual meaning, of neutral public spaces for a community to connect and establish bonds, becomes a technologically enabled transformation of third spaces as places that are public, open, accessible virtual environments where community and personal relationships are formed and explored.

Within the library the notions of information, resources and stacks is shifting, too, as material is digitized and physical books are less the centrepiece of the library – with the important and telling exception of heritage and historical collections, and the legal deposit obligations of libraries (though legal deposit of digital artefacts remains a work very much in progress). And reference sections are shrinking in physical size as they expand hugely in conceptual and information senses. At SLQ reference librarians are no longer anchored to the reference desk, but move around the library with iPads, answering users' questions as they arise in situ.

The notion of the Library as a technology crucible also involves creativity and the creative arts. SLQ has established The Edge (http://edgeqld.org.au/), a laboratory where scientists, artists, journalists and multimedia specialists meet to collaborate. Libraries are emerging as laboratories for creating content of many kinds. The shift is from collecting, organizing, curating and making accessible content to the facilitation of its creation, particularly in the digital realm. And because of their community engagement and outreach, libraries are able to include, train and nurture talent from all parts of the community. Teenagers, for instance, can be guided through the creation of a musical recording, captured on DVD, and then helped with its marketing and strategies for the public exposure of their work. The Edge has groups of what it calls 'catalysts' and 'residents', experts who join the work space and contribute to making such things happen.

The outreach and interconnectivity of libraries in Australia will be radically enhanced by the National Broadband Network (NBN; www.nbn.gov.au/), a high-speech fibre-optic communication system, which is currently being rolled out, and will eventually connect 92% of Australia's population (the other 8% will have either fixed wireless or satellite connections). Libraries, as prototypically 'open' institutions, will be ideally placed to exploit its information, education, innovation and social benefits. The greater the distance, and therefore the greater the tyranny of distance, the greater the correction that can be provided by a high-speed national network. Although subject to some political to-and-fro among the major parties, Australia expects to have a high-speed national network operating by 2020. ▪

Queensland's indigenous knowledge centres: indigenous culture, learning and spatial connectivity

---

Keywords: outreach, inclusion

Among Australia's more isolated habitations are Aboriginal and Torres Strait Islander communities, the former on the mainland and coastal islands, and the latter on the islands of the Torres Strait between Australia and Papua New Guinea. These communities, numbering from 200 to about 3000, can find themselves separated from provincial or urban centres not only by raw kilometres, but by circumstances where travel can be long and problematic. Travel to islands in the Torres Strait, for instance, may require both air and sea travel, the latter in small boats, and may be impossible during the summer cyclone season.

SLQ, based in the capital Brisbane in the south-east corner of the state, is the hub of a network of 340 libraries spread across the state. SLQ has established a network of libraries to address the special needs of these Aboriginal and Torres Strait Islander communities. This is the Indigenous Knowledge Centre (IKC) Network. There are currently 23 IKCs, and more are being prepared. The northernmost IKC is on Boigu Island, within eyesight of Papua New Guinea, 2600 kilometres north of Brisbane.

The IKC Network is a co-ordinated attempt to provide more remote communities with a range of communication, education and cultural benefits, centred on the library. IKCs belong to the local council, who also pay half the salary of the co-ordinator. SLQ pays the other half, and provides funds for collection building, training, advice, and IT support and connectivity to collections, advice, information and databases. IKCs are not just local libraries, though they fulfil that role with energy and imagination. Their role in education and schooling has dramatically increased the range and quality of learning available to library users. Some of the smaller communities which they serve, especially in the Torres Strait, are geographically extremely isolated. Microwave networks link them to the Australian mainland digital network, and the IKC is the key connection point in many of the communities. There are immediate gains in education, literacy, commerce and information access. In addition, social tasks like banking are enormously accelerated and facilitated. Banking used to require paperwork to be sent by air or sea to a mainland bank, with substantial costs. Islanders can now log on to their internet bank via the IKC, and do their banking free and in minutes. Image 6.4 shows the IKC on Palm Island off the Barrier Reef in North-East Queensland, 1200 kilometres north of Brisbane. The size of the sign indicates its importance to the community. 'Bwgcolman' is the name of the Indigenous inhabitants of Palm Island.

The integration of social tasks and community communication around IKCs is working out very productively in a number of ways. A key role for IKCs is to document and record the culture of the community. Until recently, older members of the community died without recording their stories, rituals, songs and dances. Now the programme Culture Love seeks to capture and record these aspects of the local culture. Younger members of the community acquire the necessary skills in driving the multimedia equipment, editing and presentation at the Culture Love Children's Workshop (www.slq.qld.gov.au/resources/atsi/contemporary-stories/retold/culture-love-childrens-workshop). A

Image 6.4 *The IKC on Palm Island off the Barrier Reef in North-East Queensland (courtesy State Library of Queensland)*

serendipitous corollary is that older community members acquire digital skills as they work with the younger folk on these projects. Septuagenarians learn how to operate a computer, acquire an e-mail address, and become active internet users. Through SLQ's network they can access other communities and share cultural events. And younger people not only learn the kinds of digital skills which are increasingly expected for all kinds of employment, which also reinforce literacy, numeracy and graphic arts; they also capture, preserve, share and celebrate their cultural values and practices as digital literacy meets cultural literacy. ▪

National and State Libraries of Australasia

Keywords: co-ordination, consolidation

National and State Libraries of Australasia (NSLA; www.nsla.org.au/; formerly CASL, the Council of Australian State Libraries) is the umbrella organization of the National and State Libraries of Australasia. It includes the National Libraries of New Zealand and Australia, the six state libraries of New South Wales, Queensland, South Australia, Tasmania, Victoria and Western Australia, and the two territory libraries in the Australian Capital Territory and the Northern Territory. It was established in 2008 on the basis of a shared sense of the need to co-ordinate and consolidate resources and expertise across Australia and New Zealand, and to maximize access and usability, involving a distributed and enriched library store, for the 27.5 million people within its ambit.

NSLA brings together the two national librarians (Australia's in Canberra, New Zealand's in Wellington), six state librarians and two territory librarians for meetings three times a year. This general co-ordinating structure is not unique to Australasia, though it is internationally more unusual in spanning more than one country.

NSLA has a number of projects and initiatives, which make it operationally much more than a sharing of information and policies, and it actively works both to minimize the disadvantages of distance, and to maximize resources, holdings, expertise and services to its clients in Australia and New Zealand. Under the umbrella of a vision statement *Re-Imagining Libraries 2012–2016* (National State Libraries, 2012), specialized focus teams chosen from the participating libraries are working on topics like:

- archival collections
- digital collections and preservation
- collaborative collections
- community created content
- indigenous material
- literacy and learning
- open borders and open access in a wider sense
- storage management (what hardware and software are suitable for continuous use into the future?).

NSLA is committed to co-ordinating expertise and maximizing resources across space. A reader in Wellington, New Zealand, with an online question about 18th-century maritime cartography, could find themselves transferred to the appropriate expert in Perth, Western Australia. NSLA's strategies are: 'One library', 'Enabling people' and 'Accessible content'. ■

Conclusion

In the 1983 revised edition of *The Tyranny of Distance* Blainey reflected: 'Distance has been visibly tamed in the last quarter century but it has not been conquered. Distance has been tamed more quickly on the map than in the mind' (1983, 341).

The advent of electronic networks has begun to turn this judgement on its head. The physical distances of Australia remain, despite substantial improvements in surface, water and air transport. But for people who live outside the cities and larger provincial centres, distance persists as a constant background, when one needs specialist medical attention, for example, which can only be accessed in a larger hospital after many hours of driving or a flight provided by Royal Flying Doctor service (www. flyingdoctor.net). But the notion of Australia as a flat, communicable space is taking hold, and libraries are among the leaders. As the high-speed NBN rolls out, subjective distance will shrink even further. Already distance education is bringing opportunities to people living in 'the bush' (outside the urban areas) that were either unthinkable or impractical before, because of delays enforced by slow mechanical communications.

It's not easy to capture the various competing directions for the library of the 21st century. As JISC's 2011 *Scenarios for 2050* noted, we can imagine three scenarios for 2050 in higher education, the focus of their report:

- 'the wild west': uncontrolled capitalism and competition
- 'the beehive', with highly developed social sharing and structure, based on openness
- 'the walled garden', where intellectual property is protected behind barriers.

Our view is that the scenario that best fits the developing public library in Australia is 'the beehive', which 'is a world in which society and [higher education] have open values and the state is the primary funder and controller of [higher education]. Its overriding aim is the production of a skilled workforce' (JISC, 2011, 1.6.4). Our concern in this chapter is not specifically with higher education. Indeed, we believe that the membrane between 'higher' and 'other' education will be progressively blurred by lifelong learning, and the many kinds of 'openness' that will accompany, and catalyze, this development (Suber, 2012). But the key beehive elements of openness and state funding, plus digital networking, provide libraries with a huge opportunity. As the most developed and community-integrated instrumentality, libraries are ideally placed to share and propagate knowledge, culture, creativity and innovation. And they will do this from a spatial location, to an aspatial audience, which could be anywhere on the planet. This overlaps with the domain of the aspatial library in extended, extensive geographical space. Apart from the inconvenience of different time zones, synchronous usage of library facilities, as we have outlined them, is growing steadily more distance-neutral in Australia. Asynchronous access is even more effective. Given access to a cellular network, everyone in Australasia is able to use substantially the same resources online. This capacity will become even richer as NSLA makes progress with its various projects.

But at the same time as it is becoming aspatial, the Australian library is also reinforcing its spatial, social role, suggesting that libraries may well become one of the last free public spaces. Libraries are moving fast to fill new needs, arising both directly and indirectly from the information revolution. Far from withering as the conventional printed book and other print media decline, libraries are reinventing not only their roles, but also the space where they sit, and the way they relate to it in social and geographical terms.

References

Biskup, P. (1994) *Libraries in Australia*, Centre for Information Studies.

Blainey, G. (1983) *The Tyranny of Distance: how distance shaped Australia's history*, 2nd edn, Sun Books.

Brisbane Writers Festival (2013) *Every Side of the Story*, http://bwf.org.au (accessed 1 July 2013).

Hanspul (2012) *Places. Aarhus' Mediascape Library: new concepts for an old institution*, http://blog.inpolis.com/2012/07/23/aarhus/ (accessed 1 July 2013).

JISC (2011) *Scenarios for 2050: rethinking library scenarios*, www.futurelibraries.info/content/page/scenarios-2050-0 (accessed 14 August 2013).

Johnstone, L. (2012) *Small Rural Libraries: alternative service delivery models*, www.plconnect.slq.qld.gov.au/__data/assets/pdf_file/0006/229911/small-rural-library-services-models-20120530.pdf (accessed 14 August 2013).

Local Government Association of South Australia (2012) Jim Crawford Award, www.lga.sa.gov.au/page.aspx?u=579 (accessed 1 July 2013).

Mount Gambier Public Library (2013) *Learn, Connect, Explore*, www.mountgambier.sa.gov.au/library/ (accessed 1 July 2013).

National State Libraries (2012) *Re-Imagining Libraries 2012-2016*, www.nsla.org.au/reimagining-libraries (accessed 1 July 2013).

Oldenburg, R. (1989) *The Great Good Place: cafés, coffee shops, community centers, beauty parlors, general stores, bars, hangouts, and how they get you through the day*, Paragon House.

Oldenburg, R. (1991) *The Great Good Place*, Marlowe & Company.

RN Big Ideas (2013) *Vision for Libraries in a Digital and Multicultural World*, www.abc.net.au/radionational/programs/bigideas/vision-for-libraries-in-a-digital-and-multicultural-world/4279650 (accessed 1 July 2013).

SGS Economics and Planning Pty Ltd (2012) *The Library Dividend Technical Report: a study of the socio-economic value of Queensland public libraries* (2012) www.slq.qld. gov.au/__data/assets/pdf_file/0009/225864/the-library-dividend-technical-report.pdf (accessed 14 August 2013).

Suber, P. (2012) *Open Access Overview*, www.earlham.edu/~peters/fos/overview.htm (accessed 5 January 2013).

The Seattle Public Library (2013) *About the Library: Libraries For All: investing in experiences*, www.spl.org/about-the-library/libraries-for-all/lfa-plan (accessed 1 July 2013).

Wright, J. and Peasley, J. (1995) *Bushtrack to Superhighway: public access to electronic information*, State Library of New South Wales.

Background references

For population density data, see www.infoplease.com/ipa/A0934666.html (accessed 17 March 2013).

For airline data, see http://en.wikipedia.org/wiki/List_of_airlines_by_foundation_date (accessed 13 March 2013).

Summary to Part 1

Les Watson

It is striking that in describing the case studies above, all authors, without prompting, have felt the need to include, in some cases considerable, information about the locality of the libraries that they describe. Each is to some extent a response to its locality and inseparable from it. Not surprisingly, then, in their chapter on Europe, Joyce Sternheim and Rob Bruijnzeels conclude from their cases that 'no one size fits all' in library and learning space design. All authors also refer to the need for these buildings and their spaces to respond to the issues of technology, flexibility of space, variety of environment, and development of community and culture. Local diversity and variety of emphasis plays an important part in the overall picture here, too. For example the technology focus for Australasian libraries is an external one to overcome the tyranny of distance in addition to the more general focus on technology-rich environments being created within buildings – illustrating again that 'no one size fits all' even within these common threads. And nor should it. Creating a standard formula-driven library replicated across the world would do little to serve local communities and would be agnostic to diversity of culture.

The overall key trends in library space development implicit in these case studies include responses to the impact of ubiquitous technology and its effect on information availability and study habits, the use of open plan space, and integration of services through co-location with the library or assimilation into it. These trends lead to community development around service provision or learning activities, and the resulting ideas of participation and co-creation of new knowledge transforming the concept of 'the collection'. There is also a recognition that space is not isolated and cannot be divorced from service provision so that ultimately reformulation of space inevitably leads to rethinking roles within the library.

The Jisc (Future Libraries) beehive model mentioned in Chapter 6, with its 'highly developed social sharing structure', provides a concept that is shared between all the libraries featured in the academic and public sectors. It focuses on those using libraries and their activities as producers of new information and knowledge. Underpinning this is the attraction factor of library space. It is suggested that a strong concept is important and that 'powerful conceptual design is an inestimable factor in the successful development of new libraries' – the 'wow' factor mentioned in the Introduction is at the heart of this. Developing that 'wow' requires all those representing the library in new space design projects, particularly project leaders and managers, to be bold about library design and prepared to risk failure. However, a space that works well can also be designed by learning from others. Bob Fox and Peter E. Sidorko point out in Chapter 4 that it is wise to be a follower and selectively implement measures that are likely to work in the local cultural context. Although judging by the online image of the Mini Theatre at the City University of Hong Kong, even in this scenario there is still opportunity for experiment and creativity. It is the importance of experimentation with library and learning space design that is at the heart of this book. In Part 2 we explore some of the factors that have influenced the buildings and spaces described in Part 1 that are pertinent to designing better library and learning space.

PART 2

Trends and ideas

PART 2

Introduction

Les Watson

In this part there are four chapters, covering important aspects of the development of better library learning space. The importance of technology to the library was clearly evident in the case studies in Part 1, and this is discussed in Chapter 7. Technology is without doubt one of the most important factors to be considered in the development of new buildings and spaces. Because of its rapid developmental trajectory, it requires constant horizon scanning and some degree of risk taking in order to implement the most appropriate technology in a timely fashion. Chapter 7 looks at the relationship between the library and technology, what we really mean by rapid change, and suggests how technology should fit with overall strategy and what features technology-rich library space has today and may be like tomorrow.

In Chapter 8 aspects of literacy and learning that are most relevant to the development of the informal learning space commonly found in libraries are discussed, with an emphasis on the central importance of conversation to the construction of our knowledge and understanding. The growing acceptance of the importance of informal learning is considered as is societal change and the need for diversity, variety and flexibility of space provision.

Chapter 9 contains a range of ideas about space and the tangible and intangible factors that make it work well. Among these are the emotional impact of space and the importance of experiences. Open plan space is considered along with strategies such as zoning and the ideas of semi-private space, balance of spaces and the flow between them.

The importance of intuitive approaches to library space and the professional insight of expert intuition in the planning of library learning space are discussed in Chapter 10. Other topics include imaginative approaches to the consultation process, evaluation processes and the importance of experimentation and modelling.

CHAPTER 7

Library space and technology

Les Watson

Introduction

Over the years libraries have used technology to improve operational efficiency adopting systems to automate library functions and services that focus on the acquisition, management and circulation of resources, more recently extending these activities, somewhat imperfectly, to digital resources. In contrast to an operational view of IT, this chapter is concerned with the technology of the library in relation to library space. Extensive hardware provision, networking (wired and then wireless) and self-service facilities have been the most noticeable aspects of technology-rich space along with some investment in electronic signage and display screens. The idea of the commons (see Chapter 2), as IT commons and information commons and then learning commons (Watson and Anderson, 2008), has featured the creation of ever larger installations of serried ranks of networked desktop machines, particularly in higher education, reminiscent of battery chicken farms. There is a real threat that such unpleasant environments, increased availability of digital resources, remote access, personal ownership of devices and the inadequate variety of the technology response that is the 'commons' will make visiting the physical library become much less likely. Reduced footfall is taken as a key factor in the irrelevance of the library as a place – particularly in public libraries – and an indicator of library ineffectiveness, and adds to the apparent destruction of library as place. So a key question is, Will technology kill the library as a place? For those providing the funding, especially in times of austerity, the technology factor is often a neat excuse to close a library rather than retain it, access to electronic resources and services being viewed as more pertinent making the library as a place less relevant in the rapidly developing electronic information environment.

Change we expect – revolutions we don't

That technology and change are as inseparable as identical twins is widely accepted but generally the speed with which technology drives change is not so well understood. As a first stage, in the time of relatively slow technological development, in the last century merely adopting technology to automate processes was sufficient. Then came a phase of adapting technology to gain service improvement such as modifying the user interface of systems by amalgamation into the ubiquitous portal. The reality, however, is that the rate of technology change itself is accelerating so we often fail to see what is coming next. Seeing where technology is going is therefore not easy, and spotting which technology innovations are likely to become ubiquitous, and of real importance to library space development, is a much bigger challenge than it has been in the past. How will driverless cars, Google Glass, 3D printers, cloud computing, the social web, the web of things, wearable devices, robots, machine intelligence or the products of nanotechnology affect the library? And which of these, if any, could ensure a bright future for libraries over the coming years? This incomplete short list includes just the technologies that we have now – the reality is that the continuing development of technology at a rate that is 'change squared' (the rate of change itself increasing exponentially) will have more fundamental effects than we can currently imagine.

Just a quick look at recent technological history puts this in perspective: 1997 – IBM's Big Blue beats the world chess champion, then goes on a few years later to be the champion of the TV quiz show *Jeopardy* and is currently to advise doctors in the US on cancer diagnosis. The year 1997 was the first time a machine outperformed a human being in a complex cognitive task and now the same machine is advising professional doctors. Ray Kurzweil (2006) predicts that by the end of the 2020s computers will pass the Turing test – a machine will be able to participate in a conversation so competently that it will be indistinguishable from a human being. Will we continue to need staff in libraries to provide guidance and deal with queries? When this and other unimagined developments happen it surely takes us beyond adoption or even adaption to a need for libraries to embrace and assimilate technology. Computers are certain to be self-repairing, self-replicating and responsible for their own further development not too far into the future, making 'change squared' even more challenging. The consequence of this increasing pace in the rate of change and our failure to see it is that the impact of technology on all aspects of life, including libraries and the work of librarians, will be enormous, deeply important and largely unexpected. 'Change squared' brings uncertainty and suggests that we need to fundamentally rethink the form and function of the library as a place. Why will people choose to go the library? To answer this question in the context of technology, libraries need to start by closely evaluating the library-technology relationship.

What is technology?

Technology is anything that was invented after you were born.

Alan Kay (in Kelly, 2010)

Libraries have responded to the technologies of information and communications following a long history of responses to previous technologies – microfiche, audio recording, print and tablets of stone for example – these responses are often to bolt new technologies on to existing facilities and services. Kevin Kelly (2010), co-founder of *Wired*, likens these individual technologies to species in a rapidly evolving technological ecosystem that he calls the technium. Kelly's technium is a technology system that 'extends beyond shiny hardware to include culture, art, social institutions, and intellectual creations of all types' and consists not just of all the tools that have been invented by the human race but also all the systems that enable us to manage, develop and use these tools. Kelly believes that over the centuries the technium has evolved in parallel with biological evolution. From this perspective the library itself is clearly a technology, a system within the technium invented to enable continued use of information technologies such as tablets (of stone), books, multimedia materials, blogs and tweets. The question then is not 'Will technology kill the library?' but 'What is the next form of the technology that is the library?' Such a question is more fundamental than considering the tactics of technology adoption and adaption by libraries. Parking technology in an area that we call the commons, or using it to automate what we already do, just doesn't meet this challenge. What is needed is for the library to internalize and assimilate technology using imagination to take the technology that is the library to its next technological stage, rather than continue the current position in which libraries bolt on technologies as they emerge.

One of the directional characteristics of Kelly's evolving technium is that as it evolves it creates greater opportunity – specifically opportunities for human betterment through the extension of our intellectual and creative capability. The consequence of greater opportunity is more choice and Kelly believes that 'we [as humans] need the full spectrum of choices won by the technium to unleash our own maximum potential'. In Kelly's view we should 'always act to increase choice'. The idea of library as a technology system and of developing the library as a system that works to increase choice provides a powerful perspective, which takes us beyond those bolt-on automation solutions and puts the focus firmly on the members of the library.

Tactics to strategy

A bolt-on approach is a tactical one and can never take the library to its next technological level. Bolt-on approaches tend to adopt technologies only when safe to do so, for example. For technology to be internalized and assimilated by any organization it has to be future focused and integral to the strategic framework of the organization. Technology has to enhance the work of the people of the organization and be integrated into the organizational environment, as shown in Figure 7.1.

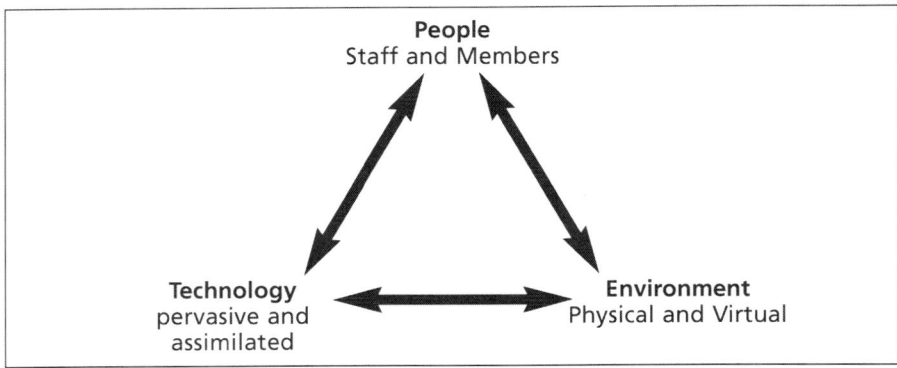

Figure 7.1 *Technology in strategic context*

While this strategic approach will not predict the future it does provide a clear framework for thinking about technology and specifically how it interacts with other factors within the technology system that is the library. An important aspect of this framework is that it highlights the assimilation and integration of technology with other key resources. Considering these factors together within this framework is more likely to ensure that they work in synergy to add value to each other rather than work against one another. Thinking, strategizing and planning around any one of these three factors must embrace interaction and impact with the others and in doing so is more likely to produce additive effects and benefits as compared with considering them separately. For example, in the past it has been common for libraries implementing self-service solutions to site the machines on or near the desk, with the effect of cluttering the space on or around the desk and creating uncertainty for staff and library members on when to use the new facilities. Thinking about the real purpose of the technology, how we want the space to work and what our expectations are of staff and members holistically would suggest that placing machines away from the desk, as a first intervention, and with others distributed throughout the building would be a solution that not only enhances the environment but also makes the choice to use the technology more obvious to members and staff of the library.

At a more strategic level perhaps the staffing structures we currently have may be unfit for purpose in the technology that is the library – the current focus on resource management needs to shift to process management. Where is the head of socio-technology, or enviro-technology or socio-environment to lead the thinking and change required? The complex issue of our approach to technology problems, particularly in the context of the networked society, is discussed by Chris Batt in Chapter 16. He is clear that this problem affects all libraries and requires a dialogue across sectors to develop a strategic approach. Sector-wide approaches have previously had value as the successful work in higher education, in particular on e-resources, journal subscriptions and digital repositories, shows – the complex issues around what's next for the technology system that is the library go beyond sectors to affect all libraries.

As a technology system the 21st-century library, through the activities of its staff and the environments that it creates, should strive to provide access to knowledge and understanding and engage its community in the processes of learning so that new knowledge and understanding can be created in the community and beyond. One key objective of an integrated technology strategy is the creation of the environments – technology-rich physical and virtual library spaces – that can provide users with services, options and choices to enable them to be effective information seekers and lifelong learners.

Technology-rich library space today
Ubiquity

Current technology-rich library space has ubiquitous networking both wired and wireless, enabling library members to use technology devices throughout the space. Some of these devices are 'owned' by the library and include desktop computers arranged for individual and group use but increasingly many of the devices are owned by the user. The current bring your own device (BYOD) trend prevalent in higher education and public libraries lending e-books frees up users to bring their own laptops, tablets and smartphones to work in the library. This is a welcome change from requiring library users to use library 'owned' desktop machines, partly because it acknowledges the personal nature of technology (as identified in the name of PCs – personal computers) and also because it enables users to work with their preferred application software with real-time access to their personal cloud storage. Importantly the use of these devices enables users to choose where they work within the library, selecting those environments that best suit their current needs and emotions (see Chapter 9). Jenkins (2013) observed:

> What a person can achieve with an outdated machine in a public library with mandatory filtering software and no opportunity for storage or transmission pales in comparison to what a person can accomplish with a home computer with unfettered Internet access, high bandwidth, and continuous connectivity.

Mobility is still restricted by the occasional need for access to power, however. A well equipped technology-rich library has an extensive under-floor power grid and power sockets mounted in clusters and/or on tables and informal furniture such as sofas. The technology-rich library also reinforces the theme of ubiquitous distributed technology by the loan of mobile devices for use throughout the building. Alongside BYOD technology-rich libraries will continue to provide some devices for those in their community who would not otherwise have access to them. In the future providing greater technology choice involves exploiting wireless power as it becomes available in the next few years and new types of mobile wearable devices such as Google Glass as they become the norm. Librarians have always been early adopters of technology (for example, using punched-cards and microfilm for activities such as issue systems, indexing and newspaper preservation in the early 1960s) and the library role of horizon scanning and showcasing new technological possibilities continues in the technology-rich library – expect early use of 3D smartboards and 3D printers, holographic displays and gesture computing in the technology-rich library for example.

Technology management

Like most technology systems the technology-rich library currently has both emerging and legacy technologies, including books. The technology-rich library will have taken a carefully considered approach to the balance between space for books and space for users, adopting strategies such as annual stock reviews and deletion of items no longer required. Detailed knowledge of stock use (informed by borrowing stats for example) is essential as base data for this strategy and also to extend the strategy into an active management policy, taking a strategic approach to the use of open access shelving, compact shelving and remote book stores to free up space for users. Imaginative solutions for holding books in the library should also be part of the technology strategy, for example using books to create zones within the library, book walls to provide privacy and sound proofing, and books to create inspirational features within the library, such as the Book Mountain described in Chapter 5. The adoption and use of electronic resources and digitization enable the technology-rich library to extend the space for people while at the same time increasing the scope of the collection. Careful and imaginative management of legacy resources is an essential first step in a library refurbishment or new build to ensure that maximum space can be provided for users, and is part of the technology strategy.

A conversational journey

In Chapter 9 I outline the importance of experiences, including how users experience the library. Technology can be used to have an ongoing conversation with members of the library as they move from space to space within the building. At a basic level electronic signage can be used to provide information for users on the library, its events and services. As in museums, some libraries use quick response (QR) codes that can be accessed from smartphones to access deeper information, or local information points can send information to mobile devices using Bluetooth connections as users walk past them. Interactive displays based on surface technology can be used to take electronic signage to the next stage, providing novel ways of experiencing information such as those used in the Hive (see Chapter 1) that provide information on the history of Worcester. Many of the libraries described in the case studies in Part 1 of this book make extensive use of lighting technology to enhance the look and feel of library spaces – using light to modify the colour of a space throughout the day can have powerful effects on mood and behaviour and is a real alternative to fixed colour décor. Similarly graphics can be used to create a range of environments within the library to encourage active group work or quieter behaviour – the quieter floors of the Saltire Centre are designed as a garden and a living room, for example (for more on metaphors see Chapter 10). Audio devices, also used by the Hive (see Chapter 1), can provide variety to the way that information is presented. In the Saltire Centre sounds were used at doorways to add to the user experience such as a 'Ssssh' as users enter a quiet zone or the sounds of the marketplace as they enter the interactive group space.

Enhancing technology-rich space: using technology to create the environment

The experiential and interactive nature of the library is being extended through immersive technologies. Interactive displays can add a sense of fun and excitement to the library, such as the koi carp pond at the entrance to the Bedford library at Royal Holloway, University of London, where fish 'swim away' as visitors walk through the pond. Social software, holographic displays and haptic interfaces offer further potential for engaging users with the library, and its resources and staff.

Understanding and supporting the library community

All libraries strive to obtain data on how members use the library and how the facilities and services can be improved. Simple data is easy to collect (such as the footfall mentioned earlier in this chapter) and to understand, but the real 'user experience' of the library is complex and difficult to understand. The dilemma is that if we stick with simplicity we can collect and analyse the data, but if we seek a more in-depth understanding of our users and dig deeper, collection and analysis become complex and burdensome. Enter big data – recent developments in the ability to not only collect large volumes of data but also use the technology itself to understand it. It is becoming possible to analyse and synthesize this data by using complex algorithms and greater computing power. For the technology-rich library this presents the opportunity to get a much better understanding of the 'library experience'. In the late 20th century Mihaly Csikszentmihalyi developed the technique of experience sampling. Using pagers Csikszentmihalyi's researchers were able to collect data in real time on how people felt, leading to the development of his now widely known theory of flow (2002). How much more powerful could this technique be using today's mobile devices combined with big data to get a genuine understanding of the library experience. The experience sampling method has the potential to provide real insights as it overcomes the tyranny of our current time-lapse feedback methods. Collecting real-time data, which rather than focusing on what happened in the past tells us what is happening in the present, and analysing and synthesizing the results using big data techniques, could enable us also to understand how users really feel about our facilities and services.

Big data

In 2013 Jisc launched the Jisc Library Analytics and Metrics Project (JISCLAMP) in the UK, which was aimed at enabling libraries to capitalize on the opportunities of big data. Efforts such as this, if they concentrate not just on quantitative data but also explore qualitative information, could address another developing trend in technology-rich libraries by enabling the collection and curation of information and knowledge produced by those who use the library. As library users migrate from being passive consumers of information to active producers of knowledge the need to ensure that all the electronic documents, blogs and tweets are not transient becomes more urgent. The potential of big data is that it could make this happen. Determining user journeys and designing real-time information services has been an aspiration of libraries for some time; could big data give the push needed to make this a reality?

Robots – removing routine

My mention of robots earlier in this chapter may have been met with disgust or disbelief by many readers but the robots are coming and will have uses in the technology-rich library. Robots are already playing a role in book repository retrieval using radio-frequency identification (RFID) and robotic arms are used to offload book hoppers onto conveyers. At present librarians are still picking individual books, guided by RFID scanners, and may do so for some time – at least until the standalone mobile robot that can search the shelves arrives. According to the UK Foresight Horizon Scanning Centre (2012), 'The principal markets for service robotics include defence, healthcare, manufacturing, transport, energy, entertainment and education' (I'm also thinking libraries here). The report states that service robots 'have the potential to transform the competitiveness of service industries . . . just as industrial robots have transformed the competitiveness of engineering manufacturing' but sees a large barrier in the lack of social acceptance of such robots. The form that future robots will take and when they will become socially acceptable is at present unknowable. However, technology-rich librarians should be thinking about what they would wish them to do. Providing the best environment for library users depends on making the best use of all resources – human and robotic. Arthur C. Clarke (1980) said, 'A teacher that can be replaced by a machine should be.' A librarian that can be replaced by a robot should also be – librarians have more meaningful work to do in the 21st-century library.

Conclusion

This chapter suggests that, for libraries, the strategic development of technology is an important aspect of thinking about library space. Viewing the library as a technology, as part of the technium, that works to increase choice for library users shifts our thinking about technology from operational to user needs. Adopting this strategic stance combines the physical and the virtual, the book and the computer, into a single system of information and learning. The promise is that using technology to understand how users really feel about services and facilities provides opportunities for development of the physical library to ensure its continuation as a place that exceeds expectations and is a source of inspiration and delight for those that use it.

References

Clarke, A.C. (1980) Electronic Tutors, *Omni Magazine*, http://archive.org/stream/omni-magazine-1980-06/OMNI_1980_06#page/n1/mode/2up (accessed 15 August 2013).

Csikszentmihalyi, M. (2002) *Flow: the classic work on how to achieve happiness*, Rider.

Foresight Horizon Scanning Centre (2012) *Technology and Innovation Futures*, Technologie Annexe, www.bis.gov.uk/assets/foresight/docs/general-publications/10-1252an-technology-and-innovation-futures-annex.pdf (accessed

23 April 2013).

Jenkins, H. (2013) *Confronting the Challenges of Participatory Culture: media education for the 21st century*, occasional paper from the John D. and Catherine T. MacArthur Foundation, MIT.

Kelly, K. (2010) *What Technology Wants*, Penguin.

Kurzweil, R. (2006) *The Singularity is Near: when humans transcend*, Gerald Duckworth & Co Ltd.

Watson, L. and Anderson, H. (2008) *The Design and Management of Open Plan Technology Rich Learning Space in Further and Higher Education in the UK*, Joint Information Systems Committee, E-Learning Program, www.jisc.ac.uk/whatwedo/projects/managinglearningspaces.aspx (accessed 4 May 2013).

CHAPTER 8

Library space and learning

Les Watson and Jan Howden

Introduction

Libraries have always been places of learning, supporting personal exploration of the information and knowledge held in their collections and also being a place for researchers to learn and for the learner as researcher. Equally instruction on how to make best use of the resources held by the library and how to access its services has always been part of the work of the library, through either documentation distributed to users or specific training courses. This role has further developed with the growth of e-resources, with libraries acting as information brokers. In these ways libraries are already part of the national and international learning landscape, but can play a greater role in community, societal and individual learning support for learners and their learning by developing better library learning space.

In the late 20th and early 21st century theories and models of information literacy have been developed – for example in the UK both the Society of College, National and University Libraries (SCONUL), supporting libraries in the higher education sector and national UK libraries, and CILIP: the Chartered Institute of Library and Information Professionals, providing support to all member librarians, developed structured models for the provision of information literacy training and education. Some of these models were informed by current learning theories, for example, the SCONUL seven pillars model (2011) (with the recent addition of a cyclical representation of the pillars) is strikingly similar to Kolb's model of learning (1984), acknowledging that for learning to occur the learner requires a phase of reflection, to then learn from the experience, and then plan and conceive the next experience. However, in practice most users of these models do not consider all of these aspects but tend to focus on information finding. Making the shift from an operational 'consumer view' of access to learning resources towards the process of learning is one of the challenges for models of information literacy and the library's wider involvement in learning.

In the 21st century technology has become a key component of the skills environment required to access and handle information and develop new knowledge. Inability to use technology effectively is an insurmountable barrier to information access and use. Up to 30 years ago many libraries led the way in IT training, refocusing their efforts on IT literacy as a necessary precursor to information skills. Unfortunately much of this work, as in school systems, took something of a cul-de-sac by focusing on instruction in the use of commercial software rather than the generic transferable understanding of IT as a tool for personal creativity and production. Emerging new technologies are fortunately enabling users to move beyond this episode by providing intuitive interfaces and applications. As we move to the next stage of digital and media literacy (see Chapter 19, by Kyle Dickson) and a 'participatory culture' (Jenkins, 2013) we need to rethink our library and learning space provision, the contribution that the library can make to communal and individual learning, and revise our view of learners as consumers of information to one of constructors and producers of knowledge (see Chapter 21, by Mike Neary and Sam Williams).

We live in a conceptual age

Ken Robinson (2013) claims, 'Current systems of education were not designed to meet the challenges we now face. They were developed to meet the needs of a former age. Reform is not enough: they need to be transformed.'

Continuing to educate using only an 'industrial' approach is highly questionable at the current stage of societal development. In his book *A Whole New Mind*, Daniel Pink (2005) describes society's transition over the past 200 years from an agricultural to an industrial age and, eventually, to an age of information and knowledge. Much of what we currently read, what determines how we configure our libraries, and what we 'teach' in our libraries relates to this information society and the methodologies we use to teach it are informed by the instructional approaches of the industrial age. In these early years of the 21st century Pink sees a new significant societal shift with the emergence of a conceptual society – one that values personal attributes such as creativity and empathy as the most important individual and collective societal assets. This conceptual society is about creative capacity and the ability to generate new thinking and ideas, providing the new basis for global individual participation and national competitiveness.

Education is the only resource that we have in order to be competitive in any economy, not least an ideas economy. Rethinking how we can shift our education systems from their focus on instruction to enable learners to develop broader skills is the challenge. Developing new library learning space requires an awareness of the changing nature of the activities of both teachers and learners in order to ensure that services and resources are used to the best effect. Freeman (2005) sees the library 'as an extension of the classroom' concluding that 'library space needs to embody new pedagogies, including collaborative and interactive modalities'.

There has been increasing emphasis on how learners develop through the informal learning that occurs outside the classroom in recent years; for example, in Chapter 14 Jo Dane explores the impact of massively open online courses (MOOCs), which are taking hold in higher education worldwide. When lectures are 'delivered' online en masse the 'real' learning occurs outside these lectures. Libraries of all types, and their spaces, consequently have a more important role than ever before as places of learning in a truly mass education system. In such a 'flipped' education system, libraries in the education and public sectors need a vision and purpose about people and how to make a real contribution to the learning landscape of the conceptual society. Extending the idea of the library to be a '21st century library that recognizes the importance of a participatory culture' (Jenkins, 2013) and embraces not just the information but also the ideas economy demands that we develop library space to support new learning activities.

Focus on the experience

In Chapter 9 I outline the importance of experiences to the creative people that populate the conceptual society. Making our buildings 'an experience' is a fresh perspective that demands we think about their look and feel in considerable detail. Richard Florida's work (2003) illustrates that place remains important to members of the conceptual age, and the importance of thinking of our buildings as experiences cannot be underestimated. The designer Karim Rashid expresses this well in point number 43 of a 50-point manifesto: 'Experience is the most important part of living, and the exchange of ideas and human contact is all there really is. Space and objects can encourage increased experiences or detract from our experiences' (Design Log, 2013). Such thinking takes us beyond customer service to a requirement for intimate knowledge of those who use our facilities, which translates into an understanding of how they experience, and how they feel about how they experience, our libraries and learning spaces (see Chapter 10).

What's happening with learning?

Seely Brown and Duguid (2000) believe that 'learning is a remarkably social process. In truth, it occurs not as a response to teaching, but rather as a result of a social framework that fosters learning.' This social framework encompasses the orality and sociality of learning and sees knowledge as both a social construct and a result of social interaction. It is rooted in a Vygotskian social constructivist view of the world (Pass, 2004). Our common understanding of 'social' is normally devoid of a learning perspective and focuses on the importance of interactions with others in informal get-togethers. The main activity in such gatherings, however, is conversation and as Seely Brown and Duguid note: 'All learning starts with conversation' (Seely Brown and Duguid, 2000).

This simple statement presents a far-reaching and deeply important idea that extends our view of what 'social' is – it is not merely interaction but a sociality of learning. Many types of conversation play a role in learning (and teaching) activities. Interactions involving materials and resources, peers and teachers, technologies and activities can all be considered to be conversational. The conversational framework developed by Diana Laurillard (2002) shows a spectrum of learning activities that include acquisition of and inquiry about knowledge and information, discussion, practice, concept development, collaboration and production. Conversation is the central process in a wide range of current learning theories, including social constructivism (peers checking their understanding through conversation), instructionism (teachers presentation and explanations), constructionism (conversations with ourselves that modify our conceptual frameworks) and situated learning (co-creating knowledge in the situation you intend to use it). This view of learning has a broad, unrestricted view of conversation: including the one-way 'conversation' of the lecture or presentation as well as the multi-channel conversations of team and peer group work, but also, importantly, the private conversations with ourselves inside our heads, as Feynman (2000) observed,

> When I was a kid growing up in Far Rockaway, I had a friend named Bernie Walker. We both had 'labs' at home, and we would do various 'experiments'. One time, we were discussing something – we must have been 11 or 12 at the time – and I said, 'But thinking is nothing but talking to yourself inside.'

The importance of conversation to effective learning is clear in both social and personal contexts as is the point that the current focus on social learning is not a replacement for all that has gone before. The opportunity is for libraries, as learning places, to contribute to these activities. The challenge is to rebalance education systems that have for too long focused too heavily on instruction, through what we create in our libraries and learning spaces. In considering the nature of learning to inform our libraries of the future, we should avoid overt enthusiasm for social learning, recognizing that learning is socio-personal and diverse. New library and learning space should reflect the diversity of conversational possibility, redressing the balance between social construction of understanding and the instructional acquisition of information. Libraries should provide environments and experiences for learners that enable them to challenge and develop their frameworks of understanding through as rich a variety of conversations as possible. Carefully constructed social learning space with a variety that supports all types of conversation from active engagement with others to solitary reflection enables learning – the creation of social space alone will not. Given appropriate space, how people supporting learning in the library participate in conversations and create the experience is crucial to the effectiveness of the space. Librarians can play a significant part in learning because they understand resources, which are the primary material of the learning process, and when used effectively can transform it. Also the range of open education resources is expanding rapidly (Bonk, 2009) and provides a basis for librarians to build further on their key skills and find their place as learning facilitators in the learning library.

It's diversity

Howard Gardner's research (1993, 1999, 2006) in educational psychology makes it clear that personal intelligence is not a singular concept; learners all have a wide range of facets to their personal intelligence – and consequently are all intelligently different. The clear message from this work is again the existence of individual differences and the inherent variety of need exhibited by learners. There is also now an acknowledgement that learning has an important emotional component. Positive and negative emotions can improve or hinder learning. Jensen (2005) reminds us that not only are emotions important as drivers and barriers to learning but they are present all the time, connected to our behaviours, and transient – continuously dynamically changing. It is also clear that the dynamic nature of need is not limited to emotional or intelligence factors but also driven by extrinsic factors such as assignment or examination pressures, which vary over time, requiring flexible provision that can easily be modified to match such changes. The result is a complexity that demands we strive continually to understand in experiential terms which environments might work and which will not because the interiors that we create can improve or hinder learning through the subtle effects they have on those who inhabit them.

Italian teacher and psychologist Loris Malaguzzi, founder of the Reggio Emilia educational approach believed that children develop through interactions, first with the adults in their lives – parents and teachers – then with their peers, and ultimately with the environment around them. Malaguzzi believed that the environment is the third teacher and that 'We value space because of its power to organize and promote pleasant relationships among people of different ages, create a handsome environment, provide changes, promote choices and activity, and its potential for sparking all kinds of social, affective, cognitive learning' (quoted in Edwards, Gandini and Forman, 2012).

Conclusion

An education that acknowledges individual difference, conversational learning and emotional factors rather than ignores them demands a new approach to what it provides and how it provides it. One clear message emerges – the existence of wide ranging individual difference, the inherent variety of need exhibited by learners, and that these needs change over time. These factors demand a variety of space provision in our libraries to give learners real choice. This variety is not about separate space silos but about recognizing that we are social animals with distinctive contributions; we construct our frameworks of understanding within a powerful conversational framework, which includes a continuum of interactions with resources and technology by listening, participating, contributing, reflecting and producing. Learning will always be the responsibility of the individual; libraries currently, through their resource collections, supply the outputs of individual and group creativity; they need to do more to embrace, encourage and stimulate the producers of future knowledge. Shifting the focus of library space to the activities of people as learners in the context of the rapidly emerging conceptual age requires us to understand not just how people learn but also how space can support them through its variety and flexibility.

References

Bonk, C. J. (2009) *The World is Open*, Jossey-Bass.

Design Log (2013) Today's Dose of Design Inspiration: Karim Rahid's "Karimanifesto", http://tianickels.wordpress.com/2013/04/18/todays-dose-of-designspiration-karim-rashids-karimanifesto/ (accessed 1 July 2013).

Edwards C., Gandini, L. and Forman, G. (2012) *The Hundred Languages of Children: the Reggio Emilia experience in transformation*, Praeger.

Feynman, R. P. (2000) *The Pleasure of Finding Things Out*, Penguin.

Florida, R. (2003) *The Rise of the Creative Class: and how it's transforming work, leisure, community and everyday life*, Basic Books.

Freeman, G. T. (2005) *Changes in Learning Patterns, Technology and Use*. In Council on Library and Information Resources, *Library as Place: rethinking roles, rethinking space*.

Gardner, H. (1993) *Frames of Mind: the theory of multiple intelligences*, Basic Books.

Gardner, H. (1999) *Intelligence Reframed: multiple intelligences for the 21st century*, Basic Books.

Gardner, H. (2006) *The Development and Education of the Mind*, Routledge.

Jenkins, H. (2013) *Confronting the Challenges of Participatory Culture: media education for the 21st century*, an occasional paper from the John D. and Catherine T. MacArthur Foundation, MIT.

Jensen, E. (2005) *Teaching with the Brain in Mind*, ASCD Books.

Kolb, D. A. (1984) *Experiential Learning: experience as a source of learning and development*, Prentice Hall.

Laurillard, D. (2002) *Rethinking University Teaching: a conversational framework for the effective use of learning technologies*, Routledge.

Pass, S. (2004) *Parallel Paths to Constructivism: Jean Piaget and Lev Vygotsky*, Information Age Publishing.

Pink, D. H. (2005) *A Whole New Mind: how to thrive in the new conceptual age*, Cyan Books.

Robinson, K. (2013) *Out of Our Minds*, Capstone Publishing.

SCONUL Working Group on Information Literacy (2011) *SCONUL Seven Pillars of Information Literacy: core model for higher education*, www.sconul.ac.uk/sites/default/files/documents/coremodel.pdf (accessed 3 May 2013).

Seely Brown, J. and Duguid, P. (2000) *The Social Life of Information*, Harvard Business School Press.

CHAPTER 9

Key ideas on space

Les Watson

Introduction

In a chapter entitled 'Key ideas on space' you might expect to read about the many tangible factors to be taken into consideration in creating a new or refurbished library or learning space. Factors such as lighting, noise control, IT infrastructure, ventilation, temperature control, humidity and maintenance among many others all have to be considered and have to be right – they are often the source of complaint by users if they are not right, and occasionally even if they are. The professionals such as architects and building engineers engaged in the project will provide expert guidance on these tangible aspects and sources such as the Space Management Group (smg.ac.uk), in the UK, can provide library and learning staff with sufficient background, toolkits and guidance to enable them to participate in the consideration of these factors.

Hugh Anderson and I (Watson and Anderson, 2008) working on a project for Jisc carried out a survey of a number of further and higher education institutions to identify which of these tangible factors proved to be most problematic. By a clear margin heating and ventilation caused the most issues for the spaces in our survey, closely followed by noise. Many libraries and learning spaces are felt by users to be too hot in the summer and too cold in the winter, and users of the space often complain about the lack of local control that they have over heating and ventilation. Ensuring that temperature and ventilation controls are rigorously modelled is an absolutely essential prerequisite to project success, which must be undertaken in the planning stage of the project. Issues around noise were also often mentioned to us in our survey, particularly relating to large open plan spaces, but in spaces where strategies such as zoning and semi-private structures (see pages 125 and 126) were deployed noise was not an issue.

Among the factors that were felt to be less problematic were lighting and smells. While it appeared from the survey that there was a general satisfaction with lighting arrangements, our feeling was that opportunities were being missed to introduce additional impact into a space by using lighting, which could add interest and also provide an easily manageable way of introducing colour flexibility – a key factor in determining mood, which can also send subtle signals about the purpose of a space. The advice here is also that sufficient consideration be given to lighting not just in order to conform to standards but as an additional way of enhancing the emotional impact of the space.

With the increasing prevalence of food and drink in library and learning spaces care should be taken where possible to ensure that smells are not intrusive; the planning of ventilation systems should take food and drink into account, as it is now becoming the norm to have refreshment facilities in libraries and learning spaces.

However, despite all the things we know we know, it is the things that we don't know that can force a project off course; paradoxically, it is also these unknowns that can make a project great. Alongside the certainty of getting tangibles such as heating and ventilation right there will certainly also be some uncertainty, for example about the impact of colour and graphics used. Developing a new library or learning space is an act of creativity. Rather than retreat to a place of comfortable certainty that repeats what we already know, projects need to experiment to play their part in the evolution of library and learning spaces and provide a platform for future innovation. This chapter aims to explore some less tangible ideas and give a broader framework for thinking about space as well as some practical strategies to help configure new spaces.

Creativity and experiences

Creativity is at the heart of the conceptual society discussed in Chapter 8. In his work on 'the creative class' Florida (2003) reveals, importantly, that contrary to our expectations about connected net-aware creative people they still do value place:

> The death-of-place prognostications simply do not square with the countless people I have interviewed, the focus groups I've observed, and the statistical

research I've done. Place and community are more critical factors than ever before . . . the economy itself increasingly takes form around real concentrations of people in real places.

This indicates the need for the continuation of the library as a physical place. As a result of his work with focus groups of creative class people, Florida believes experiences are primarily important: 'Experiences are replacing goods and services because they stimulate our creative faculties and enhance our creative capacities. This active, experiential lifestyle is spreading and becoming more prevalent in society.'

Writing about the 'experience economy' Pine and Gilmore (1999) describe a progression of customer needs from commodities to goods then services and ultimately experiences. Providing excellent library experiences should be one of the primary aims of any library and learning space development. How users experience the library is dependent on the quality of the space, how it is organized and the services provided within the space – space and service are inseparable and interdependent. Where space and services are designed and managed to fit perfectly with expectations, and change over time as expectations change, the outcome will be excellent experiences.

Spaces that speak to us

Quality of space can be hard to define but is easy to recognize. Tangible factors are a baseline requirement and relatively easily measured but the intangible are more elusive, although some attempts have been made to take these into account (Hisham and Neda, 2012). Part of the experience of a space is to do with what it suggests to us either overtly or subliminally, or both. In his work on the architecture of happiness De Botton (2006) quotes John Ruskin: 'John Ruskin proposed that we seek two things of our buildings. We want them to shelter us. And we want them to speak to us – to speak to us of whatever we find important and need to be reminded of.'

Our library buildings should reflect our views about variety, choice and diversity underpinned by our beliefs and values about the importance of the library as space in the 21st century or, as De Botton (2006) says, 'the question of the values we want to live by – rather than merely of how we want things to look' should be encapsulated in the spaces that we design. The use of interior design to do the speaking in our spaces is fundamentally important, and done effectively is more than just cosmetic enhancement. We should speak to those who use the library with spaces that are designed for silence and solitude as well as those that are communal, collective and collaborative. These spaces, through the language of design, should acknowledge the diversity of user need, making it clear that both conversation and reflection have equal importance. At a tactical level we can speak to our users with 'design gestures' (Jamieson, 2013) such as choosing round tables to encourage conversation. At a strategic level deploying such tactics in an integrated way along with the use of graphics and other design elements creates a metaphor for the space (see Chapter 10) that speaks to those who use it. Integrating spaces along a continuum will avoid the disaster of 'silo' space such as the 'isolated' café in the library, which sees sociality as separate from learning. The library as a place should become a focus for association and activity, and home to a wide range of facilities and services preserving the best of the information, support, services, community and resources that have traditionally been provided – the experience should be, and feel like, more than just a library. As Loris Malaguzzi said, 'We also think . . . that the space has to be a sort of aquarium that mirrors the ideas, values, attitudes and cultures of the people who live within it' (quoted in Edwards, Gandini and Forman, 2012).

The emotional impact of space

In her book on how the brain works Fine (2007) tells us that 'seemingly trivial things in our environment may be influencing our behaviour', highlighting the fact that we are susceptible to environmental cues in our surroundings – for example, 'if someone asks you about a good friend and then asks you for a favour, you will be more willing to help'. The ability of a subtle stimulus to awaken other contextual factors in our subconscious can affect our conscious thoughts and emotions. The environments that we inhabit are, often inadvertently, rich in such subtle stimuli. Thinking in a careful and detailed way about the environments we create in our libraries and learning spaces and the contexts that they are set for those using them is deeply important. These interiors can influence behaviours through the subtle effects they have on those who inhabit them.

This context set by interior design has deep significance, affecting us psychologically and even potentially physiologically, as suggested by the work of Harvard psychologist Ellen Langer (1989). Langer took a group of elderly men (aged 75 to 80) to a retreat to see whether 'behaving' younger and reliving the past, rather than just talking about it as a control group did, could influence ageing. Great care was taken to ensure the experimental group experience was contextually authentic – environmental details, for example not just playing radio programmes of the past but playing them on old radios, were part of the authenticity of the experience. In short, the participants who 'lived' the past showed improvement in a range of physiological factors such as height when sitting, manual dexterity, improved vision and some improved performance in intelligence tests as compared with the control group who had merely talked about the past. This intriguing work hints at the possibility that the context in which we live and work, which in part at least is the environment(s) that we inhabit, can have deep and far-reaching effects on us beyond what we might expect. The use of colour and graphics in the spaces we create should not be superficial decoration but the result of careful thought, which aims to create purposeful environments. The chapters on Hong Kong and China in Part 1 of this book hint at the importance of creating spaces that speak of culture and identity – suggesting aspects of culture, identity and purpose can be made tangible through the subtle emotional impact of interior design.

The default position is that whatever environment(s) we create as we develop and refurbish our libraries and learning spaces will speak to those who use them, and they will have emotional impact. A café with bright coloured furniture and a corporate splash of orange across the wall will have impact – but what will it do for the emotional state of those using it? It is no coincidence that many fast food restaurants use red as their primary colour. A carefully constructed environment that speaks of our aspiration for meaningful, purposeful conversations and the learning that results from this may revive the purposeful air of learning of the 17th-century coffee house described by Ellis (2004):

> To scholars, both of the arts and sciences, coffee-houses became one of the most significant locations for debate and the exchange of ideas, evolving into an important research tool, somewhere between a peer review system, an encyclopaedia, a research centre and a symposium.

Such a purposeful air is a million miles away from the space equipped with flimsy second-class furniture and vending machines, which exists because people need to 'get a drink' to relieve the tedium of long hours in the library. The role of the client librarian or learning specialist is to articulate to the design professional, through the project brief and continuing conversations, what messages are to be conveyed by the interior design of the space, so they bring their skill to translate this into inspirational design.

The third place

Much has been written about Oldenburg's (1999) idea of the third place:

> Third places are neither home nor work – the 'first two' places – but venues like coffee shops, bookstores and cafes in which we find less formal acquaintances. These comprise 'the heart of a community's social vitality' where people go for good company and lively conversation.

The danger of this third place model for the library is that it talks only of sociality, company and good conversation, but not of purposeful work and learning. As a stimulus to development of informal space in libraries this concept is a step on the path and has been a useful touchstone. However, future libraries need a model that combines the third place with the productivity of the second place of work and the safety, comfort and ownership of the first place – home. Indeed an important aspect of library space is often to create a 'study home' for those users who do not otherwise have such a place.

Variety with balance

One of the messages in the previous chapter on libraries, information and learning is that libraries, if they are to support learners, need to create a variety of spaces that speak to the diversity of people using the space and to different modes of learning. Rizzo (2002) provides some useful guidance derived from exploring the expectations of academic library users for types of space that they seek. Rizzo lists four types of space:

- highly active and engaging communal places
- interactive collaborative places for individual research and group work
- quieter less active places such as reading rooms, study rooms and alcoves
- out of the way contemplative places for quiet reflection and deep thought.

While not expressed in terms of learning these general types of space give us a useful framework for thinking about what a 21st-century library can provide. These types of space are neither definitive nor exclusive but are a starting point and open to extrapolation, extension and fusion. The extent of any marketplace (or mall) (Rizzo's type 1) and monastic space (Rizzo's type 4) and the balance between them will vary from library to library. Thinking about the balance of these types of space involves considering the extent of 'noisy' social or social learning space of types 1 and 2, currently in vogue in higher education, versus the quiet and silent spaces of types 3 and 4 of the more traditional library. The reality of changing user expectations and 21st-century ideas about learning encourages a shift from types 3 and 4 to types 1 and 2. This is expressed clearly by Lankes (2012): 'Today's great libraries are transforming from quiet buildings with a loud room or two to loud buildings with a quiet room. They are shifting from the domain of the librarians to the domain of the communities.'

A successful 21st-century library, or learning space, will need to have a balance between types of space that meets the needs of the communities that use it. A really successful 21st-century library, or learning space, will have a dynamic balance that exceeds expectations and can morph over the annual cycle of use to closely match demand over time. A clear example is the increased demand in educational organizations for more quiet study space in their libraries around exam time as compared with the need for more group study space during project working. An example of dealing with this changing demand is the university of Exeter's buffer zones described in Chapter 1. Making such changes can be as simple as changing the colour of the space using lighting or deploying semi-private structures (see the section 'Semi-private space', on page 126) or partitions. Least successful are the spaces that don't match user need or are unable to be adapted to changing short-term demands. A variety of spaces that are balanced and dynamic will ensure that provision matches need over time.

Flow

The creation of space is not, however, merely about the range and balance of a variety of spaces but also about how they interrelate and flow from one space to another. Crucial is how a fragmented feel is avoided and how, in the case of a part refurbishment, the 'bolt-on' facility is integrated into the whole. Much has been written about the library as third place (Oldenburg, 1999), as mentioned earlier, those places that are not work and not home but hold special significance to those who visit and use them. According to Mikunda (2006), the creation of a third place should have a 'golden thread' (flow) running through it that encourages users to 'mall' and explore it. Using the tricks of suspense and revelation such places also often have a landmark or core attraction that arouses curiosity – the 'wow' factor mentioned in the introduction to this book that is so often found in new spaces and buildings. Examples include public works of art, impressive atrium spaces and the furniture itself deployed in the space. Flow facilitates user journeys through the space. Landmarks and core attractions provide destinations.

Open plan *vs* enclosed space

Many of the case studies in Part 1 of this book include large open spaces that we describe as 'open plan technology rich' in Chapter 1. In that chapter Jan Howden and I argue that such open plan space has the advantage of flexibility; the detail of the space is defined by furniture, fittings and equipment, and can easily be changed, enabling experimentation. Open plan originated in offices around the middle of the last century and came about partly to squeeze as much accommodation as possible from the space available, but also to address the need for flexibility arising from changed working practice and the introduction of IT (see Chapter 13, page 169 for more on this). The design of libraries and learning spaces now has similar pressures, especially in higher education, with the global growth in student numbers in universities and the current thinking about group and project-based learning demanding more space and greater flexibility. Over-simplicity in meeting this need for flexibility, for example by providing office accommodation in massive open space crammed with screened-off cells, can lead to universal dislike of such spaces, with the accompanying difficulty of worker dissatisfaction. Potentially modern open plan learning space can lead to similar problems if it lacks variety and interior design, but if planned carefully open plan space is not just flexible but also allows for variety, flow and complexity. Open plan space done well provides inspiration, stimulation, curiosity, interest, opportunities for vicarious learning, a sense of community, and choice and excitement for those who use it.

With flexibility, however, comes potential complexity. Large open plan spaces carry with them, in addition to a promise of greater potential for change and ongoing innovation, the inevitable overhead of difficulty of management. Any project must consider this tension between difficulty of ongoing management and potential for innovation at the planning stage. Open plan technology-rich space is not a panacea (otherwise the Leeds City Library described in Chapter 1 would not be the success that it is) and an important initial consideration in the development of library and learning space has to be the realities and practicalities of ongoing management of the space – there is no point building for the flexibility that open plan technology-rich space can bring if the resources needed periodically to reconfigure and manage the space cannot be made available. The issues expressed above in respect of open plan office space also warn against extreme use, particularly overpopulation, of open plan learning space. A key question to consider is which activities we wish to continue into the future that absolutely require specialist use or need to be enclosed for other reasons. Honestly addressing the question of whether fixed full-height walls are really necessary for an activity is crucial – realizing that in most situations it is always easier to argue for the status quo than for change – change is the experiment. Flexibility is a desirable characteristic of space allowing innovation and experiment making it 'fit for the future', but it does have a cost – ongoing complexity of management.

Zoning

The tendency in libraries, even most existing ones, is for space to lean towards open plan rather than be cellular. Currently such open plan spaces provide a home for the book stacks, which bring with them their own zoning strategy regularly segmenting the space from floor to near ceiling height. Collection consolidation may give the opportunity to use the remaining stacks as 'book walls' to create effective zones, or small 'rooms' within an open space. In new space carefully selected furniture can be used to the same effect and has the advantage of being more easily reconfigured for future needs. Ideally, even in open plan space, zones can, and if possible should, arise out of the natural configuration of the building with the zoning strategy enhanced further by the strategic positioning of furniture or other fit-out items. The purpose of creating zones is for each one of them to have a different environmental feel and purpose. The degree of separation can vary depending on the height of furniture and fit-out items used, but even minimal structures such as the 'street umbrellas' shown in Image 9.2 (page 128) can have a surprising effect. Zoning does have its limitations, however, so when planning a new library learning space it is important to ensure that the architecture of the building provides separation between extremes of environment – noisy and silent do not collocate well. What is important is that zoning is another route to choice, providing the kind of flexibility that enables people to move about the building and activities to be undertaken in different parts of the building without the need for constant physical adaptation of the space. A well zoned space will provide choice for users that is part of the conversation with the building and easily understood, support interaction and also work against ownership of different parts of the building by different interest groups.

Semi-private space

Included in the category of 'other fit-out items' mentioned in the paragraph above I include items that provide semi-private space. These items can be used for two reasons. First, to shield the users of the library from the less tidy parts of library operations such as self-service machines, printers and book trolleys. Second, to partly separate members of the library from others in the large open space.

In the first category structures can be constructed such as printer pods, trolley bays and self-service machines housings that not only serve to screen off these items but also enhance the environment. For example the 'printer pods' used in the Saltire Centre serve to contain the noise and untidiness of the photocopy points and create opportunities for interest through the use of graphics inside the pod, on an otherwise open plan floor.

Secondly semi-private structures can also provide some separation for members of the library who want to work individually or in a small group. Most new developments include some form of banquette, or diner, seating, for example, and book walls have been mentioned above. Again in the Saltire Centre extensive use has been made of semi-private structures to provide varying degrees of enclosure and sound separation such as the inflatable igloos shown in Image 9.1 and the canopies shown in Image 9.2 (on page 128).

These temporary semi-private structures are recognizably different from other furniture and fittings in the space and, as their continuous use and popularity suggest, appeal to users in other ways than just their ability to reduce noise. They serve to structure the space and provide a tool for flexibility. This recognition of the importance of the ability of structures to start to act as furniture and furniture to start to structure a space provides a significant opportunity in the dynamic design of open plan spaces.

Creating a 21st-century library

It is my view that rather than being of reduced importance libraries in the 21st century now have a greater role to play than ever before. They need to

Image 9.1 *Igloos used in the Saltire Centre (copyright inflate.co.uk)*

continue to develop their role as centres of learning and community by rethinking the space and services that they offer. The 21st-century library goes beyond gratuitous social space, defies categorization as a third place, and is an essential part of 21st-century learning infrastructure within both universities and the public sector. A 21st-century library is necessary not merely 'for good company and lively conversation' but enables, through a broader provision of services, links to the unexpected encounter and the chance conversation that are at the heart of what Johanssen (2004) described as a 'Medici effect' – enabling the emergence of new ideas for the conceptual age. It is a space that is flexible and responsive, dynamic not static, for users not librarians and more art than science. The 21st-century library is not a third place but a subtle combination of Oldenburg's first and second places,

Image 9.2 *Canopies used in the Saltire Centre arranged to form a 'street' and provide a feeling of 'semi privacy' (image courtesy Les Watson)*

providing a place for work, leisure and learning with the feeling of home.

Conclusion

A 21st-century library is itself an act of creativity – artists can paint over their work to change it; the 21st-century librarian erases lines and creates new vistas through the flexibility afforded by open space and the imaginative reconfiguration of the contents of the space. Engaging continuously with the creation and re-creation of the space we have in our libraries is an essential part of the 21st-century library, a library that does not stop experimenting at the first successful space configuration but is dynamic, constantly pursuing a better library environment.

References

De Botton, A. (2006) *The Architecture of Happiness*, Penguin.

Edwards, C., Gandini, L. and Forman, G. (2012) *The Hundred Languages of Children: the Reggio Emilia experience of transformation*, Praeger.

Ellis, M. (2004) *The Coffee House: a cultural history*, Weidenfeld and Nicolson.

Fine, C. (2007) *A Mind of its Own: how your brain distorts and deceives*, Icon Books.

Florida, R. (2003) *The Rise of The Creative Class: and how it's transforming work, leisure, community and everyday life*, Basic Books.

Hisham, E. and Neda, A. (2012) *Development of a Tool for Evaluation of Academic Library Spaces (TEALS)*, www.srhe.ac.uk/conference2011/abstracts/0242.pdf (accessed 18 May 2013).

Jamieson, P. (2013) Reimagining Space for Learning in the University Library. In Matthews, G. and Walton, G. (eds), *University Libraries and Space in a Digital World*, Ashgate Publishing.

Johanssen, F. (2004) *The Medici Effect: breakthrough insights at the intersection of ideas, concepts and cultures*, HBS Press.

Langer, E. (1989) *Mindfullness*, Lifelong Books.

Lankes, R. D. (2012) *Expect More: demanding better libraries for today's complex world*, CreateSpace Independent Publishing Platform, 32.

Mikunda, C. (2006) *Brand Lands, Hot Spots and Cool Spaces: welcome to the third place and the total marketing experience*, Kogan Page.

Oldenburg, R. (1999) *The Great Good Place*, Marlowe and Company.

Pine, J. B. and Gilmore, J. H. (1999) *The Experience Economy*, HBS Press.

Rizzo J. C. (2002) Finding Your Place in The Information Age Library, *New Library World*, **103** (1182–83), 457–66.

Watson, L. and Anderson, H. (2008) *The Design and Management of Open Plan Technology Rich Learning Space in Further and Higher Education in the UK*, Joint Information Systems Committee, e-learning program, www.jisc.ac.uk/whatwedo/projects/managinglearningspaces.aspx (accessed 4 May 2013).

CHAPTER 10

Thinking it through

Les Watson

Introduction

The tension between the certainty that is required by project delivery and the imagination that is needed to conceive and vision a project is mentioned in several places in this book (for example in the introduction and Chapter 21). There can be no argument that on-time and on-budget delivery is not just a highly desirable outcome of any project; it is essential, but it should also be recognized that imaginative solutions that make the project fit for the present and future are at least equally important. In a chapter titled 'How little we know' in his book *The Halo Effect* Phil Rosenzweig (2008) quotes social psychologist Eliot Aronson who observed that 'people are not rational beings so much as *rationalizing* beings. We want explanations. We want the world around us to make sense.' Creating that 'sense' certainly means building on what we know, but to create something new and amazing can only be achieved by taking a 'both and' approach, which combines the best of what we know, from our professional expertise and experience and research, with the best of what we can create by imagination.

Chapters 8 and 9 touch on the importance of creativity, experiences and emotions in respect of space. In this chapter I continue these themes by discussing some common ways of thinking about projects, and emphasizing tools and techniques for planning creatively. Thinking outside the box is something of a cliché but it is required at the outset of a project from all concerned. De Bono (2000) argues that we should be concerned with 'skills as a thinker' if we are to create the future – and one of the most important, and often neglected, aspects of our thinking skills is intuition. Albert Einstein once said, 'The intuitive mind is a sacred gift and the rational mind is a faithful servant. We have created a society that honours the servant and has forgotten the gift' (quoted in Staes, 2008).

The idea of 'both and' means that we need to strike a balance between the rational and the intuitive minds. Currently this balance is strongly tilted towards the rational mind in most organizations and building projects. Shifting the emphasis to the intuitive mind opens up thinking, making it more likely that a project will have the elusive 'wow' factor.

Acknowledge the past – think future

Those managing any project, and especially the project leader, must have a clear, well articulated vision, must own that vision, and ensure that it is widely communicated. By consulting as widely as possible the project manager(s) should aim to capture new ideas that enhance the core purpose of the project. And as the project will be building for the future, focusing on the future is crucial. Library professionals, users of library spaces, learners, and indeed anyone else all bring a wealth of expertise, knowledge and their own perspective, which can inform the project. A 'both and' approach takes all of this into account and refines and filters information through a future view developed by projection of the contextual factors discussed in these chapters in Part 2. Making the future the reference point is essential. Land and Jarman (1992) call this a creative world view approach to strategy and planning: 'The reference point is the future, not the past. We don't need to fall back on the past for our decisions. Choices are based on alignment with our purpose and our vision for a different world.'

The past is not ignored in this view but using the past to prevent the growth of new ideas at an early stage in their formulation is avoided by focusing on the future. The data we hold in our databases and spreadsheets is about the past, and although it is helpful in providing us with 'lessons learned', in a general sense, it can only be used to make decisions about the future if it is extrapolated. Any extrapolation of past data brings uncertainty. It is important therefore that we do not rely on data alone to create the future. It is more important that we use our professional insight, understanding and intuition to develop our creative world view. This view should be a rich descriptive picture of the future, which can be easily understood by others and used to inform decision making during the course of the project. When reaching a decision past data can help but more important is the question, 'Which choice is more likely to lead to the creative world view that we have developed?'

Space is strategic

In the strategic framework discussed in Chapter 7, I included the environment as one of the factors along with people and technology. There is no doubt that investment in new library and learning space is an important part of strategy. The four-stage approach to strategy – anticipation, insight, imagination and implementation – mentioned in the introduction works well when thinking about developing new spaces. Anticipation involves knowing as much as possible about what is happening in the internal environment of the organization and the external world. Gathering information and ideas from a wide variety of sources should be a constant activity even before a project is on the horizon (see the section 'Evaluate' later in this chapter) and when a project becomes a reality this information gathering should continue all the way to project completion (and beyond). The rest of this chapter provides ideas about the anticipating stage of a project and the use of insight and imagination to bring new ideas into the frame.

Anticipate

Information gathering analysis and, importantly, synthesis form the natural part of the anticipation phase of a project. No matter how much we already know we know that there is more to learn. That is what is behind the feeling of information anxiety that I mentioned in the introduction. We don't know what we don't know and anxiety comes from the feeling that we will complete an expensive building project and then discover something that is a game changer. The fact that we are not actively aware of the totality of our own knowledge can add to these feelings of anxiety. Our subconscious absorbs the many stimuli that bombard us every day and carries the greater part of our experiences. Unfortunately these are not easily accessible to us.

Writing about our ability to think and make choices, Daniel Kahneman (2011) describes two types of thinking: System 1 (fast and intuitive thinking) is based on information that is retrieved quickly, and System 2 (slow thinking) requires attention, as it is evaluative and rational. System 2 thinking is 'slow' because its role is to analyse and reassure us that the intuitive suggestions of System 1 thinking are right. Kahneman points out that not all information and ideas that we have in System 1 thinking are always activated leading us to make decisions on a 'what you see is all there is' (WYSIATI) principle. Increasing the range of ideas available and active in associative memory is an attractive idea, which serves to increase our awareness, enable subconscious synthesis of information and maybe reduce information anxiety. A broad exposure to ideas from as many sources as possible is essential for innovative ideas to emerge. I suggest some ways to do this below, but also recommend that you explore the concepts of predisposition, priming, illusions and cognitive ease that Kahneman (2011) describes in relation to System 1 thinking, which can bring personal bias into decision making – which in my view is acceptable as long as it is acknowledged.

In Chapter 8 we suggested that conversation is at the heart of the learning process. To fuel personal learning (through internal 'conversations') we should exploit valuable sources of ideas from reading materials, online resources, visits to places (not just libraries and learning spaces but also other types of space in as wide a variety of organizations as possible), attending meetings and conferences and having conversations with others. The objective of this information gathering is to expand our knowledge of possibility. As Peter Drucker (1955) observes: 'The most common source of mistakes in management decisions is the emphasis on finding the right answer rather than the right question.'

Information gathering will not provide a 'right' answer but will raise many questions and stimulate thinking. It will also provide opportunities for what Tom Peters (1989) calls 'creative swiping'. What Peters means by this is taking ideas from elsewhere and not simply copying them but rearticulating, twisting, tweaking and modifying them to be an integral part of your overall vision (you could use Michalko's Thinkpak for this – see the section 'Imagineering – an attitude', below).

A useful structure for making sure that as many perspectives as possible are covered in the scanning phase of the project is a PEST analysis. This is a commonly used tool for providing structure to an environmental scan. PEST involves the exploration of the political, economic, social and technological context of the project. PEST can be extended to include other factors, for example a framework suggested by Jisc infoNet (2013) in their Learning Spaces web resource is PESTLEV, which adds pedagogical, legal, environmental and values of the organization to the PEST framework. This extended PEST is useful in guiding the information search before developing the project vision, ensures that a broad view is taken of the project (for example by including values) and can also be used with a simple SWOT (strengths, opportunities, weaknesses and threats) analysis to make links between the external and internal contexts for the project.

Continuous thinking

There is significant pressure from project professionals to finalize all of a project's details at the earliest opportunity. Any subsequent changes during the course of the project can be expensive. For a two- or three-year project, a new build for example, there is a danger that the completed project is potentially two or three years out of date on completion. However, project management, implementation and all that this entails can to some extent run in parallel with the consultative processes, workshops, conversations, discussions and daydreaming required to develop a great project, recognizing that any significant changes in the project at a late stage are expensive and must be avoided if at all possible. In *The Clock of the Long Now* Stewart Brand (2000) talks about the presence of fast and slow components in systems. For example he describes a coniferous forest as a spectrum of scale from pine needle to tree crown, patch, stand, whole forest and biome. These components are scaled in size and, more importantly, time from the eternity of the biome to the short lifetime of a year or less for the pine needle. Each layer has its own speed of change and it makes sense to locate the capacity for change in those items with the potential shortest life span. This idea when applied to buildings translates into the concept of pace layering shown in Figure 10.1.

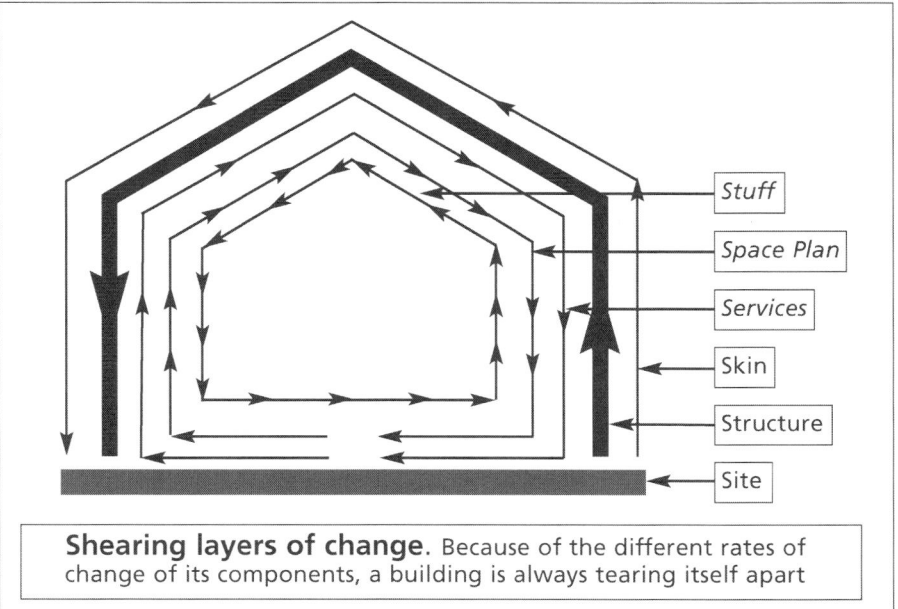

Shearing layers of change. Because of the different rates of change of its components, a building is always tearing itself apart

Figure 10.1 *Pace layering (Brand, How Buildings Learn, p.13, courtesy Stewart Brand)*

For buildings and new spaces this means avoiding creating some layers, such as internal dividing walls, that have a medium-term life span and are a potential barrier to accommodating changing activities. In Chapter 9 the idea of pace layering is encapsulated thus: 'This recognition of the importance of the ability of structures to start to act as furniture and furniture to start to structure a space provides a significant opportunity in the dynamic design of open plan spaces.' The suggestion is that investing in furniture, fittings and equipment as the way of creating the internal environment provides greater opportunity for future flexibility. The idea of pace layering also serves as a guide to when each aspect of the project needs to be finally decided and become unchangeable – the least permanent and most rapidly changing items such as furniture and technology, which are potentially most important in creating the environment, can be finalized relatively late in the project.

Insight

> Information's pretty thin stuff unless mixed with experience.
>
> Clarence Day (author)

The role of professional expertise cannot be underestimated in developing insight into the information gathered in the anticipation stage. The synthesis of personal knowledge, experience and intuition, rather than analysis, can create new ideas for space and service. The information gathered through the anticipation stage combined with what can be imagined – using some of the approaches below, and subjecting this to professional scrutiny from a wide range of perspectives – enables the fusion of the known and imagined to create something new. William Duggan (2002) describes the insights that occur at the interface of knowledge and experience as a *coup d'oeil*: 'Modern science has its own name for coup d'oeil: expert intuition. Psychologists see it as a form of déjà vu, a sixth sense based not on dreamy visions but on solid knowledge and past experience.'

Tools for thinking with
Imagineering – an attitude

Projects that have significant impact 'break new ground' and have some innovative and exciting aspects that come from imagination. The potential of imagination is described in *Out of Our Minds* by Ken Robinson (2011):

> Imagination is the primary gift of human consciousness. In imagination we can step out of the here and now. We can revisit and review the past. We can take a different view of the present by putting ourselves in the minds of others: we can try to see with their eyes and feel with their hearts. And in imagination we can anticipate many possible futures.

The experts on imagination are Disney Corporation (The Imagineers, 2003). They changed the noun into a verb. The staff at Disney invented the term 'imagineering' and consider themselves to be imagineers. For Disney this is a state of mind, not a simple recipe to be followed. According to Disney's imagineers, to be a successful imagineer you need to assume that you will be, and this means avoiding being constrained by traditional thought processes. In particular you shouldn't worry about everything fitting together perfectly early on in your planning, and you must be prepared to challenge every assumption that you come across.

Imagination is a crucial starting point for anything new as it is the source of creativity and essential for innovation. Robinson (2011) analyses the difference between imagination and creativity:

> Imagination, which is the process of bringing to mind things that are not present to our senses; creativity, which is the process of developing original ideas that have value, and innovation which is the process of putting ideas into practice.

A useful stimulus for imagination and for challenging the status quo is Michael Michalko's (2001) book *Cracking Creativity*, which provides a rich source of approaches to thinking differently. Michalko's *Thinkpak* (2006) is a practical tool for getting groups to experiment with ideas. The 56 Thinkpak cards support group-based idea generation using the SCAMMPERR structure for looking at topics from a wide range of different angles. SCAMMPERR is an acronym for nine ways of modifying ideas to generate new ones – substitution, combination, adaptation, magnification, modification, repurposing, elimination, rearrangement and reversal. It's simple to use – take an idea and then pick a card and apply what it says to the idea, for example, what would be the reverse of the idea?

Metaphors and stories

Although much transmission of knowledge is through text and print, communication about culture has largely been transmitted through the spoken word. Two important constructs for the transmission of culture that have been used since humans first learned to communicate are metaphor and story. These are powerful tools, which can be used to articulate the aspects of a project and help develop ideas. Often, particularly at the outset of a project, it is a struggle to articulate what the real hopes, aspirations and intentions are – what Lakoff and Johnson (1980) describe in *Metaphors We Live By* as the objectivist myth. This difficulty is partly due to the western system of thinking, which attempts to deal with uncertainty by identifying concrete targets and milestones, often too early in a project, when thinking is incomplete. At the other extreme we intuitively know what we are trying to achieve but often have deep insecurity from our inability to articulate and validate our intuition and our worries about the consequences of being wrong. Lakoff and Johnson (1980) suggest that metaphor can help us clarify imperfect emergent ideas:

> Metaphor is one of the most important tools for trying to comprehend partially what cannot be comprehended totally: our feelings, aesthetic experiences, moral practices, and spiritual awareness. These endeavours of the imagination are not devoid of rationality; since they use metaphor, they employ an imaginative rationality.

This 'imaginative rationality' provides an alternative to both objectivist and subjectivist points of view. By taking an experiential approach to developing ideas that acknowledges both what is known and what we learn during the course of the project our 'understanding emerges from interaction, from constant negotiation with the environment and other people' (Lakoff and Johnson, 1980).

Metaphor is particularly useful for developing thinking at the top level of the project to inform the brief. For example, consider the project as a journey – a journey with a clear direction but perhaps with an unknown destination. Metaphor is also a way of understanding components of the project, for example considering what the service desk might be like – an ice-cream cart, a dining table or a bus shelter? What is important here is the need to focus on not merely how things will look but how they will work and how experiencing them will feel.

Biological concepts such as symbiosis, speciation, mutation, ecosystems and others have much to offer in the understanding of systems and processes that may support innovative thinking about space development and the services offered in the space. *It's Alive* by Christopher Meyer and Stan Davis (2003) covers ideas on the convergence of information technology, biology and business, and Brand's (1994) book *How Buildings Learn* touches on concepts of evolution and natural selection in the context of buildings – for example, those perfectly formed and lacking the flexibility to change are unlikely to survive for long.

We can use stories to combine metaphors (and analogies) into engaging descriptions of the project and how it will work. For example, it is worth considering writing a 'day in the life' account for each type of user, or member of staff, in the new space, which shows how that person will make use of any new features. Specific scenario stories of alternative futures are a good method of helping decide what type of spaces are required for the many different types of learning and other activities that are expected to take place, and ensuring that the needs of library members and staff are met. Imagination is also needed here, otherwise new spaces will look and operate just like the old spaces – 'Some people think that the future is just like the past – but bent a little!' (Peter Day, 2005). It is impossible to predict the future; it can only be based on what we know today, but scenarios can help paint plausible possibilities for the future.

Consult across domains

In Part 3 of this book there are 14 chapters, only some of which are written by authors with a library or learning background. The aim of Part 3 is to introduce what Johanssen (2004) calls the Medici effect (mentioned in Chapter 9): 'When you step into the intersection of fields, disciplines, or cultures, you can combine existing concepts into a large number of new ideas.'

The idea of a Medici effect provides a rationale for getting the broadest mix of ideas and opinion in the consultation phase of a project. By seeking out and mixing a wide spectrum of people with differing interests and know-how new ideas are likely to emerge. Thinking carefully about who to involve and at what stage in the project is important, as only some people will be able to contribute from the earliest ideas stage, whereas others will have more to contribute once there are some concrete proposals on which they can comment. In Chapter 22 Stephen Heppell describes the involvement of children and young people in the design process as rich sources of imaginative ideas that have yet to be dulled by experience – it works for school design and undoubtedly will work for ideas for library space design.

Much of the consultation process is likely to occur in face-to-face meetings but it is also useful to use more imaginative ways of soliciting feedback – for example by issuing disposable cameras, or asking people to use their phone cameras, to collect images of things that they like or dislike to inform the project. Collecting comment through social media such as Twitter and Facebook is also useful.

Evaluate

Behavioural observations of the way in which current resources and facilities are used can be helpful not only to inform the project but also to provide baseline pre-project information that provides comparison data for post-project evaluation. By using similar techniques post-project real improvements or issues can be more easily identified and it is possible to understand some of the softer cultural impacts of the new facilities. The design of new spaces and development of existing ones requires an evidence base that should contain not only numbers of users but also information about what they do and how they feel about the spaces they inhabit (see Chapter 23 by Val Clugston).

Techniques such as social network analysis, experience sampling and day reconstruction can all contribute to in-depth understanding of the softer cultural impact of the project. For example, social network analysis can be used to compare the diversity of pre- and post-project human interactions using observation and/or video, and show who is talking to whom and whether the complexity and extent of interactions has increased. The experience sampling method that I mentioned in Chapter 7, used extensively by Hektner, Schmidt and Csikszentmihalyi (2007) to record how subjects were feeling at a number of points in the day, uses a series of alerts sent to subjects over one or more 24-hour periods, which prompt them to record their experiences and how they feel about them. In the original work pagers were used for the alerts, but with smartphones and tablets now widely available the method is more easily used in a wide variety of situations, including discovering what library users feel about the environment, facilities and services. The great advantage of this method over others is that it collects data in real time and removes the need for subjects to remember the experience and what it made them feel like, and hence is likely to produce more accurate information. Day reconstruction studies involve subjects recording their activities and how they feel about them at intervals throughout the day and then participating in a conversation with a researcher to review the information. Used in combination all of these methods can provide insights into not just who is in the learning space and what they are doing but also how the experience of the space feels to them.

Kelly (2010) points out that the problem used to be that we never had enough information quickly enough to evaluate successfully whether things worked or were safe to use, whereas now we can easily have too much information in many situations. The issues of information quantity and the fact that much of the information collected by the methods mentioned above is qualitative means that we will need to rely on computing power and algorithms to analyse and find meaning from it as suggested in the section on big data in Chapter 7. If there isn't a library evaluation app yet, there will be. For the only way to find out what works is to try it, continuously evaluate it and use the information created to model the user so that we can design the next innovation.

Model the user

Painter et al. (2013), reporting on research into the effectiveness of learning space design, including informal spaces in libraries, conclude that 'the field of learning space research lacks systematic, longitudinal research'. A programme of continuous collection of information on the way people use and feel about a library or learning space informs us of the range and diversity of users, their wants and needs, and how they feel about the space. Such information provides a good basis for understanding the user but is insufficient to make the link between the user and tomorrow's successful space or to link the success of a space to learning outcomes. For their book *Predictable Magic*, Prahalad and Sawhney (2011) studied a range of products with commonly agreed stunning designs that had not sold well and ultimately failed in the market place. They used this information to develop a psycho-aesthetic approach to design, based on the idea that it is not how you feel about a design that is important but how a design makes you feel about yourself that matters. Considering the success of top brands they conclude: 'There is a consistency to their quality and the unique and consistent experience they provide – in short, in the way that they tend to the well being of their customers.'

We have discussed elsewhere the importance of such emotional connections with the users of library and learning spaces and the importance of emotions in respect of learning. Prahalad and Sawhney (2011) see two barriers to be overcome in developing designs that connect emotionally with users – information overload and inadequate models of collaboration within the organization. Their psycho-aesthetic approach to design aims to overcome these issues through a framework of collaboration within the organization and a 'systematic understanding of the emotional reactions of consumers [users] to products, services and experiences'. The idea that we can predict the emotional impact of a space, or any other product or service that we create, is attractive. Employing a 'design strategy' for a new library or learning space, such as predictable magic, has potential. As Prahalad and Sawhney (2011) point out, 'The key . . . can be found in first understanding the consumer experience and then innovating meaningful ways of transforming it' and importantly 'the best innovations transform both the experience and the customer'. As educators we need to add a further parameter and find ways of exploring how space affects tangible aspects of learning.

Experiment

In Chapter 5, on libraries in Europe, Joyce Sternheim and Rob Bruijnzeels concluded with a question:

> Should we take less time in library building development and adopt a more experimental approach that produces temporary solutions enabling us to come up with more innovative designs – and throw away the ones that don't work?

This idea of 'temporary solutions' as experiments to see what works, especially if the experiments do work, can be very useful. For example, before embarking on the Saltire Centre, Glasgow Caledonian University developed a small learning café space in the existing library, which provided informal study space in a café setting to promote conversational learning. This successful pilot paved the way for the bigger project. Such experiments are to be recommended and are of equal importance if they succeed or fail as long as something is learned that can be carried into the next project. Even small-scale experimentation is to be welcomed. Using the idea of 'semi-private' space pop-up learning venues can be constructed quickly in corridors, within larger spaces or outdoors using inflatable structures or screens to assess the usefulness of the location for the intended purpose. The increasing availability of mobile computing facilitates mash-ups of different activities presenting some potential for exploring new combinations of facilities, for example bringing together exercise and learning facilities, that might bring new benefits. There is evidence that physical exercise, or simply movement, can enhance cognition (Ratey and Hagerman, 2009). Simply using furniture that moves sufficiently to facilitate adjustment of body position, therefore providing subtle exercise for the core muscular system, may also serve to extend time on task, or improve concentration for some users.

Conclusion

The aim of this chapter was to provide ways of thinking about library and learning space development that redress the current imbalance between the rationality of project definition and management and the imagination required to develop and capture new ideas that work. The discussion also demonstrates the need to start to apply a more rigorous approach to data and information collection, the range of data and information collected and its analysis and synthesis so we can identify what works. What makes a great library or learning space is not just the architecture or interior design, it is the ideas that are realized in the building. Most importantly the ideas that make libraries and learning spaces work best come from the insights of educators, learning specialists and librarians.

References

Brand, S. (1994) *How Buildings Learn: what happens after they're built*, Penguin.

Brand, S. (2000) *The Clock of the Long Now: time and responsibility – the ideas behind the world's slowest computer*, Basic Books.

Day, P. (2005) World of Business, BBC radio 4, 15 January.

De Bono, E. (2000) *New Thinking for the New Millennium*, Penguin.

Drucker, P. (1955) *The Practice of Management*, Heinemann.

Duggan, W. (2002) *Napoleon's Glance: the secret of strategy*, Nation Books.

Hektner, J. M., Schmidt, J. A. and Csikszentmihalyi, M. (2007) *Experience Sampling Method: measuring the quality of everyday life*, Sage.

Jisc infoNet (2013) *Learning Spaces Infokit*, www.jiscinfonet.ac.uk/infokits/ learning-spaces/design/developing-vision/ (accessed 24 April 2013).

Johanssen, F. (2004) *The Medici Effect: breakthrough insights at the intersection of ideas, concepts, and cultures*, Harvard Business School Press.

Kahneman, D. (2011) *Thinking Fast and Slow*, Allen Lane.

Kelly, K. (2010) *What Technology Wants*, Penguin.

Lakoff, G. and Johnson, M. (1980) *Metaphors We Live By*, Chicago Press.

Land, G. and Jarman, B. (1992) *Breakpoint and Beyond Mastering the Future – Today*, Harper Business.

Meyer, C. and Davis, S. (2003) *It's Alive: the coming convergence of information, biology and business*, Texere Publishing.

Michalko, M. (2001) *Cracking Creativity: the secrets of creative genius for business and beyond*, Ten Speed Press.

Michalko, M. (2006) *Thinkpak: a brainstorming card deck*, Ten Speed Press.

Painter, S. et al. (2013) *Research on Learning Space Design: present state, future directions*, Society for College and University Planning, www.scup.org/page/pubs/books/rolsd (accessed 14 August 2013).

Peters, T. (1989) *Thriving on Chaos*, Harper Business.

Prahalad, D. and Sawhney, R. (2011) *Predictable Magic: unleash the power of design strategy to transform your business*, Wharton School Publishing.

Ratey, J. and Hagerman, E. (2009) *Spark: how exercise will improve the performance of your brain*, Quercus.

Robinson, K. (2011) *Out of Our Minds*, Capstone Publishing.

Rosenzweig, P. (2008) *The Halo Effect: how managers let themselves be deceived*, Pocket Books.

Staes, J. (2008) *My Organisation is a Jungle*, LannooCampus.

The Imagineers (2003) *The Imagineering Way: ideas to ignite your creativity*, Disney Editions.

Summary to Part 2

Les Watson

This part of the book has looked (in Chapters 7 and 8) at aspects of technology and learning in the context of library space development. Switching the technology system that is the library from a focus on technology for operational management to a more strategic focus on user need and user choice links closely with the ideas in Chapters 8 and 9 on variety and flexibility, in both space and service provision, to support learning. Chapter 8 argues for a new approach to education, shifting from an industrial model to one based on individual capability and performance that acknowledges difference, conversational learning and emotional factors. The 21st-century library has a key role to play in this shift becoming a more important place of learning than ever before by providing variety and giving learners real choices – of space, technologies and services. This variety is not about separate silos but about a continuum of experiences and interactions with resources, technologies and people, understanding not just how people learn but also how space can support them through its variety and flexibility. Finding out what works with space and technology is an essential part of the 21st-century library, requiring continuous experimentation.

This experimentation needs imagination and in Chapter 10 I covered some ways of thinking about library and learning space development that can help develop for the imagination needed to come up with new ideas that work. Exposure to a broad range of ideas is important to feed the imagination and in the final part of this book there are 14 chapters from a range of perspectives to provide some food for thought.

PART 3

Ideas and futures

Introduction

Les Watson

Part 3 of this book has 14 chapters, written by authors from a wide range of backgrounds, that look at the potential for future library space. These chapters stand alone as individual essays on how the authors see the library from their professional perspective, giving glimpses of their version of the future. There is remarkable consensus in their view that we will continue to have places that do what libraries currently do and more – though they may not be called libraries and they may be physical or virtual, or both. My reasons for inviting such a variety of authors to contribute their ideas, as mentioned in the introduction to the book, were:

> Those close to and deeply involved in the work of the library often have answers
> to questions about the future of libraries that are bounded by the realities of
> day-to-day library operations – it is, in my view, more likely that the fresh ideas
> for future library and learning space will come from unexpected places.
> Understanding the broadest range of perspectives is at least helpful and possibly
> invaluable when faced with unknown possibilities.

CHAPTER 11

Beyond space: access is all – or is it?

David Baker

Introduction

This chapter considers the future of physical library space from a higher education perspective and questions the future need for libraries – other than virtual ones. Reference is made to the work done in recent years by Jisc, though the views expressed here are those of the author and not the organization.

Out with the old; in with the new

Traditional academic libraries, their buildings, collections and services face an uncertain future, as demonstrated by the following quotation from a report by the University Leadership Council (2011), which enumerates the key drivers behind a fundamental change in thinking about 'the library':

> Decreasing use of both traditional collections and the spaces in which they are contained has been combined in recent years with significant rises in the main costs associated with library provision. This is particularly evident in the dwindling importance of the library's collection size as an indicator of value in universities and the very low footfall by academic staff and research students, for whom 'the library' is – or is expected to be – at their fingertips. Increasingly, the creation, ownership, management and access to content rests outside the direct sphere of library-type services.

The University Leadership Council (2011) report also neatly summarized future requirements for what is increasingly being described as the 'edgeless'[1] university:

> Today's users require a new set of services and accommodations from the
> academic library that necessitate a strategic paradigm shift: from building and
> maintaining a collection to engaging with students and faculty, as well as
> providing space for study, collaboration, and creativity. Traditional
> organizational boundaries are likely to fade and the word 'library' will cease to
> adequately describe the suite of both virtual and physical academic support
> services offered to patrons.

> There is little doubt that the major changes in the delivery and receipt of
> education are changing the ways in which library space is designed, built, used,
> re-used and refurbished. Hardly an academic year goes by without some new
> development that is likely to alter the education landscape. The recent advent of
> massive open online courses (MOOCs) is one of the more radical, with the
> potential to change the current distance and face-to-face teaching models
> irrevocably. While the business and pedagogical models for such developments
> are not yet clear, it is already possible to assert that the work of 'the library' in
> these contexts is unlikely to require space other than perhaps for core staff
> providing facilities to users who are online and perhaps at a distance from the
> sources of information and content or as a locus for student and staff discussion
> of the materials delivered through the MOOC sessions and the tasks coming
> from them.

Jisc and space

Already, then, information provision is often digital and users expect digital
access as the norm. Libraries now spend more on electronic access than
physical ownership and storage. Mobile technologies in particular have the
potential to make old-style library buildings and services largely irrelevant.

Jisc has long been at the forefront of technology development and
application in further and higher education within the UK. Recognizing the
significant changes likely to take place in library building design, Jisc
launched *Designing Spaces for Effective Learning* (JISC, 2006) at its 2006
conference. This publication aimed to promote better understanding of what
makes an effective design for the 21st century and to summarize the key
points to consider when approaching a refurbishment or new-build project.
The emphasis was on 'technology-rich' spaces, for Jisc recognized early on
the relationship between technology and space, and the significant drivers
(noted earlier) that were then already changing the ways in which buildings

are used. In 2008, the organization published an 'overview' of its work in helping institutions 'develop physical spaces that anticipate the pervasive use of technology in learning and teaching, enable innovative, learner-centred pedagogies and inspire and motivate wider participation in learning'.[2]

The document recognized both the need for a strategic approach to space management that integrated it with all aspects of academic activity, embraced the culture of the institution as much as its formal objectives, and developed new ways of evaluating the effectiveness of library space.[3] Investment in estate and learning technologies was making it more important than ever that longer-term return on investment – financial and academic – was considered, especially at a time when environmental as well as financial sustainability was coming to the fore as a major challenge in higher and further education. In 2008 Jisc infoNet[4] developed a web-based resource linking tools for project management and process review with key principles in designing for 21st-century learning spaces, noting:

> Good design and effective management are fundamental to the success of a new-build or refurbishment project. With the chance to influence the future direction of learning and teaching in an institution, much is at stake for directors of estates, project managers, academic and library staff embarking on a large capital project.

More recently, the emphasis within Jisc has again been on reducing cost, especially through shared development, services and digital collection building (including the digitization of existing – special – collections), all activities that further impact on the future of physical library space while recognizing that the physical campus will 'remain at the core of educational provision for the foreseeable future'.[4]

Recent developments in UK universities[5] also suggest that there is a substantial continuing need for a central campus location where certain activities, including socializing, can take place (Usherwood et al., 2005; Lippincott, 2010; Loder, 2010). In his book *The Great Good Place*, Oldenburg (1989) writes of a 'third place': somewhere that is neither work nor home but situated in the middle. In other words, neutral territory where people can gather freely, learn and socialize; where they are encouraged and spontaneity is supported. The academic library building is changing in the direction of Oldenburg's 'third place', and in many ways becoming unrecognizable from the physical space that it was only one or two decades ago, even though, for now, books can still be found on shelves in these new 'learning environments' (Carnegie and Abell, 2009; Darnton, 2009).

The latest received wisdom suggests that academic library design should facilitate the provision of physical places and digital spaces. In both the physical and digital arenas, libraries involve a constant interaction between collections, services, spaces and people. The physical library is increasingly about flexible, technology-enabled, supported environments in which users can interact with high quality content, each other and staff. Users also want libraries to be friendly, welcoming places, where they can meet, study, communicate and, perhaps, relax. The digital library is about the provision of powerful search and navigation facilities, which enable access to and use of an extensive array of information materials.

Physical and virtual library services should be complementary and highly integrated. For example, the best physical spaces are configured to enable optimum access to digital resources, while online search services should be designed to encourage the use of both digital and physical content. David Vogt (2011) describes one example in Vancouver where an integrative approach, which combines physical and virtual across a continuum of diverse yet complementary services and collections and is 'built around the needs of people', offers one future model for the physical library, success being 'measured in how flexible they can be as those needs evolve' (Keiser, 2010).

Making such a contribution by successfully adopting this new emphasis depends on recognizing the prerequisite of a clear understanding of what makes facilities effective for users. Such places also typically have a landmark or core attraction that arouses curiosity – the 'wow' factor – which feedback, including in the case of UK universities the National Student Survey scores,[6] shows to be important and valuable to users and the institutions that fund their construction.

Space, the final frontier

Recently, the author carried out an internal, in-depth study for a major research university. The aim was to develop a long-term strategy for the institution's library system. The existing space-based provision of stock, services and digital access was seen as outmoded and likely to have a deleterious effect on the reputation of both library and parent organization. Analysis of student and staff opinions, needs and usage patterns, in the context of the trends outlined earlier in this chapter, strongly suggested that what was needed was:

- provision of high quality core services anytime, anyplace, anywhere
- digital provision as the norm
- vibrant collections supporting learning, teaching and research in a global top 100 institutions
- information literate students and staff
- continuous innovation in provision.

Ultimately, the institution was looking for:

- an outstanding and highly skilled focus for the delivery of excellent collections and services
- the support of research, knowledge creation, learning and teaching
- a hub for discourse, sharing, access, creation and reflection.

Could and should all this be provided physically as well as virtually? Does it need to be? Certainly, if the university's aims are to be fully met, then the existing approaches to library provision in general, and space management in particular, need to be completely rethought. Otherwise, physical considerations will get in the way of future developments. As a result, the institution is looking to create high quality physical space of high value and relevance to all. This fits in with the broader trend – already discussed – for university campuses to have core central spaces where students and staff can go to study, research, learn and be taught, both individually and collectively. But is that space a library? Longer term, say over the next 15–20 years, the likelihood is that digital access will not just be the norm; it will be the sole means of provision for all but very specialist need and usage. Already, the vast majority of core requirements, as described and discussed in Table 11.1 (see pages 156–7) – with the exception of working space and special collections storage (and to a lesser extent access) – can be satisfied without a building, other than somewhere to house the staff and servers. Managers in the institution to which I have already referred are currently debating what to call the entity that will be responsible for this provision. The word 'library' is unlikely to feature in the title.

Table 11.1 *Key strategic drivers for the university and challenges for 'THE LIBRARY'*

Strategic driver for the university	Challenges for 'THE LIBRARY' (not mutually exclusive to each goal)
Maintain a strong research focus	Maintain access to high quality resources from a range of subject areas
	Acquire and maintain specialist collections
	Manage and promote research outputs, including university's research publications, through an accessible and flexible repository infrastructure or set of repositories with the capability to interface with national and international repositories
	Integrate new research tools that support the researcher's work from anywhere on or off campus so they can be used by research groups that cross institutional boundaries – 'THE LIBRARY' systems – with tools that are being adopted, either by research departments or centrally
	Provide a single information source to provide simple access to all required resources: licensed, open access and in-house
Attract most able students and postgraduates	Provide specialist, high-end support, specialist resources, high-end technology and storage space
	Integrate systems of 'THE LIBRARY' with tools that are being adopted, either by research departments or centrally; this requires co-ordination with other departments in order to meet expectations
	Provide specialized study areas for individual and group work
	Provide real and virtual dedicated work and collaborative spaces for postgraduates only
	Provide high specification computers for personal research
	Co-ordinate with other departments in order to meet expectations; offer departments guidance on how to manage information resources if needed
Recruit and retain large numbers of students	Provide high quantity easy availability and fast access to most popular, heavy usage resources; 'THE LIBRARY' platforms may need to be upgraded or replaced in order to interface with new systems and be able to deliver content in formats suitable for the devices that students wish to use; there will be a need to interface with student record systems and possibly other systems such as financial data
	Make it possible to access resources using mobile devices
	Offer online learning platforms that can be accessed remotely and provide a single point of entry to all resources
	Work with other departments to establish the ownership and responsibility for personalized learning support systems; conduct user needs analyses and alter or replace systems so they can meet needs
	Provide fast, efficient services that can cope with heavy demand
	Provide flexible opening hours
	Provide zoned working spaces to cope with large numbers and a wide range of students
	Ensure there is social space as this is important

Table 11.1 *(Continued)*

Strategic driver for the university	Challenges for 'THE LIBRARY' (not mutually exclusive to each goal)
Develop partnerships with businesses and other organizations	Offer professional, high quality working spaces
	Provide extended licensing arrangements for on and off site access, which allow other users to access resources of 'THE LIBRARY'
	Offer expertise in key subject areas that are most relevant to partner organizations
	Create an interface between a genuinely personalized learning system and a number of other existing institutional systems; this may require the acquisition or licensing of new systems
Develop learning management systems and virtual learning environments	Make digital resources of 'THE LIBRARY' available to students through their Moodle module pages
	Make it possible for students to search 'THE LIBRARY' resources (or be automatically directed towards them) from their learning system or portal rather than having to use separate systems
Develop the institutional repository for research outputs and data	Ensure staff of 'THE LIBRARY' have the knowledge and experience to build good information and resource management systems; they will not always be considered as the best place to store research outputs, so this needs to be achieved through partnership
Develop customer relationship management	Use information about 'customers' and provide information about their users into a Customer Relationship Management system

Notes

1 P. Bradwell (2009) *The Edgeless University: technology and higher education institutions,* Demos, www.jisc.ac.uk/publications/research/2009/edgelessuniversity.aspx (accessed 19 August 2013).

2 JISC (2008) *Technology-Rich Physical Space Design: an overview of JISC Activities.*

3 JISC (2007) *Planning and Designing Technology-Rich Learning Spaces* – 'an applied infoKit following the life cycle of a project from vision to post occupancy, with an image gallery, virtual campus tour and links to related resources', www.jiscinfonet.ac.uk/infokits/learning-spaces/ (accessed 1 July 2013).

4 JISC (2008) *Technology-Rich Physical Space Design,* www.jisc.ac.uk/media/documents/publications/bpelearnspacev1rtf.rtf (accessed 4 July 2013).

5 Aberdeen is currently constructing a flagship new £57 million library. Edinburgh is undergoing a radical reconstruction process for its library. Queen's University Belfast has recently opened a major new £50 million library facility. Leeds has built library extensions to all of its main libraries. University College London has completed a major new fit-out of its libraries, including a major overhaul of its Science Library. Warwick continues to invest in its Information Grid and has also added a research exchange facility to its portfolio. Sheffield opened a new

£23 million information commons student library and resource centre three years ago, and Leicester opened a major extension to its library (including refurbishment and redesign of the original 1970s library, at a total cost of £31 million) in 2008–2009.

6　See www.thestudentsurvey.com/ – informal research carried out by the author comparing relevant scores for Russell Group universities against their recent capital spend.

References

Carnegie, T.A.M. and Abell, J. (2009) Information, Architecture, and Hybridity: the changing discourse of the public library in *Technical Communication Quarterly*, pp. 242–258, Routledge.

Darnton, R. (2009) *The Case for Books: past, present, and future*, Perseus Books.

JISC (2006) *Designing Spaces for Effective Learning: a guide to 21st century learning space design*, Higher Education Funding Council for England, www.jisc.ac.uk/media/documents/publications/learningspaces.pdf (accessed 14 August 2013).

Keiser, B. E. (2010) Library of the Future – Today!, *Searcher*, **18** (8), 18–54.

Lippincott, J. K. (2010) A Mobile Future for Academic Libraries, *Reference Services Review*, **38** (2), 205–13.

Loder, M. W. (2010) Libraries With a Future: how are academic library usage and green demands changing building designs?, *College and Research Libraries*, **71** (4), 348–60.

Oldenburg, R. (1989) *The Great Good Place*, Marlowe.

University Leadership Council (2011) *Redefining the Academic Library: managing the migration to digital information services*, http://utlibrarians.files.wordpress.com/2012/01/23634-eab-redefining-the-academic-library1.pdf (accessed 14 August 2013).

Usherwood, B. et al. (2005) Relevant Repositories of Public Knowledge? Libraries, museums and archives in 'the information age', *Journal of Librarianship and Information Science*, **37** (2), 89–98.

Vogt, D. (2011) Islands in the Cloud: libraries and the social life of information. In Baker, D. and Evans, W. (eds) *Libraries and Society: role, responsibility and future in an age of change*, Chandos.

CHAPTER 12

Thinking inside the box

Colin Allan

Introduction

Much is said about transforming education. As architects and designers it is debatable as to whether we can influence pedagogical outcome . . . but we are eager to try. Through placemaking and the creation of better learning environments we can influence activity and behaviour in a creative, exciting and innovative way.

Since Socrates sat under a plane tree in ancient Greece, Cistercian monks occupied their monastic cells in the 11th century, merchants discoursed in the coffee houses of 17th century London and pupils were fearful in foreboding Victorian school houses . . . learning has been serendipitous. We learn, despite the space or building.

This chapter will illustrate how form and space provide 'a wrap' for learning environments – intentionally or otherwise – and how it can be improved. The architecture can work much harder to encourage the activity within the space – creating the joy of space and an exciting environment in which to learn.

I believe that as architects we need to establish objectives, then work within defined parameters. This should be considered as a creative challenge rather than a restrictive convention. It is a fundamental multi-dimensional assessment of light, space and technology and how they can best be combined architecturally . . . it is about 'thinking inside the box'.

Many learning spaces now excel through designing from the inside out. We are not talking about simply interior design but true architecture where the inside of the building form and function is expressed in an intrinsic rather than superficial way – for example the Saltire Centre at Glasgow

Caledonian University, where a range of learning spaces has been created, in part through orientation, circulation patterns, the permeability of the building and the environmental strategy. More recently some of the most exciting, imaginative environments have been created for technology and media-based companies such as Apple, Google, Microsoft, Pixar and Disney, embracing dynamic architectural spaces, the latest information and communication technology, smart furniture solutions, minimal storage, and bold use of colour and art to create a sense of place, which encourages inspiration and creative learning, and makes for a joyful working environment. An essential ingredient in all of this is the injection of a choice of spaces conducive to creative activity . . . while being fun!

Library – an outmoded type of building?

Libraries traditionally contained material made of paper, lots of it. For architects this created the challenge of designing storage for a considerable number of books and periodicals in such a way that was efficient and accessible to the browser and researcher. Books also needed a controlled environment that protected and preserved these sensitive paper-based products – particularly with temperature, humidity and light control. This led to a certain way of designing libraries – the physical layout, height of rooms and ultimately the overall form of the building. Stacked books generate considerable static weight, so structure became much more onerous than normal. From this a building typology developed.

In Finland a recent international architectural design competition (Helsinki Central Library, 2012) for a major new library had a brief that required a design as follows:

> The objective is a high-quality, eco-efficient and timeless building…
>
> …forms a symbolic and architecturally significant building that resonates with society as a whole and expresses the operational concepts of the building in an intriguing way
>
> …offers a functionally high-quality and technically and spatially flexible framework for cutting-edge and adaptable library operations.

In summary, it should be an impressive and contextual building, energy efficient, with a flexible interior. Curiously books are not mentioned specifically in the headline brief. For me the interesting aspect was that the design should express 'the operational concepts of the building in an intriguing way'. How we engage, communicate, research and learn.

This is about rethinking the needs and aspirations of what we want from our libraries of the future and not about continuing traditional ways of operating. We need to challenge convention in the way we do things and the technology we need to achieve them. Perhaps we should no longer think of our buildings as libraries, but more as mediatheques?

Beware of ICT!

There is a general assumption that technology is the panacea for the future of learning. Don't worry about removing book stock, you can always get the information downloaded from a handy computer and the building will be the better for it. While this is in part true, it has become apparent that technology can isolate and de-socialize space.

Relaxing within a coffee shop recently I looked around and was intrigued to find that most people around me were not conversing with their friends or colleagues but instead were quietly focused on technology – their smart phone, tablet or laptop. They may well have been communicating, but in a virtual way. Free wi-fi facilities generally available in coffee shops are encouraging their use as a place not only to drink espresso but also to gather globally. This is genius, encouraging people to use coffee shops as a meeting place draws parallels with their antecedent in 17th-century London. But what is happening to the joy of conversation and discovery of knowledge through discourse?

It's good to talk as 'all learning starts with conversation'.[1] Sadly the silent coffee shop phenomenon is now international. While it is likely that most of these people were using convenient technology and comfortable venues for productive working or social networking, something is missing.

How can architecture respond to and assist in placemaking that encourages learning and conversation, now and in the future?

Why do we prefer one pub, restaurant or theatre to another? It's not just about the beer, food or performance. It is more often ephemeral things such as atmosphere, space and people that determine choice. Expectations of students and staff are ever increasing and educational institutions need to be competitive. They seek the best. By providing buildings and environments that are inspiring, comfortable and adaptable, as well as functional, there is a far greater chance of the building being used regularly and maintaining its popularity. By creating learning communities in buildings with atmosphere and space, so people will engage and return, again and again.

How to be popular

The indicators are that new libraries or 'mediatheques' will be considerably different from the model currently understood by most. They need to be more accessible, provide a wide range of study environments, encourage social engagement, be flexible and future proof, and offer enlightenment. Community engagement no longer brings about bespoke libraries for the elite but access for all.

So as architects, how do we design for such a diverse and intangible brief?

Architects can be at their most creative when faced with constraints. Consequently we should focus on getting the very best out of what could be a limited brief, restricted site or tight budget. In building terms we need to consider the spaces, events, wayfinding, environment and choice contained within the building envelope – the learning landscape. We need to stimulate the senses by the use of light, colour, touch, sound and even smell – all contribute to the identity of place, encouraging engagement and potential creativity.

Thinking inside the box is about maximizing efficiency and effectiveness through innovative design. This best use of space will be achieved through fresh thinking, ideas and experimentation – challenging the status quo in order to achieve added value. It also involves looking hard at every aspect of the brief and in particular the accommodation schedule, which will likely be based on past experience or previous examples rather than necessarily consider future needs and aspirations. There is a limit to how far you can manipulate room functions, space allocation, circulation, storage and so on. Challenging convention will inevitably reap greater rewards within set financial and physical constraints than endlessly tinkering with area schedules.

Spaces on the edge

People watching is fascinating. How do people use spaces – as individuals, pairs or groups – how do we naturally interact with each other? In deeper plan social spaces, the natural tendency of most occupants is to gravitate to the edge – whether in a restaurant, bar or library. We tend to feel more comfortable on the edge – whether because it is nearer natural light or a view, or because it offers privacy or defensible space. This personal space is highly valued. Consequently it could be argued that as architects we should consider the real value of small or shallow planned spaces. However, deeper planned space containing a series of 'events' or 'landmarks' can provide identity and a sense of place as well as feeling welcoming and 'safe' for conversation, learning and creativity.

Rooms or spaces

The question we often pose on receipt of the client's brief is do we need to create actual rooms or are spaces acceptable? Creative use of space and its sub-division can encourage greater interaction of users and increased flexibility. Environmental controls don't need to be as sophisticated when dealing with bigger volumes of space as elsewhere; for example, heat gains from a large number of computers can be dissipated within a large volume space rather than be dependent on air-conditioning within a confined room. High volume spaces, light wells and atria can assist in improving environmental qualities by admitting natural light into a deep space as well as providing natural ventilation through the stack effect.

Circulation

Corridors are often seen as wasteful but necessary, providing nothing more than a circulation route between a series of rooms. Corridors are expensive – they need to be lit, heated, ventilated and finished in appropriate materials. However, there are opportunities to convert or inhabit this circulation space, creating attractive places to meet, sit or present. But where possible, corridors should be avoided in favour of gallery access or open circulation. Gallery access can work well with single-sided accommodation and outdoor or balcony space opposite. Opportunities for the creation of interventions such as small booths or 'pop-out' balconies add variety and offer additional choice. Open circulation deals with access routes within a general space, allowing it to change and adapt to suit shifting functional demands.

Staircases can extend their primary role from purely vertical circulation to something much more. A main access staircase can also serve as an informal seating or gathering space, or form part of a temporary venue for a presentation or performance.

Designing for people not books

Books and related reading material demand a vast amount of space for access and storage. As demand for hard copy reduces as items are made available electronically, so space can be freed up within libraries for alternative and higher value use of space. This fundamentally shifts the architectural approach to design, so liberating the interiors and changing the environmental parameters, which in turn can influence overall building form and the external building envelope.

Flexibility

'The only constant is change' – this might not have been an issue for libraries in the past but now we have to be far more forward thinking in anticipating future trends and demands. Consequently when considering a new design we must look at the physical planning and structural implications of the building.

Structure

Developing a pragmatic approach to structure makes sense. Structural grids of columns and beams rather than load-bearing walls liberate internal planning.

Building services

A passive approach to library design is attractive but not always possible. Natural or mixed mode ventilation should be considered over air conditioning. Designing building services to be modular and controlling zones within the building contributes to efficiency and flexibility.

Fabric

The internal fabric of the building including walls, partitioning and ceilings can be planned for ease of removal or relocation. Modularity, non-load-bearing walls and 'dry' construction all contribute to future flexibility.

Connectivity

Creative use of space and physical adjacencies between spaces can inspire. This should be considered as a three-dimensional exercise in placemaking. Shaping space with an interplay of low single volume space with contrasting high volume single or multi-level space can add drama, offer a real choice of informal or social spaces, and improve wayfinding. Besides simply considering functional spaces, the connectivity between these spaces can create opportunities for a range of formal or informal activities.

Art space

Often in the past the selection of art in libraries has been inappropriate or uninspiring. Whether from political and academic precedent or pressure from an influential benefactor, the choice of art is often alien to students and consequently has no value. Careful consideration of the type and form of art in libraries, including consulting students about what they find relevant and appealing, is so important. As architects, in defining space we can provide a range of spatial opportunities for art simply by keeping in mind how people will navigate the building. Consider where the horizontal and vertical routes, intersections and gathering places are likely to occur so we can provide clear wall space, void space and suspension or projection points for different forms of media, which can be easily applied, accessed and changed.

Conclusion

In conclusion, the value and enrichment of library space is within our gift. The reinvention of the library into something much more appropriate and creative than in the past is happening. It needs everyone involved in the project to adopt a can-do, forward thinking mindset, particularly in light of economic constraints, in order to challenge, explore and deliver something that is truly innovative and wholly appropriate for learning in the future – it's about thinking inside the box!

Note

1. Quote by John Seely Brown (former CEO of Xerox Palo Alto Research Center).

Reference

Helsinki Central Library (2012) http://competition.keskustakirjasto.fi/ (accessed 1 July 2013).

CHAPTER 13

Nothing has changed/everything has changed – the enduring aspects of learning

Hugh Anderson

The limitations of 'library'

It is sometimes depressing when talking to clients about libraries that they lapse into traditional notions of what these spaces might be. But it is easier to pigeon-hole a concept into a traditional building type than deal with the socio-technical complexity that the concept involves.

Thus on the one hand 'library' is a misleading shorthand for something ever-changing and far more complex than it once was, but to suggest, on the other, that it does not include enduring aspects of the process of learning and working is equally wrong. What is important is to understand the fundamental human processes at work in the new concept of 'library' and not be confused by either traditional or futuristic images. Image, when we come to it, will be critical, especially in establishing the attitudes of users to what is possible, but image is only 'image'. In adopting instead a fundamentalist, 'space usability', activity-led approach to library design one can avoid becoming a 'style monger' and free oneself up for a more creative approach. At haa design we have applied an activity-led approach to the design of various building types and found this liberating. It may not be dramatic but it enables us to look into the future in a way that can provide genuine clues of what might lie ahead. It is an approach that has worked within the evolution of other building types where, far from inhibiting the development of ideas, it has led to massive, liberating change and an escape from either traditional or futuristic cliché.

Activity-led design

What is 'activity-led design' and why is it key to developing an idea of the library of the future? Da Vinci's and Le Corbusier's icons of 'modular man', a man whose physical proportions underlie the appropriate design of all usable spaces, will be familiar to many, but these icons draw attention only to our anthropometric needs, to the way that the design of spaces to be used by humans requires ultimately to relate to the proportions of the human body. What is less celebrated (and also less succinct) is an analysis of man's basic psychological and emotional needs, our ways of behaving and operating, and yet these needs constitute the corresponding building blocks of good design.

Thus working by oneself, locked in thought and reading, or being engaged in 'reflective learning', represents one particular desire and is one such activity. Talking to one other person, or with a group in formal or informal circumstances, are others, as are computer work and technologically sophisticated presentations. These are all 'modes of work' or 'modes of learning' that have been affected by technology over time but are as valid now as ever. What is different now, and what will continue to change as technology and pedagogical practice evolve, is how, where and when these activities might take place. To this extent 'nothing is different'; we continue to need to design for these activities. However, a rather limited range of activities tended to define the library of the past and define its physical boundaries, and to the extent that these boundaries have now been blown apart, 'all is different'. Our preconceptions deserve complete revision.

Already the concept of work and learning as 'placeless' is commonplace; what the future might hold in new forms of information-transfer is anyone's guess, but insofar as all activities remain place-related, by definition they always take place in a physical context, the range of characteristics that these different places will require to meet will remain the same.

Thus the difference between then, now and the future is likely to depend not so much on completely new ways of behaviour as on the degrees of complexity of the activity modes that will constitute working and learning. And it is this 'richness' of types of place and 'richness' in types of behaviour that will characterize the nature and effectiveness of the 'libraries' of the future. This might not add up to a clear image of what lies ahead but is likely to be truer than any particular 'futuristic' image.

What can libraries learn?

In seeing how this works and how library design might learn from the evolution of other building types, let us examine what has happened elsewhere.

The modern office, or at least one that relied on the use of electric light and the telephone, was until recently a pretty traditional affair. There were private offices, meeting rooms, typing pools, catering for a variety of activities; and the whole was organized in a standard arrangement of corridors and rooms, rooms that had taken on titles that described their status as much as their physical characteristics. Thus 'board room' or 'typing pool' or even 'library' described who might use these rooms as much as the kind of function they might usefully support. Similarly, to use an educational analogy, 'classroom' or 'refectory' defined a type of generalized activity, but did not sufficiently describe the kinds of activity that were taking place within them. Worse still they had started to limit the concept of the kinds of activity that might take place within them.

In the world of work, technology eventually put the strain on these definitions and the standard concept of 'office', and eventually forced a revision. But the new notion of an effective workplace has involved more than a breaking down of barriers and a removal of individual rooms. The new 'flexible office' has involved rather a return to an appreciation of the basic work activities or 'work modes' that are called for, breaking down different persons' days into the different activities and sub-activities that business involves. It has isolated and appraised the need for quiet or privacy, for instance, or effective group communication or a place for simple touchdown, providing a series of spaces to meet these different requirements and overall a much richer mix of activities than was previously recognized. The result is an office that still has a locus and some enclosed rooms, where full acoustic privacy, for instance, is required; it is now diffuse, incorporating a host of other spaces where semi-enclosure or background noise might exist, but where awareness of and interaction with others might be more important. It certainly includes spaces that do not conform to the previous notions of a 'room'. In operational terms the result is something more dynamic and person-oriented, much richer and much more effective than the traditional office. Just so has been the change in the more progressive learning environments where the act of learning has broken the bounds of the 'classroom' and in so doing created situations for effective interaction and a far wider range of learning behaviour than was taken for granted before. And by letting go of the traditional notions of 'library' in understanding the different types of activity that add up to investigation and understanding, just so might be the library of the future.

The key change in the effective modern office and effective modern learning environment has been the rediscovery of the importance of the person, or personal interchange, and the social basis of effective communication. Gone are the days when information was only available via books, a teacher or the 'boss' imparting unique knowledge; gone too is the need for ubiquitous 'Keep Quiet' signs; gone too the regime that frowned on eating and even drinking at the workplace. No one is denying the need for quiet in some places, or anything else that might facilitate reasonable order and security, but instead we are appreciating the importance of social interaction and diversity. The change has been about the democratization of the workplace, opening up the opportunities for new types of behaviour and new attitudes to the acquisition of knowledge, enabling these different atmospheres to exist alongside and creating a context where appropriate behaviour is instinctive rather than enforced, creating an enjoyable experience for different people, all in one location.

The parallels between library and general workplace relate therefore at different levels, both in the physical conditions which we now recognize as being conducive to effective working and learning and in the way that we might go about re-imagining the workplace, seeing it as a blend of different component parts and activity modes, not just a one-off 'thing'.

Highlighting these parallels however raises the essential question 'What makes the new "library" or "learning centre" different from the general workplace?' Both want to be flexible, diverse, fit for individual concentration and group work. So where does the one end and the next start? Does it matter or is this very blurring in itself significant? The blurring of boundaries implies a democratization of space. In the same way as the formal office reflected a rigid organization and the privilege of management, the formal library reflected privilege in the acquisition of knowledge. A blurred boundary and a blurred definition open up the opportunities of management and the acquisition of knowledge to all.

More questions than answers

In some ways the answer is immaterial. Why should there not be a convergence? What intrinsically is the difference between work at home, in the office or in the library? Why should the one not start to look like the other, the office becoming more relaxed and domestic, the home more business-like, the library like a blend of the two? The answer, if there is one (and trying to understand this is important, because it gives a clue to what is special about a 'library'), possibly lies in the nature of the 'clientele', not necessarily its interest, age or style of working but possibly its purpose.

The spirit of a 'library' lies in its provision of knowledge and understanding as objectives in their own right, opportunities which are the right of anyone. It is a place (yes, its physical location allows it to embody this spirit) where learning, though sometimes conducted singly, thrives in being part of a common pursuit, an exploration conducted with fellow travellers. To this extent its doors are metaphorically open, its spirit is egalitarian and its atmosphere social. It is a place of interaction and relaxation, but its nature is ultimately serious, understanding the work styles of different individuals, but individuals with a common purpose. Its atmosphere might not be characterized by the smell of books, but it is likely to smell of shared endeavour, more than the commercially targeted, regulated activity of even the best office. In design terms it will be about being more person-focused, with even greater variety than the best flexible office, with a greater quality of space.

Extrapolating into the future

Current examples reinforce a current trend but what do they say about the future? Does this trend mean that all we need are congenial, social areas, so long as they are wi-fi enhanced and that we have ever more effective smartphones? The trend is significant and suggests that, insofar as we are social, this change in the culture and flexibility of what we think of as the library is indicative of the kind of further change that we can anticipate. But for designers to focus solely on the congenial social areas would be to miss the point. Above all the examples illustrate the need for variety and choice.

Another trend has been for technology to become increasingly less intrusive. To that extent spaces can afford to be 'informal', but it would be a serious mistake to equate informality with lack of specificity. The different work modes, identified within an activity-led approach to design, will remain, and the need to maximize the potential of each of them will be just as great. The way that learners will want to oscillate rapidly between them will be key. Thus the juxtaposition of spaces and creation of 'clusters' of types of space will be critical; while on the one hand the locus of what is the library is getting blown apart, on the other certain types of space will like to coalesce. Thus, in the same way as the future of the office or campus (as distinct places, where people come together socially to engage in a variety of related activities) is not dead, so too is the learning centre as a destination place likely to continue. It is only that its balance of types of space will change and its interaction with other places and remote facilities will increase.

In opening up the composition of what makes a library, at the same time as realizing that a sense of place is what will give the library 'destination appeal', a word of warning is necessary to ensure that different spaces do not start to compromise one other, that those wonderful 'wow' spaces like atria do not start to become unusable, generating heat, proliferating noise, contaminating one space with the smells of another. In other words, when designing the 'completeness' of these learning spaces, preferably rich in variety, the old-fashioned, technical issues of noise control, smell control, subtlety in lighting, and preservation of fresh air, greenery and views of the outside should not be forgotten. The more complex the overall space, the more difficult becomes the execution of conventional design; it is easier to design and manage one-dimensional spaces. In liberating the design process the challenge is therefore going to be in understanding how the new library operates as a total system, including built space, technical infrastructure, learning culture and management regime. There is going to be an increasing need for full engagement between designers and users to allow for the different parts of the system to evolve in parallel, with a democratization of the management process also as a protection against reverting to that which is primarily convenient for building managers and those responsible for timetabling and the curriculum.

The way forward

Liberating the library is thus ultimately a political issue, not much less complicated than liberating society! It will progress, fuelled by new technical opportunities, pedagogical theory and the seductiveness of fashion, and is likely to suffer setbacks from reactionary management, but information is now 'out there' and information exchange is both powerful and fun; the 'library' in its expanded, blurred, exciting, changeable context is likely to remain. This diffuseness will ensure that it is unlikely to be identifiable as a particularly distinct building type, in the same way as 'offices' can now exist in almost any situation, but if a prediction of the future is called for it would be that, like the office, the library of the future will continue to have a physical centre of gravity where people actually come together to gain energy from fellow human beings.

CHAPTER 14

Books, nooks and MOOCs

Jo Dane

Introduction

Ssssshhhhhh! Don't tell anyone, but the university library is a hip and happening place. Learning actually happens there. Some even still have books in them. Do you need to work in a group? Do you need a quiet place of respite? Do you like studying in proximity to others? Do you need access to a fast computer? The library has become a spectrum of spaces to cater for every imaginable learning modality. Consequently librarians have become curators of learning, anticipating the resources, services and physical settings to support all levels of education and research.

An archaeological dig of the University of Alexandria dating to the 5th century revealed the instantly recognizable remnants of a series of lecture halls: tiered seating and a podium for the scholar (Majcherek, 2008). Some 1500 years later lectures remain the dominant mode of content delivery across the majority of universities, despite criticisms in recent decades regarding the effectiveness of learning in lectures (Bligh, 1972; Penner, 1984; Hodgson, 1997). In stark contrast, the university library represents a space typology that has adapted to new pedagogies and technologies emergent in the last 20 years, generating a distinctly different student experience from libraries of past eras (Jamieson, 2005).

21st-century library space – it's all about value

Where traditional libraries were typically centred on books and study carrels, the 21st-century library is developing as a dichotomy of spaces: quiet versus noisy (individual and group learning); hi-tech versus low-tech (digital and analogue activities); light versus dark (reading and multimedia activities); open versus closed (short and long duration). Furthermore, the role of books in the student learning experience is being seriously questioned, with librarians being forced to negotiate the value proposition of space for books. Do students get more value from space comprising book collections or places where they can access digital resources and study collaboratively?

In a recent focus group of first-year students discussing use of their university library, the students conveyed their systematic avoidance of sourcing books on course reading lists, in deference to digital resources they found much easier to source (Woods Bagot, 2012). A related survey of students at the same Australian university revealed that access to computers and quiet study spaces were valued above access to book collections, closely followed by demand for group study spaces (Woods Bagot, 2013). The tension between spaces for books and spaces for the spectrum of student learning appears to be a common dilemma for librarians, as I experienced in several university library projects in the last 12 months. The question must be asked: how long before the university library ceases to house books altogether? Macquarie University has taken one significant step to manage its book collection by locating a significant portion of it in a high-density archive, making use of an automated archive and retrieval system that delivers books on request to students, but otherwise renders them out of sight (Rosenberg, 2011). Library managers at Macquarie University argue that the automated system will make access to books easier for students, but by reducing visibility of books this nonetheless represents a significant shift in view about the importance of browsing physical books.

Libraries in the age of the 'flipped' classroom

How will the type and variety of spaces in our university libraries continue to change and adapt to 21st-century pressures such as increasing student enrolments, changing student demographics and the predicted transformation of higher education through innovations such as massive open online courses (MOOCs)? While universities are intent on increasing student enrolments, the logical solution is to manage growth by increasing lectures and timetabling them to larger lecture auditoriums. This is an unsustainable enterprise (how many squillion-dollar lecture theatres can a university build?), and students have expressed their dislike of the passive lecture experience through survey responses, research and non-attendance

(Clay and Breslow, 2006; Wesch, 2007; Oakley et al., 2011). Lectures were conceived in response to the resources available to scholars, in times before projection, computers and the internet. But that does not mean that lectures are the way forward in the 21st century.

There are six key elements that should transcend every learning encounter. Effective learning is:

- social – a social process whereby knowledge is socially constructed (Piaget and Inhelder, 1969; Vygotsky, 1978)
- contextualized and relevant (Prosser and Trigwell, 1999; Biggs and Tang, 2007; Entwistle, 2009)
- evaluative – involves continual evaluation by the teacher of student understanding and progress (Hounsell, 1997; Laurillard, 2002; Ramsden, 2003)
- perspective – involves the teacher viewing teaching from the student's perspective (Prosser and Trigwell, 1999; Ramsden, 2003)
- deep and independent – fosters a deep approach to learning that encourages student independence (Hounsell, 1997; Marton and Saljo, 1997)
- active – promotes student activity, choice and variety (Biggs and Tang, 2007; Entwistle, 2009; Skinner, 2010).

If a teacher's goal is to activate each of these elements to create an effective learning experience in a singular episode, they would surely not seek to lecture. An effective learning encounter is more aligned with the notion of the 'flipped classroom' (Bergmann and Sams, 2012), but applied in a higher education context. The 'flipped classroom' concept essentially involves students accessing lecture content online in their own time rather than in a lecture theatre, and reinforcing new concepts by then engaging in learning activities in the classroom. In this sense the classroom encounter becomes social and active, fosters independence and enables teachers to develop more meaningful relationships with students. But the dilemma of flipping the classroom in a higher education context is that it demands a different spatial typology that is not commonly available on the university campus. While some universities are exploring learning spaces that support more active modes of learning (Van Note Chism and Bickford, 2002; Dori et al., 2003; Radcliffe et al., 2008) such spaces are far from commonplace. Therefore the provision of active learning spaces frequently becomes the domain of the university library, more so than formal timetabled learning spaces.

A word on MOOCs. Love them or loathe them, the concept of the MOOC is compelling and fascinating. They are 'massive', with some courses boasting enrolments in the tens of thousands. For example, a MOOC on artificial intelligence run by Stanford University in 2011 attracted 160,000 people to enrol, of whom 20,000 completed (Bremer, 2012). They are 'open', in the sense they are free and do not require any formal prerequisites to participate. They are 'online', commensurate with the 'learning anywhere, anytime' philosophy. They are organized as bona fide 'courses' with lectures, assignments and computer-aided assessment. Successful participants receive a certificate of completion at the end, although debate is currently raging over whether MOOCs should attract a formal accreditation, with some degree of inevitability surrounding the pro-accreditation argument. Universities are supporting MOOCs as a strategy to encourage participants to follow their MOOC experience by enrolling in a fee-paying course. However, MOOCs are essentially an isolated learning experience for the majority of participants, without a formal structure of engaging with peers or communities of learners. Retention and completion rates are typically low. They do not meet all and sometimes meet none of the criteria for 'effective learning' as described earlier.

Putting the library at the heart of the campus experience

However, the weakness of MOOCs could render an opportunity for universities to exemplify the fundamental element that MOOCs cannot provide: an effective on-campus experience. Why pay for expensive on-campus courses that are dominated by lectures – typically available online anyway – when MOOCs provide almost the same experience for free? The antidote is to provide a higher quality on-campus experience that engages students in authentic 'effective learning' practice. Instead of simply flipping the classroom, I propose that we flip the entire university:

- Broadcast lecture content online and timetable active learning classes on campus.
- Instead of having one teacher in a room of 30 students, have four teachers in a room of 120 students.
- Teach in teams; learn in teams.
- Discourage students from engaging with lecture content in a solitary manner.
- Encourage small groups to get together to watch instructional content so

that students can build meaning and understanding together. Media can be paused and replayed as required.

• Online lectures introduce concepts; active classrooms enable understanding and knowledge to be constructed.

Small group engagement with online instructional content and collaborative learning places greater emphasis on campus-based informal learning spaces, avoiding issues of geographically dispersed cohorts and groupings. This is where the university library has a key role to play. While the university library is emerging as a field of learning spaces to meet various student learning requirements, it will also need purposeful media nooks to enable engagement (watch, listen, discuss, understand) with content. Nooks may be enclosed for acoustic privacy, or with the use of wireless headphones could be in semi-open caves, curtained nooks or open corners. While student centres and other informal learning environments may be equipped with similar nooks, the library is the natural place for such media-centred engagement.

Furthermore, library spaces support many of the key elements of 'effective learning' as presented earlier in this chapter. University libraries are increasingly providing social learning spaces such as lounges, where students can meet informally but segue into synchronous learning encounters. They provide relevant and contextualized experiences through the availability of relevant, up-to-date resources and technologies. Libraries foster independence and a deep approach to learning through the variety of spaces that provide choices for students to study in places of their choosing. (This morning I will work with my group in the 'sandpit'; this afternoon I need a quiet study space.) Active learning becomes a natural extension of the library experience as students move to different learning settings in response to their immediate needs.

Conclusion

The 21st-century library – at least in the foreseeable future – will build on the current spectrum of learning spaces to provide students with a truly effective learning environment: a place for books, nooks and perhaps even one for people to engage in MOOCs.

References

Bergmann, J. and Sams, A. (2012) *Flip Your Classroom: reach every student in every class, every day*, International Society for Technology in Education.

Biggs, J. and Tang, C. (2007) *Teaching for Quality Learning at University*, 3rd edn, Open University Press.

Bligh, D. A. (1972) *What's The Use of Lectures?*, Penguin.

Bremer, C. (2012) *New Format for Online Courses: the open course future of learning*, www.bremer.cx/vortrag67/Artikel_elba2012_opco_bremer.pdf (accessed 15 August 2013).

Clay, T. and Breslow, L. (2006) *Why Students Don't Attend Class*, http://web.mit.edu/fnl/volume/184/breslow.html (accessed 14 May 2013).

Dori, Y., Belcher, J., Bessette, M., Danziger, M., McKinney, A. and Hult, E. (2003) Technology for Active Learning, *Materials Today*, **6** (12), December, 44–9.

Entwistle, N. (2009) *Teaching for Understanding at University*, Palgrave Macmillan.

Hodgson, V. (1997) Lectures and the Experience of Relevance. In Marton, F. , Hounsell, D. and Entwistle, N. (eds), *The Experience of Learning*, Scottish Academic Press.

Hounsell, D. (1997) Understanding Teaching and Teaching for Understanding. In Marton, F. , Hounsell, D. and Entwistle, N. (eds), *The Experience of Learning*, Scottish Academic Press.

Jamieson, P. (2005) Positioning the University Library in the New Learning Environment, *Planning for Higher Education*, **34** (1), 5–11.

Laurillard, D. (2002) *Rethinking University Teaching: a conversational framework for the effective use of learning technologies*, 2nd edn, RoutledgeFalmer.

Majcherek, G. (2008) Academic Life of Late Antique Alexandria: a view from the field. In El-Abbadi, M. and Fathallah, O. (eds), *What Happened to the Ancient Library of Alexandria?*, Koninklijke Brill NV.

Marton, F. and Saljo, R. (1997) Approaches to Learning. In Marton, F. , Hounsell, D. and Entwistle, N. (eds), *The Experience of Learning*, Scottish Academic Press.

Oakley, G., Lock, G., Budgen, F. and Hamlett, B. (2011) Pre-service Teachers' Attendance at Lectures and Tutorials: why don't they turn up?, *Australian Journal of Teacher Education*, **36** (5), 30–47.

Penner, J. G. (1984) *Why Many College Teachers Cannot Teach*, Charles C. Thomas.

Piaget, J. and Inhelder, B. (1969) *The Psychology of the Child*, Basic Books.

Prosser, M. and Trigwell, K. (1999) *Understanding Learning and Teaching: the experience in higher education*, Society for Research into Higher Education and Open University Press.

Radcliffe, D., Wilson, H., Powell, D. and Tibbets, B. (2008) *Designing Next Generation Places of Learning: collaboration at the pedagogy-space-technology nexus*,

University of Queensland.

Ramsden, P. (2003) *Learning to Teach in Higher Education*, 2nd edn, RoutledgeFalmer.

Rosenberg, J. (2011) Full-metal Dust Jackets and Wi-fi in Uni's Space-age Library, *Sydney Morning Herald*, 2 August, www.smh.com.au/technology/technology-news/fullmetal-dust-jackets-and-wifi-in-unis-spaceage-library-20110801-1i88g.html (accessed 15 August 2013).

Skinner, D. (2010) Effective Teaching and Learning in Practice, Continuum International.

Van Note Chism, N. and Bickford, D. J. (eds) (2002) *The Importance of Physical Space in Creating Supportive Learning Environments*, Jossey-Bass.

Vygotsky, L. S. (1978) *Mind in Society: the development of higher psychological processes*, edited by Cole, M., John-Steiner, V., Scribner, S. and Souberman, E., 14th edn, Harvard University Press.

Wesch, M. (producer) (2007) *A View of Students Today*, www.youtube.com/watch?v=dGCJ46vyR9o (accessed 15 August 2013).

Woods Bagot (2012) UNE Dixson Library Master Plan student focus group conducted by Jo Dane at the University of New England on 24 July 2012.

Woods Bagot (2013) UNE Dixson Library Master Plan Report. Unpublished report commissioned by the University of New England, dated 21 May 2013.

CHAPTER 15

The researcher's view: context is critical

Sheila Corrall and Ray Lester

Introduction

Our ideas about future models of the library focus on the needs of researchers. Our thinking is informed by our own experiences as both users and directors of library and information services in research institutions, and by debates on future roles for library and information professionals in the network world – a world where automation, digitization and socialization of data, information and knowledge, and disintermediation, are transforming the scholarly landscape. We begin with three reasons why library support for research is a critical issue, and then reflect on the current situation and environmental forces shaping provision for researchers, before setting out our thoughts about future services and spaces for research.

The library and research

First, higher education institutions across the globe continue to identify teaching and research as two distinct missions (Scott, 2006), and most academic libraries similarly define their roles in education and research as related, but separate, elements of their mission (Aldrich, 2007). Second, surveys in several countries show that researchers' experiences and perceptions of libraries are not altogether positive (Daniels, Darch and de Jager, 2010; Schonfeld and Housewright, 2010; MacColl and Jubb, 2011) and their views about future priorities often differ from librarians' views (RIN, 2007). Third, while changes in teaching and learning have largely driven spatial transformations of academic libraries over the past 20 years, we expect changes in research and scholarship to have a more central role over the next two decades in transforming and re-engineering libraries to meet the needs of both researchers and learners (Lyon, 2012).

Current provision and usage

For most people, the idea of a library is inseparable from a collection of books and periodicals, a perception that has continued into the network world, despite the arrival of digital technologies, new media and online services. Library requests for research assistance have given way to self-help and mutual support; few people use ask-a-librarian services and information seekers rarely start their search on library websites (OCLC, 2010). Academic researchers mainly use electronic resources, which they access remotely, with only arts and humanities researchers visiting libraries regularly, but less often than before (RIN, 2007). Faculty members rarely consult a librarian or use the library catalogue to begin their research, preferring network-level services, including general-purpose search engines, as well as services targeted at academics (Schonfeld and Housewright, 2010).

Library services for research range from the simply reactive to highly creative (Webb, Gannon-Leary and Bent, 2007), but most researchers seem to have little interest in the support offered (MacColl and Jubb, 2011). Many perceive university libraries as geared towards teaching and learning, prioritizing undergraduates (RIN, 2007; Daniels, Darch and de Jager, 2010) and 'a dispensary of goods (books, articles) rather than a locus for badly needed, real-time professional support' (Jahnke, Asher and Keralis, 2012, 16). Libraries are currently moving into more specialized higher-end research support roles that are aligned with institutional concerns and have the potential to enable strategic repositioning on campus. Scholarly publishing is a growth area, with many American libraries now publishers of journals, monographs and conference proceedings, and well placed to lead experiments with open access business models (Crow et al., 2012). Bibliometric analysis is increasingly used to evaluate and manage research activities at institutional, departmental and individual level, creating opportunities for libraries to deliver valued support to senior research administrators, and input to grant applications and promotion cases (Corrall, Kennan and Afzal, 2013).

The library role most valued by researchers is apparently the traditional collection stewardship function, which now includes digital content as well as print material, along with the procurement and administration of electronic resources. There are positive, though less consistent, messages about institutional repository development: many researchers support the concept of open access to scholarship, but have not actually deposited their work, or used content from their own or other repositories (RIN, 2007; Schonfeld and Housewright, 2010). The role of librarians in information skills is also recognized, though more care may be needed to ensure support is geared towards researchers' needs and pitched at the right level (RIN, 2007, 2011). In addition, despite visiting them less frequently, many researchers continue to be inspired by the creative and contemplative atmosphere of research libraries, particularly valuing the 'scholarly nature' of library space (Gannon-Leary, Bent and Webb, 2008, 4), but noise levels from mobile phones and group work in contemporary library buildings often make working conditions no longer conducive to individual quiet study (RIN, 2007; Daniels, Darch and de Jager, 2010). Researchers also see the library as a place to access up-to-date technology (RIN, 2007).

Current trends, implications and opportunities

Looking ahead, the trends expected to have the biggest impact on libraries are changes already under way for more than a decade in scientific research and scholarly communication – specifically, the emergence of networked data-intensive science (also known as cyberscholarship and e-research) as the dominant research paradigm, and the parallel elevation of data, rather than publications, as the valued product of scientific enterprise (Michener, 2012). E-research developments have major implications for library activities in digital and data stewardship, digital and data reference and digital and data literacy. Data here can originate from observation, simulation or experiments; it can take many forms (such as text, numbers, audio, still and moving images), and relate to any discipline, including the arts and humanities (Martinez-Uribe, 2007; Williford and Henry, 2012).

The data revolution and corresponding revolution in scholarly communication and publishing will have an impact on the library comparable to the education revolution in the 1990s, which replaced 'sage-on-the-stage' pedagogy with student-centred resource-based learning and enabled librarians to develop and professionalize their educational role as learning facilitators, learning advisers, instructional designers and teachers of information literacy (Breivik, 1999; Bewick and Corrall, 2010), and also reposition their services and spaces as 'learning resource centres', 'learning centres' and, latterly, 'information commons' or 'learning commons'

(Roberts, 2007; Lewis, 2010; Weiner, Doan and Kirkwood, 2010). E-science uses high-capacity global networks to access very large-scale shared resources, including high-performance simulation, observation, computation and visualization equipment and massive distributed datasets. E-research has been described as 'collection-based science' (Beagrie, 2006, 5), highlighting potential synergies with traditional library activities and a clear opportunity for libraries to develop their research role from support service to project partner and more – though few researchers see the library as a research partner at present (Jahnke, Asher and Keralis, 2012).

While technically challenging and requiring a deeper understanding of research processes and workflows than other library activities, data management fits logically with established library responsibilities and in many ways simply extends the scope of existing activities; for example, teaching data discovery skills and citation practices as part of information literacy education, as well as incorporating data into collection development, repository management, metadata creation and digital preservation (Cox, Verbaan and Sen, 2012). Mandates from research funders for open access to datasets mean that institutional repositories and data curation are now required elements of university infrastructure that need professional management by a central service, and the library is the obvious candidate for this stewardship role. Data-intensive science is giving libraries the opportunity for a more visible role as a partner in the knowledge creation process, by contributing to obligatory data management plans, data description and preservation (Tenopir, Birch and Allard, 2012; Witt, 2012). As data management becomes the 'new statistics', students will need training in all aspects of the data life cycle so they can handle massive volumes of complex data and use new analytical and visualization tools to interpret underlying patterns and processes (Michener, 2012, 50). Libraries will accordingly need to build services and facilities around the knowledge creation cycle of scholarly research workflows (Jahnke, Asher and Keralis, 2012; Ohio State University Libraries, 2012).

University libraries are already offering or planning services to help researchers with data problems (Corrall, Kennan and Afzal, 2013). At Purdue University, subject librarians are dealing with data in their collection, instruction and reference activities (Witt, 2012), and also partnering three other research libraries, all working with experienced researchers, to develop training in data information literacy for science and engineering research students (Jahnke, Asher and Keralis, 2012). Librarians and researchers have both spotted the opportunity for spaces freed up by collections going virtual to be repurposed for research collaboration and computing facilities (Michener, 2012), particularly for research students and early career researchers who may not have their own labs (Jahnke, Asher and Keralis, 2012). Several US libraries have opened or are planning 'research commons' facilities as renovations or new builds designed to support interdisciplinary data-intensive scholarship, offering services in partnership with other campus units, to assist researchers in areas such as grant writing, research conduct, copyright and open access publishing; for example, the University of Washington Libraries (2010).

Future space and services

The research commons model emerges as the preferred strategy globally for promoting library support for research. A consortium of research libraries in South Africa collaborated in an innovative programme to improve research support by creating new research commons facilities, along with customizable web-based research resources and advanced training for subject librarians (Daniels, Darch and de Jager, 2010). In the UK, the University of Warwick Library opened its Wolfson Research Exchange in 2009 as a highly visible dedicated research space in a prime location on campus, combining traditional quiet study places, with collaborative and social areas, in a technology-rich environment with mobile equipment that can be reconfigured for different types of meetings – from poster sessions, through project meetings and reading groups, to summer schools and academic conferences. Facilitating cross-discipline research interactions and 'fostering a sense of community' are key aims of the service, which includes events on topics such as funding opportunities, grant application tracking, data management, bibliometrics, journal impact, patents and spinout companies (Carroll, 2011, 91). Some research commons facilities provide access to specialized hardware and software for data and textual analysis; others are collocated with digital humanities institutes and interdisciplinary research centres or offices (Ohio State University Libraries, 2012).

Commentators emphasize that researchers want and need physical facilities that are separate from undergraduates, because they are engaging in knowledge creation and production at a quite different level. Another clear message is the critical need for librarians to understand the day-to-day working contexts of the researchers they aim to support, including their academic ambitions, disciplinary differences, institutional imperatives and political pressures that drive or constrain their efforts. Partnerships, marketing and empathy emerge as key library requirements for delivering relevant and valued services (Webb, Gannon-Leary and Bent, 2007). The subject, reference and liaison librarian role is the traditional model used for supporting research in academic libraries (Holland, 2006), but has evolved in some institutions into the more specialized role of 'informationist' or 'information specialist in context' (Shipman, 2007), which requires deeper knowledge of the subject domain and its research methods to enable more extensive input to research projects. The 'embedded librarian' concept is a variant that similarly emphasizes closer engagement with stakeholders and location of assistance in academic departments or equivalent settings (Dewey, 2004; Shumaker, 2012). Embedded librarianship is also a potential model to support research data management, where a librarian is embedded into research group or specific research projects (Carlson and Kneale, 2011).

An interesting feature of emergent data management and bibliometric services is the way they are extending library service partnerships beyond typical partners in the information or learning commons model, through collaborations with research offices and graduate schools, and (to a lesser extent) planning departments, human resources and records management and legal services, and adding new dimensions to collaborations with technology services, including high-performance computing and e-research units (Corrall, Kennan and Afzal, 2013). Partnerships between research libraries and external institutions to promote long-term preservation and access to scholarly resources are also becoming an essential dimension of stewardship responsibilities in the network world and liberating space for repurposing, through distributed reserve collections and collaborative storage facilities for low-use print journals and monographs, shared digital archives and open access repositories for digitized books and digital data (Boyle and Brown, 2010; Demas and Miller, 2012; Williford and Henry, 2012).

Future services for research will continue to focus on the library's stewardship responsibility, but emphasize a rich array of digital data. Collections will be planned and managed collaboratively through internal and external partnerships, but based on a mix of federated, licensed and open access resources with a greatly reduced physical presence in library buildings. Spaces for people and technology should be expanded and reconfigured to provide more visible, effective and efficient support for research across the institution by adopting the research commons model. Our vision of the research commons is a one-stop shared space-as-service facility for researchers, similar in its design philosophy and staffing model to leading examples of information and learning commons, which have demonstrated how careful and innovative user-centred design aligned to institutional needs and pedagogies can successfully integrate resources provided by the library into the working and social lives of students with support from other campus units (Lewis, 2010; Weiner, Doan and Kirkwood, 2010) and rebrand the library as a central, essential and vital facility.

The research commons should similarly reflect campus needs and priorities, including research methodologies and researcher preferences, but should be designed and managed by a different set of service partners, to accommodate more specialist hardware and software, and multi-professional teams with the research, subject and technical know-how to provide in-context end-to-end support for both discipline-based and interdisciplinary projects and programmes. Research offices and graduate schools have emerged as key partners for libraries delivering innovative higher-end research support, along with information compliance units and research computing teams in campus technology services (Carroll, 2011; Lyon, 2012; Corrall, Kennan and Afzal, 2013). The presence of staff from such units will provide complementary expertise and credibility for librarians moving into areas such as calculations of research impact indicators and guidance on data management planning for grant applications or peer review of online scholarship and publication advice for digital datasets after project completion (Williford and Henry, 2012; Witt, 2012). University presses, which are increasingly library-based operations, could also have a presence here, along with knowledge transfer and innovation units.

The overarching goal is to create a place that is viewed as a research facility – not a traditional library or learning centre – which offers expert help for all stages and phases of the research process from ideas generation, through problem definition, project design and bid writing, data acquisition, analysis and interpretation, to publication and archiving of findings. Repurposing one or more floors of a library building is one option, but is likely to be most successful if it is clearly differentiated from undergraduate facilities and has substantial physical presence of cognate services. A prominently positioned facility could also support the strategic objectives of many institutions to showcase their research to wider audiences, by hosting public lecture series, Café Scientifique meetings and citizen science events – another area envisaged as a future interest for libraries (Lyon, 2012; Williford and Henry, 2012).

Our proposed model is compatible with the current trend towards embedded librarianship (Dewey, 2004; Carlson and Kneale, 2011; Shumaker, 2012), which places information specialists with domain understanding in locations where they can anticipate and deliver point-of-need assistance geared to the work context. Dividing research liaison librarians' time between academic units and a central commons facility is more likely to be scalable and affordable than having liaison librarians wholly located in academic departments or schools. The design of user-centred high-tech expertly staffed research facilities on a collaborative space-as-service model will elevate libraries from invisible infrastructure to vital partners in the work of researchers.

References

Aldrich, A. W. (2007) Following the Phosphorous Trail of Research Library Mission Statements into Present and Future Harbors, *ACRL 13th National Conference*, Baltimore, MD, March 29 – April 1, 2007, American Library Association, Association of College and Research Libraries, 304–16, www.ala.org/acrl/conferences/confsandpreconfs/national/baltimore/baltimore (accessed 16 August 2013).

Beagrie, N. (2006) Digital Curation for Science, Digital Libraries, and Individuals, *International Journal of Digital Curation*, **1** (1), 3–16, www.ijdc.net/index.php/ijdc/article/viewFile/6/2 (accessed 16 August 2013).

Bewick, L. and Corrall, S. (2010) Developing Librarians as Teachers: a study of their pedagogical knowledge, *Journal of Librarianship and Information Science*, **42** (2), 97–110.

Boyle, F. and Brown, C. (2010) The UK Research Reserve (UKRR): machinations, mayhem and magic, *Interlending & Document Supply*, **38** (3), 140–6.

Breivik, P. S. (1999) Take II: information literacy – revolution in education, *Reference Services Review*, **27** (3), 271–5.

Carlson, J. and Kneale, R. (2011) Embedded Librarianship in the Research Context: navigating new waters, *College & Research Libraries News*, **72**, 167–70, http://crln.acrl.org/content/72/3/167.full (accessed 16 August 2013).

Carroll, D. (2011) Fostering a Community of Scholars at the University of Warwick: the Wolfson Research Exchange, *New Review of Academic Librarianship*, **17**, 78–95.

Corrall, S., Kennan, M. A. and Afzal, W. (2013) Bibliometrics and Research Data Management: emerging trends in library support for research, *Library Trends*, **61** (3), 636–74.

Cox, A., Verbaan, E. and Sen, B. (2012) Upskilling Liaison Librarians for Research Data Management, *Ariadne*, **70**, www.ariadne.ac.uk/issue70/cox-et-al (accessed 16 August 2013).

Crow, R., Ivins, O., Mower, A., Nesdill, D., Newton, M., Speer, J. and Watkinson, C. (2012) Library Publishing Services: strategies for success, final research report (Version 2.0), SPARC, www.sparc.arl.org/resource/library-publishing-services-strategies-success-final-research-report-march-2012 (accessed 20 August 2013).

Daniels, W., Darch, C. and de Jager, K. (2010) The Research Commons: a new creature in the library, *Performance Measurement and Metrics*, **11** (2), 116–30.

Demas, S. and Miller, M. E. (2012) Rethinking Collection Management Plans: shaping collective collections for the 21st century, *Collection Management*, **37** (3–4), 168–87.

Dewey, B. I. (2004) The Embedded Librarian: strategic campus collaborations, *Resource Sharing & Information Networks*, **17** (1/2), 5–17.

Gannon-Leary, P., Bent, M. and Webb, J. (2008) A Destination or a Place of Last Resort? The research library of the future, its users and its librarians, *Library and Information Research*, **32** (101), 3–14 (accessed 16 August 2013). www.lirgjournal.org.uk/lir/ojs/index.php/lir/article/view/65/112.

Holland, M. (2006) Serving Different Constituencies: researchers. In Dale, P., Holland, M. and Matthews, M. (eds) *Subject Librarians: engaging with the learning and teaching environment*, Ashgate, 131–47.

Jahnke, L. M., Asher, A. and Keralis, S. (2012) *The Problem of Data*, Council on Library and Information Resources & Digital Library Federation, www.clir.org/pubs/reports/pub154/pub154.pdf (accessed 16 August 2013).

Lewis, M. (2010) The University of Sheffield Library Information Commons: a case study, *Journal of Library Administration*, **50** (2), 161–78.

Lyon, L. (2012) The Informatics Transform: re-engineering libraries for the data decade, *International Journal of Digital Curation*, **7** (1), 126–38, www.ijdc.net/index.php/ijdc/article/view/210/279 (accessed 16 August 2013).

MacColl, J. and Jubb, M. (2011) *Supporting Research: environments, administration and libraries*, OCLC Research, www.oclc.org/resources/research/publications/library/2011/2011-10.pdf (accessed 16 August 2013).

Martinez-Uribe, L. (2007) Digital Repository Services for Managing Research Data: what do Oxford researchers need?, *IASSIST Quarterly*, **31** (3–4) 28–33, www.iassistdata.org/downloads/iqvol313martinez.pdf (accessed 16 August 2013).

Michener, W. (2012) Five New Paradigms for Science and an Introduction to DataONE, *Educause Review*, **47** (2), 50–1, http://net.educause.edu/ir/library/pdf/ERM1225.pdf (accessed 16 August 2013).

OCLC (2010) *Perceptions of Libraries, 2010: context and community*, OCLC Online Computer Library Center Inc, www.oclc.org/reports/2010perceptions.htm (accessed 16 August 2013).

Ohio State University Libraries (2012) *Overview of Research Commons in Academic Libraries: a white paper*, Ohio State University Libraries, http://library.osu.edu/staff/administration-reports/ResearchandEducation/ResearchCommonsVision.pdf (accessed 16 August 2013).

RIN (2007) *Researchers' Use of Academic Libraries and Their Services: a report commissioned by the Research Information Network and the Consortium of Research Libraries*, Research Information Network, www.rin.ac.uk/system/files/attachments/Researchers-libraries-services-report.pdf (accessed 16 August 2013).

RIN (2011) *The Role of Research Supervisors in Information Literacy*, Research Information Network, www.rin.ac.uk/news/role-research-supervisors-information-literacy (accessed 16 August 2013).

Roberts, R. L. (2007) The Evolving Landscape of the Learning Commons, *Library Review*, **56** (9), 803–10.

Schonfeld, R. C. and Housewright, R. (2010) *Faculty Survey 2009: key strategic insights for libraries, publishers, and societies*, Ithaka Strategic Consulting and Research, www.sr.ithaka.org/research-publications/faculty-survey-2009 (accessed 16 August 2013).

Scott, J. C. (2006) The Mission of the University: medieval to postmodern transformations, *Journal of Higher Education*, **77** (1), 1–39.

Shipman, J. P. (2007) Informationists or Information Specialists in Context (ISIC): six years after conception, *IFLA Journal*, **33** (4), 335–9, http://archive.ifla.org/V/iflaj/IFLA-Journal-4-2007.pdf (accessed 16 August 2013).

Shumaker, D. (2012) *The Embedded Librarian: innovative strategies for taking knowledge where it's needed*, Information Today.

Tenopir, C., Birch, B. and Allard, S. (2012) *Academic Libraries and Research Data Services: current practices and plans for the future, An ACRL white paper*, Association of College & Research Libraries, www.ala.org/acrl/sites/ala.org.acrl/files/content/publications/whitepapers/Tenopir_Birch_Allard.pdf (accessed 16 August 2013).

University of Washington Libraries (2010) Research Commons to Open in Allen Library, *UW Libraries e-News*, September, www.washington.edu/alumni/partnerships/libraries/201009/commons.html (accessed 16 August 2013).

Webb, J., Gannon-Leary, P. and Bent, M. (2007) *Providing Effective Library Services for Research*, Facet Publishing.

Weiner, S. A., Doan, T. and Kirkwood, H. (2010) The Learning Commons as a Locus for Information Literacy, *College & Undergraduate Libraries*, **17** (2), 192–212.

Williford, C. and Henry, C. (2012) *One Culture: computationally intensive research in the humanities and social sciences, a report on the experience of first respondents to the digging into data challenge*, Council on Library and Information Resources, www.clir.org/pubs/reports/pub151/pub151.pdf (accessed 16 August 2013).

Witt, M. (2012) Co-designing, Co-developing, and Co-implementing an Institutional Data Repository Service, *Journal of Library Administration*, **52** (2), 172–88.

CHAPTER 16

Libraries in the network society: evolution, revolution, extinction?

Chris Batt

The Internet has become a vital part of our lives and our society.

Dutton and Blank (2011, 8)

Welcome to the network society

The Oxford Internet Institute's biennial study (Dutton and Blank, 2011) reminds us just how important the internet now is to every aspect of life. Three-quarters of the UK population are regular internet users (ONS, 2012), who invariably use broadband, and the web is now an essential information source in support of the daily routine. Most searched-for topics include travel information (86% of users), local information (86%), news (79%) and health information (71%). The web is an online shopping mall (86%) and bank (60%), a place of communication and interaction (e-mail 96%, social networking 60%) and entertainment (music 61%, games 51%) (Dutton and Blank, 2011, Chapter 3). Dutton and Blank (2011) report that almost half of internet users expect 24/7 access from multiple platforms, and these next generation users are of all ages.

Attaching simple labels to something as complex and heterodox as a whole society risks oversimplification, but they may be helpful to understanding general patterns of change. The agrarian, industrial, post-industrial and information society all highlight significant change both in social behaviours, values and expectations and in the conventions and structures that sustain a society. In his seminal study *The Rise of the Network Society*, Manuel Castells (2010) argues that the defining feature of the network society is that digital networks become 'the predominant organizational form of every domain of human activity', and it is within Castells' definition that this chapter considers the future for libraries as agents of learning. The evidence within the Oxford Internet Survey certainly demonstrates significant behavioural changes. Furthermore, in the private sector radical structural change has already taken place in sectors such as the recorded music industry and retailing (Naughton, 2012). Traditional industries have frequently struggled to respond to the speed of market evolution and to competition from start-up entrepreneurs and innovators. Google and Facebook grew from student ideas to become global phenomena, while it took an innovative organization to see what the recorded music industry could not see, that the chemistry of Napster and the MP3 player was not a threat, but a catalyst for the market-changing iTunes service. The net result is an ever-increasing rate of change with greater competition, rapid innovation and unstoppable market demand for new platforms and services. By the end of 2012 it was expected that there would be more mobile phones on the planet than there are people (Cisco, 2012). Welcome to the network society.

Libraries in the network society

Where might the library fit within the emergent landscape of a network society? In my research I argue that the unique service proposition (USP) of libraries is that they build and curate collections and disclose the objects in those collections to people in support of public policy, specifically to disclose knowledge to users to enable learning in its many forms. The additional things that libraries do – in providing user education and improving information literacy, and as places of learning and encounter, and so on – all derive from the USP. Such a definition may not be acceptable to all. Public library managers especially may point towards the important role of the public library as a physical focus for a community, a ubiquitous place of discovery, while school librarians might argue that there is value in the school library as an informal space away from the formal context of the classroom. These are perfectly valid positions to adopt, but I suggest that unless such functions clearly connect back to the library's USP, the complex, fast moving and uncertain environment that is the network society will increasingly put at risk the unique identity and, therefore, the value of the library.

Where once the library was the essential place of destination in the search for information and knowledge, the next generation user now expects resources to be at their fingertips 24 hours a day, seven days a week. Where once the learner (formal or informal) had to be a hunter-gatherer, they are now harvesters in a digitally agrarian ecosystem. Products such as Wikipedia, Amazon, Google Books, e-books, iTunes, iTunes U, YouTube, LibraryThing and many more challenge the library's uniqueness as store of information and knowledge. In the space of less than two decades the library has shifted from being an unchallenged monopoly to being one player in a highly contested space. Of course, the skills of the librarian as link between collection and learner are not so easy to provide online. Yet, libraries are generally not open 24/7 and may not always have either the right material in the collection or the member of staff able to help. As more and more use is made of online services, it may be harder to sell to the next generation user the value of the library as a place that they have to go to when online everything is at hand.

Not only are the changes wrought by digital technologies beginning to alter fundamentally the materials that users find online, they are steadily challenging traditional formats. Where once stable objects were fixed and physical, now digital culture is fragmenting knowledge into mash-ups, blogs, data services, electronic art, e-books, digital archival records, peer production and digital simulacra of artefacts. In the digital space authenticity may be open to challenge and the same material may appear in different formats with different attributions (Tredinnick, 2008). More than most other public service sectors, libraries face challenges not only from the expectations of users to have 24/7 access to services, but also in choosing the right response to these changing formats and the changing nature of the market. User expectations and loyalties shift more quickly as the time between good idea and mass-market, blockbuster service gets shorter. No sooner does the university adopt iTunes U as a route to new users than the massive open online course (MOOC)[1] hits the streets. How can anyone judge what is transient and what will endure?

Evolution, revolution, extinction

Libraries have been essential to formal and informal learning across the whole of the modern age, and today, despite the changes brought about by digital technologies and the internet, they continue to deliver benefits through access to their collections, supporting information literacy and encouraging the value of reading. Libraries of all types have been eager to adopt digital technologies in support of their missions, from the use of automated management systems and CD-Rom technology to, more recently, offering online access to electronic services and the use of social networking tools to encourage user engagement. However, over the past ten years, while there has been an increase in the provision of all types of knowledge and information online, libraries generally have taken up digital technologies within the traditional institutional paradigm. Technology has been adopted and adapted to support existing processes within the vertically integrated institutional structure – self-checkout to improve efficiency, an OPAC to improve accessibility to collections, social networking in support of communication and engagement – yet the library as destination has remained paramount. This is not surprising since there is clearly still demand, but also the structures of public service are traditionally hierarchical and slow to change, and for good reasons. Until now policymakers and practitioners have inclined to what Schön refers to as 'dynamic conservatism'; 'a fight to remain the same' (1973). Unlike the innovator in the private sector, the public sector is rarely able simply to stop doing service A to do B when there is a risk of disadvantage to sections of the community depending on service A. Consequently, evolutionary change is the norm.

At the heart of my research I question whether an evolutionary approach born of stable collection formats and uncontested services will remain relevant. In an age when long-established organizations in the private sector are facing fundamental challenges to their business models, what ought the library do to retain its position as the trusted route to knowledge in support of learning? How important will the library as destination be for people's learning needs in the future? Indeed, how far over time will the physical collection become a less significant part of the library offer? What will be the defining métier of the librarian if there is a sustained shift to virtual knowledge resources? Will there be an increasing distinction between the library as a place, and 'libraryness' (service forms and professional practice) embedded in the digital space? How might a national library service based on the Amazon model work, guaranteeing any item to any letterbox in 48 hours? Or why not explore the development of a knowledge for learning app for smartphones that opened a user-friendly window onto all public collections with just one click?

These are fundamental questions calling for reflection and debate. Yet, in my research, while there are many voices defending the status quo – such as save our library campaigns – and conferences galore on techie things like metadata, standards, repositories and opening up access to research resources, debate on radically new ways of thinking and doing is pretty much absent. Two recent studies in the UK on the future of libraries reflect similar views, that the physical library will continue its current centrality (JISC and British Library, 2011; Arts Council England, 2012). Many libraries are still held in high regard by the communities they serve and are still popular places for learning, discovery and encounter. At the same time, for many informal learners YouTube continues to be the destination of choice. The reality of budget cuts means access to libraries as destinations is worsening while peer production sites such as Wikipedia and knowledge engines like Wolfram|Alpha are able to answer serious questions at the click of a button. Social networking tools are empowering communities of interest to apply significant pressure to change or to challenge government policy, as well as bringing together like-minded people to share ideas. If the apparently unstoppable trajectory towards the mature network society that has already radically changed other sectors threatens the evolutionary progress of public service, will libraries, traditionally great engines of learning and knowledge creation, be pushed into backwaters? What a loss that would be. Yet, as more and more learners expect to harvest rather than hunt for information and knowledge, and as more and more of the content traditional to libraries shifts to digital formats, questions about the long-term role of the library will need to be addressed. Even in a good financial climate public service should demonstrate social value and in today's tough climate the case must be overwhelmingly compelling.

Of course, the service manager must argue for the value of what exists, what is in the best interests of the community currently served. There is, however, a very different agenda between the short-term challenge of budget cuts and the long-term strategic role of public collections in the network society. I do not argue that libraries as places will not continue to be important social agents, not least since all resources will not be digital for a long time and access to physical collections will need to be provided in some form. I do suggest strongly that without long-term strategic thinking the backwater and perhaps extinction may loom. In today's landscape of increasing networked connectivity, libraries are less networked than ever before. Co-operative schemes of regional collection building and resource interlending are in decline and lack national co-ordination. In public libraries different models of management are being implemented that may reduce further a national collective mission supportive to learning in all its forms at a time when learner expectations demonstrate clearly the need for simplicity and integration (Nicholas and Rowlands, 2008).

Today's reality is hundreds of uncoordinated library websites and only very limited tools for aggregated search across all services. There is a significant difference between the extensive digital resources available to those in formal education and what is generally available to everyone else, at a time when reskilling and learning are expected to be lifelong activities. Although innovative projects such as the Digital Public Library of America and Europeana are beginning to increase accessibility and linking across collections, such projects have not yet had significant impact on the broad spectrum of libraries.

The long-term future of the library will depend on walking the dialectical tightrope between the demands of supporting learning in physical space and learning in digital space, and understanding the nature of the 'libraryness' (service forms and professional practice) that emerges from that balancing act. My key concern is that a steady process of 'adopting and adapting' technical innovation into the traditional institutional paradigm may be inappropriate in the present climate of change, complexity and uncertainty. If other agents are able to deliver knowledge and information in support of learning to all, 24/7, as a one-stop, user-friendly experience, will the library ever be more than a building and a source of resources for others to exploit in the digital space? Or should the creation of a virtual library be the collective mission of library workers? Naturally, the answer to this latter question could only be 'yes' if professional attitudes change, service paradigms are reviewed radically and policies reformulated. Creating an online library service need only be done once (the one-stop shop), not hundreds of times. It should integrate the resources of all collections (museums and archives and libraries) and make them transparently searchable for users of many different types; the knowledge for learning app. Simplicity and total integration is what has made services such as Google, Facebook, Wikipedia, iTunes and others world beaters.

It is self evident that in an age of uncertainty there can be no safe and sure route into the future, but that does not mean that nothing can be done. In *Managing in Turbulent Times* Peter Drucker (1980) wrote, 'The greatest danger in times of turbulence, is not the turbulence; it is to act with yesterday's logic.' My case is this: in an age when networking is, 'the predominant organizational form of every domain of human activity' (Castells, 2010), it is time for professionals involved in collecting and disseminating knowledge in support of learning themselves to get better networked; to set aside today's significant financial challenges, professional practices and service paradigms; to go 'back to basics' and ask how is it possible to exploit fully the value of the library in the mature network society? How best to design and manage a new relationship between the collection and the user through the lens of the user rather than of the institution? That is the lesson that sectors such as the recorded music industry have learned the hard way.

So, set aside the current traumas, to work out what services might be in the best interests of society. Let public, school and university librarians begin collective and reflective discussion. Let them all talk to museum directors and archivists about how the totality of knowledge assets might fit together. Let them study how people behave and what they need to survive and prosper in the network society, whether that is physical libraries as learning spaces or a personal virtual learning space for everyone superintended by your own virtual librarian depending on need. If the latter comes to the fore, what should be the nature of the 'libraryness' that supports it? Revolutionary thinking and debate is needed. As Abe Lincoln put it, 'The dogmas of the quiet past are inadequate to the stormy present . . . as our case is new we must think anew and act anew' (Lincoln, 1862).

Note

1   See for example the Wikipedia entry for further information. http://en.wikipedia.org/wiki/Massive_open_online_course (accessed 15 November 2012).

References

Arts Council England (2012) *Envisioning Libraries of the Future,* www.artscouncil.org.uk/what-we-do/supporting-libraries/libraries-consultation/ (accessed 26 September 2012).

Castells, M. (2010) *The Rise of the Network Society,* Vol. 1, 2nd edn, Wiley-Blackwell, xliv.

Cisco (2012) *Cisco Visual Networking Index: global mobile data traffic forecast update, 2011–2016,* Cisco, 3.

Drucker, P. F. (1980) *Managing in Turbulent Times,* HarperBusiness.

Dutton, W. and Blank, G. (2011) *Next Generation Users: the internet in Britain,* Oxford Internet Institute.

JISC and British Library (2011) *Academic Libraries of the Future Project,* www.futurelibraries.info/content/ (accessed 26 September 2012).

Lincoln, A. (1862) Annual message to Congress, 1 December. Quoted in Basler, R. P. (ed.) *The Collected Works of Abraham Lincoln,* Vol. 5, Rutgers University Press, 537.

Naughton, J. (2012) *From Gutenberg to Zuckerberg: what you really need to know about the internet*, Quercus.

Nicholas, D. and Rowlands, I. (eds) (2008) *Digital Consumers: reshaping the information profession*, Facet Publishing.

ONS (2012) *Statistical Bulletin: internet access quarterly update*, Office for National Statistics, May, www.ons.gov.uk/ons/rel/rdit2/internet-access-quarterly-update/2012-q1/index.html (accessed 20 August 2012).

Schön, D. A. (1973) *Beyond the Stable State*, Norton, 32.

Tredinnick, L. (2008) *Digital Information Culture: the individual and society in the digital age*, Chandos.

CHAPTER 17

Powered by learning: developing models of provision to meet the expectations of new generations of students

Graham Bulpitt

Libraries at the heart of campus life

At a time when discussions about academic libraries attract headlines about the impact of electronic publishing (Harris, 2012; Reisz, 2012, reporting on a round-table discussion held in April 2012), and the financial cuts resulting from the UK Coalition Government's new funding regime for English universities, it is easy to overlook the library's role at the heart of the campus.

This role has been evolving steadily. Building on their established strength of placing students at the centre of their work, libraries have embraced a range of services which go well beyond printed collections: audiovisual materials in the 1960s and 1970s, computing in the 1980s, educational development in the 1990s, and, most recently, one-stop shops which provide a single point of contact with a range of student support services.

Libraries are well placed to help universities tackle the challenges that lie ahead. As institutions seek new ways of working to deal with reductions in funding and to meet the increasing expectations of students who are paying (in England at least) substantial fees, services are being reorganized to make them more accessible and to drive down costs. This integration or 'super-convergence' of services has generally been led by librarians, who use campus library buildings as the focus for activities.

The move to integrate services affects all aspects of provision, including staff roles, organizational structures and the design of space. Integration can also create the right conditions for educational innovation, encouraging staff to work together on course developments and allowing specialists to share their skills to offer high quality support to students.

A key issue here is the social dimension of learning. The future of libraries will continue to be shaped by interactions between students, and with staff, building on their established roles and culture and also new ways of working together.

Integrated services are also being developed in other settings used by students. Public libraries are collaborating with universities and colleges, as well as arts and heritage organizations, to develop a wide range of facilities that place them at the heart of their communities. Learning centres, which bring together help, resources, innovative space and support for study, are being developed to provide a focus for learning in organizations of all kinds. Shared space is the key ingredient which attracts learners and will shape the development of services for the future.

Students, learning and libraries

Speculation about the future of learning emphasizes the pervasive use of computers for information searching, knowledge integration and learner as producer with many activities delivered through managed learning environments. Programmes that are delivered through distance learning are often highly regarded – the Open University, for example, consistently receives high scores in the National Student Survey (HEFCE, 2012).

However, most students will continue to be attracted by the opportunity to study on campus – they wish to see academic staff who are at the leading edge of their fields, to meet other students and to use the facilities and physical resources that a campus can offer. Even distance learning students, who appreciate the flexibility to fit studies around work and family commitments, like to spend time with tutors and other students from their university. Being part of the university community is important to students: a government task group looking at the future of learning noted that 'it is the view of the group – and research studies reinforce this – that effective learning takes place in a social environment' (Foresight, 2000).

Libraries are a focus for students' time on campus. Many students use the library as their base for the day's work at the university, returning to the library after each class. Kingston University (2012) has a typical pattern of student usage, with 38% of students visiting a learning resource centre at least once each day and 53% visiting at least once each week, making the building the busiest in the institution.

Why are libraries still so popular with students? The traditional culture of libraries is part of the answer. Libraries have a strong ethos of being welcoming and friendly, with staff who are keen to help. Libraries are also neutral: they are open to everyone, and adopt a non-judgemental stance – on information content as well as users. This is a key attribute of both public and academic library settings.

The resources on offer also explain the attraction. The variety of books and multimedia allows students to engage intellectually with their disciplines in ways which suit them, and provide alternatives to standard lectures and textbooks. The range of facilities and study areas also allow individuals to work in ways which suit their personal learning styles.

The social dimension is evident here: students work in libraries because they enjoy being part of a community of learners. Successful library buildings allow individuals to find a space that meets their needs and which provides the right degree of privacy, yet allows them to see other people working in the building and feel a sense of common identity. This combination of factors makes libraries the natural base for the delivery of a range of services that support students.

The integrated student hub

The integration of services to students is a trend that has been growing in UK universities since 2007. The movement, which has been characterized as 'super-convergence', is likely to accelerate in the future in response to a sharper focus on students' experience at universities and continuing financial pressure. The one-stop shops which have been established to date are usually based in libraries and the integration of provision is likely to be a key driver for the development of libraries in the future.

The first step in super-convergence projects has been to set up a common help-desk. The space used for the integrated service is often branded as the 'hub', 'grid' or 'zone' and the remit of library staff is usually extended to cover a broad range of enquiries. Front-line staff welcome the opportunity to extend their knowledge and their job satisfaction has increased since they are able to resolve more problems on the spot, rather than having to refer students elsewhere.

In addition to library services, hubs generally co-ordinate personal support to students, such as health, counselling, careers, accommodation and finance. The relocation of specialist staff to the hub allows a full service to be available to extend the first-line support provided by the help-desk staff.

A student hub operation can often be achieved with minimum physical disruption, and often universities have been able to take advantage of the space liberated by self-service facilities to develop new accommodation where specialists can provide help and advice to students. These areas incorporate desks and seating where staff and students can talk together, and reflect a different style from the earlier counters and queues. Examples of innovative working areas can be found at Imperial College London, the University of Wolverhampton and the Library Learning Centre at Delft University of Technology.

This co-location of services brings a number of challenges for the design of the physical environment to meet the requirements of different professional working styles. While librarians spend most of their time in open areas, counsellors, health workers and financial advisers have a requirement for space which allows confidential matters to be discussed. There may even be a need for waiting areas for these services to be away from the busy traffic routes in libraries, although experience suggests that this may be overstated.

The study of super-convergence carried out for the Leadership Foundation for Higher Education (Bulpitt, 2012) noted a move away from the convergence of computing and library services. Integrated student services generally include the user support element of computing, but infrastructure, systems and other technical matters are managed separately, usually as part of the corporate services brief. It seems likely that this separation will become more common as an increasing proportion of computing services are delivered from external suppliers.

Supporting learners in the community

The focus on improving services to users is shared by public librarians who have developed a number of models of integration with other activities. The iconic idea stores in the London Borough of Tower Hamlets replaced conventional public libraries, which had been left behind as patterns of transport and movement had changed (Godowski and Dogliani, 2012). The combination of adult education classes, homework clubs, advice sessions, exhibition space, cafés and community space integrated well with library services. More recently, idea stores have accommodated one-stop shops for council services, exploiting their strong community links. Public libraries have developed integrated buildings with arts and heritage providers, such as the Discovery Centre in Winchester, and the Hive in Worcester (Hannaford and Fairman, 2011), which brings together county council and university provision.

Maintaining a physical presence in communities is a critical issue for many smaller public libraries that are having to deal with the impact of reductions in local authority expenditure. Although some services can be delivered remotely, using electronic books and information, for many users a building is important since it provides opportunities to meet people and a place for learners to work. The co-location of libraries with other services – whether provided by councils (one-stop-shops, councillors' surgeries, police stations), the voluntary sector (help and advice) or commercial operators (cafés, shops, post offices) – allows costs to be shared and community hubs to be maintained.

However, the opportunities lie in moving beyond co-location, to integration. This will be required if services are to be delivered seamlessly to meet the needs of individuals and to ensure that hubs are sustainable.

The learning centre concept has been adopted in a number of settings away from its university origins. The term is often used to describe accommodation, typically a large room, which is dedicated to learning activities. These learning centres contain space for private and group study that is equipped with PCs and a collection of learning (or training) material. They may also be supported by staff who can provide practical support and advice on learning needs. The development of learning centres in locations as varied as department stores, shopping centres, broadcasting stations, offices and factories has the potential to act as a co-ordinated network of spaces – and services – which could complement those provided in universities and colleges.

Educational innovation

The quality of the teaching and learning experience remains a major concern for universities where the challenge is to meet the expectations of students who are paying high fees and who expect to use the latest technologies for their work. Libraries have an important contribution to make and a key task is to ensure that the library's assets are fully exploited. Recent studies have emphasized the impact of libraries on students' achievement and researchers' activity (Stone, Pattern and Ramsden, 2012; Tenopir, Volentine and King, 2012).

The reorganization of services can make it easier to assemble teams with skills in curriculum design, educational technology and information resources to work with teaching staff on the development of new programmes of study. This approach, pioneered by the writer with the learning centre model (Oyston, 2003) is a feature of some super-converged operations.

Libraries provide an ideal test-bed for new learning models. These can act as a showcase, which demonstrates the institution's commitment to providing an excellent experience for students. The Adsetts Centre at Sheffield Hallam University incorporated the Learning and Teaching Institute, which led work on educational innovation and evaluation. In addition to 1400 work places for students, the building also provided workshop space where faculty staff could work on educational projects with staff from the learning centre.

The Saltire Centre at Glasgow Caledonian University and the Rolex Learning Centre at the Ecole Polytechnique Fédérale in Lausanne also have distinctive study areas which convey a strong sense of activity and support a wide range of learning styles. See JISC (2006) and CRDP (2011), which show buildings in use.

The integration of help-desk provision allows universities to offer a single point of contact for students who are remote from the university, providing the opportunity for universities to develop a competitive edge through their support of distance learning programmes.

Super-convergence: a strategic approach to working with students

Universities have adopted an evolutionary approach so far with the reorganization of services. Although changes have often been triggered by institutional imperatives, particularly the need to deal with funding reductions, the pace of change has allowed time for staff to adapt to new ways of working. However, the pressure on university funding and the increasing expectations of students may force institutions to take a more strategic – and more urgent – review of the delivery of support.

An analysis of all university activities that are in contact with students would establish a framework for the adoption of common processes and systems. This would also allow arrangements for the effective delivery of services to be developed in order to provide the seamless support that students expect. Given the well established responsibilities that are in place in many institutions, the challenge of tackling this should not be underestimated.

Although the organizational structure for student support will reflect the circumstances in each institution, libraries will remain a key element. Super-converged services will need to create the conditions where staff with different professional backgrounds can work together. New buildings designed for integrated services are beginning to appear, such as the Forum at the University of Exeter and Augustine House at Canterbury Christ Church University. The key requirement is for imaginative space that encourages innovation, which enables integration and multiple occupancy and also conveys the sense of excitement associated with learning.

References

Bulpitt, G. (ed.) (2012) *Leading the Student Experience: super-convergence of organization, structure and business processes*, Research and Development Series, Leadership Foundation for Higher Education, www.lfhe.ac.uk/en/utilities/search-results.cfm?sFormName=toolbar-search&keyword=student+experience (accessed 20 August 2013).

CRDP (2011) *Visite de l'université de Kingston avec Graham Bulpitt*, video, Centre Régional de Documentation Pédagogique de l'Académie de Versailles, http://webtv.ac-versailles.fr/spip.php?article816 (accessed 20 August 2013).

Foresight (2000) *Information Communications and Media Panel: the learning process in 2020 task force; point and click: learners in the ICT driving seat: a consultation document*, Department of Trade and Industry (UK).

Godowski, S. and Dogliani, S. (2012) *Idea Stores: the next generation*, www.designinglibraries.org.uk/index.asp?PageID=242 (accessed 16 August 2013).

Hannaford, A. and Fairman, R. (2011) The Hive: a new university/public library and history centre, Worcester UK. In *Connection and Convergence: Second International Conference on Joint Use Libraries*, 3–4 November, Adelaide, South Australia, http://eprints.worc.ac.uk/1532/ (accessed 16 August 2013).

Harris, S. (2012) *Moving Towards an Open Access Future: the role of academic librarians*, Sage, www.uk.sagepub.com/oareport/ (accessed 16 August 2013).

HEFCE (2012) *National Student Survey Results*, Higher Education Funding Council for England, www.hefce.ac.uk/whatwedo/lt/publicinfo/nationalstudentsurvey/nationalstudentsurveydata/2012/ (accessed 16 August 2013).

JISC (2006) *Designing Spaces for Effective Learning: a social and collaborative learning space*, Joint Information Systems Committee, The Saltire Centre, Glasgow Caledonian University, www.jisc.ac.uk/eli_learningspaces.html#downloads (accessed 16 August 2013).

Kingston University (2012) *Information Services*, LRC User Survey Report.

Oyston, E. (ed.) (2003) *Centred on Learning: academic case studies on learning centre development*, Ashgate.

Reisz, M. (2012) Working on Borrowed Time?, *Times Higher Education*, 13 September, 13.

Stone, G., Pattern, D. and Ramsden, B. (2012) Library Impact Data Project, *Sconul Focus*, **54**, 25–8, http://eprints.hud.ac.uk/12290/ (accessed 16 August 2013).

Tenopir, C., Volentine, R. and King, D. W. (2012) *UK Scholarly Reading and the Value of Library Resources: summary results of the study conducted*, Spring 2011, Joint Information Systems Committee, www.jisc-collections.ac.uk/News/UK-Scholarly-Reading/ (accessed 16 August 2013).

CHAPTER 18

The library has left the building

Joyce Sternheim and Rob Bruijnzeels

Introduction

In Chapter 5 we wrote about the new and more active processes of inspiration, creation and sharing that should be the main focus of future libraries. We emphasized the importance of designing new and exciting ways to present the collection, of adding valuable significance, and making it possible for people to share acquired knowledge and insights with other users. We also put forward the view that this new approach will inevitably lead to different design criteria for libraries, and concluded that we need experts from other disciplines to help draw up these new criteria. They can help us to relinquish the classical use of the building and to explore new and inspiring ways of using space, of the kind we see in BK City. For us, this is the example par excellence of a place where many forms of exploration and serendipity are possible.

In this chapter we will explore territory away from the beaten track. When all is said and done, do we really need a building? Can we work without the traditional arrangement of the library? Can modern technology liberate us from that hidebound, passive presentation of library collections? This kind of presentation does not sufficiently invite people to learn and discover, and it is this inviting quality that will be so essential in the library of the future.

We will explore these issues with reference to two sample projects. The first, the 'Context Library', focuses on designing exciting search strategies for the public library collection, appropriate to the different ways in which people absorb knowledge and information. The second project is also about the exchange of knowledge and information but it is organized in a completely different way. As we examine these projects, we not only turn our backs on the traditional presentation of (public) library collections but also on the traditional library building.

The Context Library

Traditionally, library collections are placed on bookshelves by librarians according to the centuries-old principles of organization: alphabetic (fiction) or systematic (non-fiction). It remains an effective way to store and retrieve books, but it does not really invite one to explore or to discover meaningful links in the collection. To quote Lankes (2011), 'libraries should see themselves not as grocery stores but as kitchens'. The library should therefore give visitors the opportunity to cook up something worthwhile, to 'customize' the collection to their desires, expertise and needs.

In 2005 Rob Bruijnzeels launched the Context Library. This project aims to design new search routes through the collections of public libraries. He drew his inspiration for this from the possibilities offered by radio-frequency identification (RFID) technology. Because many Dutch libraries were switching to a self-service system, all books were fitted with RFID chips from 2004 onwards, so every book had a small transmitter that made it traceable at any time as long as you had a device (at that time a personal digital assistant or PDA) to receive the RFID signal. Via instructions on this device, you could guide users to the various items in the collection. This gave rise to an entirely new way of opening up and presenting the collection, based on entirely different criteria.

In the traditional arrangement of a library, sources relating to the same subject are placed in physical proximity to each other. A book acquires meaning through its position on the shelf, among other books that fall into the same category. Keywords in the catalogue then help you to trace related sources that are located elsewhere. These keywords are assigned in accordance with predetermined rules. The Context Library gives you the freedom to escape from formal arrangement systems and to follow your own knowledge, preferences and associations. For example, you can set out a route in the library connecting all the sources which have been of major significance in your life and which, together, form a reflection of your personal development. Or you might select a theme such as 'heroes' and weave your own narrative threads through the collection: about classical and modern heroes, your personal heroes, fallen heroes, and courage and self-sacrifice. You can then share these narratives with other users to generate interaction. In essence, you thereby create new meanings:

subjective contexts that other people can explore and supplement.

In her final thesis for the Dutch Library School (www.libraryschool.nl/ LibrarySchool/English.html) José Remijn has elaborated the idea of the Context Library to produce several thematic routes for the Amsterdam Public Library (Remijn, 2012). One of these routes is intended for school students aged 12 to 16. On entering the library, each pair of school students is handed a tablet computer. They select a romantic route, a horror trail, a literary ramble or an artistic journey. The tablet leads them to the first collection item along the route. After scanning a quick response (QR) code a page opens, providing information about the item in the form of text, websites, videos, photos or games. As they progress, it turns into a genuine voyage of discovery through the collection. At each collection item the students can add something of their own: a personal association or a recommendation for a book, film, piece of music or website. At the end of this voyage of discovery, the students give feedback to the librarians. Was there anything they felt the route lacked? What did they add to it themselves? The librarians use this feedback to make modifications. In that way, the routes remain stimulating and inspiring.

The city as a library

Libraries are still being built as book depositories, places where bookcases stand in a monotonous grid, all books being of equal (un)importance. It takes some effort to relinquish this image of the library. You could say the library is haunted by its own memory. We all know from personal experience what a library is supposed to look like. This memory can be so vivid that it prevents us from coming up with new ideas. To break this thinking habit, we need knowledge and expertise from other disciplines: designers, artists and other experts who are able to look at library processes with an open mind and then come up with solutions from a completely new angle.

That is exactly what happened in the project called The Architecture of Knowledge (TAOK), which was organized in 2009 by the Netherlands Public Library Association and the Netherlands Architecture Institute (NAI) (Werf, 2010). It consisted of a series of lectures followed by a two-week workshop for an international group of students from different educational backgrounds, such as music, art, new media and industrial design. The main aim was to explore new possibilities and use them as a framework or starting point for the architects of future libraries, or both.

In connection with this project, industrial designers Jurgen Bey and Esther van de Wiel joined with students to tackle the question of whether the library can still only take the form of a building. While recognizing the importance of the library as a public space and a place for meeting and exchange, they concluded that the exchange of knowledge and information increasingly takes place at other locations or in the immeasurable space of the internet. They asked themselves: what if the city itself became a public library? Can we then keep the character of a public space while at the same time using the knowledge and information that is abundantly available in the city? The key question, therefore, was whether library processes can take place outside the building and, if so, whether collections might also be distributed over diverse locations in the city.

They chose a special area of Rotterdam as the place to visualize their ideas: a section of disused railway known as the Hofplein line, which runs straight through the city. Their new public library would thereby become a linear zone in the city. Along this line, the students designed a wonderful and multi-faceted library landscape. Everything along the line became part of the collection: the shops, the hospital, the mosque, the church, the schools, the allotment gardens and so on. Everything was based on the idea that you need a variety of institutions, people and facilities in order to accumulate knowledge, including very specific knowledge about any subject. By regarding all the people along the line as 'librarians', the local knowledge of enthusiasts, clubs, students and professionals was made visible and accessible to all. For health information, for example, you could approach the hospital, while the experienced gardeners in the allotments could tell you everything you need to know about growing vegetables.

Unlike the 'Living Library', where people take the place of books (see also Chapter 20), what we have here is a unique, location-based library, which combines place, the collection and expertise.

Implications for the future

In the future, the library may become an ideal 'other' environment for the creation of new connections between people, materials and ideas. As in the Context Library, for example, one might take the personal talents of individuals as the starting point; their ability to make their own, surprising connections in the collection and thereby create their own experiences: experiences that they can subsequently share with others. In that way, the library becomes a place for social interaction and shared experiences, a place where you can discover new perspectives and different ideas. A place where you can learn in a way appropriate to the new 'conceptual age' of which we spoke in Chapter 5 (Pink, 2006).

Does this way of learning explicitly require a library building with a collection? The TAOK project seems to indicate that it does not. Here, the library leaves the building and soars freely across the city. However, the same processes are still involved. After all, this is also an environment where people can organize their own routes, discoveries and experiences. In the TAOK project, the library has become a series of personal encounters, a journey through the city among places and people where knowledge can be found and gathered. It is a learning zone in the city, connecting people with ideas, stories, messages and other people. It shows them the culture they are part of and the culture they are not part of. It is a library that allows people to participate, to peek into other, unfamiliar worlds, to explore, to imagine, to experience and to live. This applies in equal measure to the Context Library; for however differently they may be organized, both the Context Library and the library that was created in the TAOK project offer people new and contemporary possibilities for learning and exploration; the place and time to see things they otherwise would not see.

In the future, the library will manifest itself in many forms: the invisible library, consisting of a network of interlinked information and collections, available in any form we wish and at any place or time; and the visible library, which is no longer a building by definition. The TAOK project shows us that the library can be any place where we encounter information and knowledge, where we learn and are inspired.

It is no longer a question of what sort of spaces the future library needs. The question is about how to arrange space to produce the optimally integrated environment where one can consult sources of information (in whatever form), create new knowledge and contexts, and share these with others. In the past, the space laid down what activities could take place within it. Now the processes determine the arrangement of the space – the new library processes of inspiration, creation and sharing that we write about in Chapter 5 of this book.

References

Lankes, R. D. (2011) *The Atlas of New Librarianship*, MIT Press.

Pink, D. H. (2006) *A Whole New Mind*, Riverhead Books.

Remijn, J. (2012) *De bibliotheek uit de kast!*, Dutch Library School (not published), www.libraryschool.nl/LibrarySchool/English.html (accessed 16 August 2013).

Werf, Huib Haye van der (ed.) (2010) *The Architecture of Knowledge: the library of the future*, NAI.

CHAPTER 19

Beyond analogue: the learning studio as media-age library

Kyle Dickson

Introduction

In *Cognitive Surplus*, Clay Shirky (2011) signals a fundamental transition of our post-television age. He argues that media has become 'the connective tissue of society'. No longer 'something produced by professionals for consumption by amateurs', the power of digital media is in moving culture beyond the one-way transmission of broadcasting to a two-way interaction where new ideas and ways of thinking emerge. The challenge for educators in the 21st century is in capturing this active role for our students and classrooms: 'We have to rethink the basic concept of media: it's not just something we consume, it's something we use.'

This challenge is nowhere more evident than in library spaces. Mobile devices have created new ways of connecting and learning from others through images, audio and video; our students come to us expecting to interact and collaborate in vital communities linked by new media messages. Though significant attention has been given to the transition from print to digital collections, the 21st-century library must attend to the participatory culture sparked by digital media and modes of thinking and working together.

In 2010 the Brown Library at Abilene Christian University (ACU) opened the AT&T (American Telephone & Telegraph) Learning Studio. In the last decade, library redesigns built around the information commons model attempted to move spaces beyond the analogue assumptions of the repository – curation and consumption – and connect the library to the world of the web, creating a kind of crossroads for information gathering of all sorts. The studio model takes an essential next step, seeing library spaces as sites of not only information literacy and analysis but also production, collaboration and a growing list of practices essential to learning in the 21st century.

Towards media fluency

One early voice in reframing education for the 21st century was the Partnership for 21st Century Skills (P21) project. In 2002 the US Department of Education founded this project with advocacy groups like the National Education Association and corporate support including Apple, Microsoft and Time Warner. The P21 project asked what core skills would need to complement knowledge in core subjects to allow students 'to succeed as citizens and workers in the 21st century' (Partnership for 21st Century Skills, 2002).

The third literacy

One thread that runs through the P21 framework is a renewed commitment to communication skills, old and new. Future graduates will continue to need a mastery of oral and written communication but should be ready to 'utilize multiple media and technologies, and know how to judge their effectiveness . . . as well as assess their impact'. The learning studio model supports media authoring as a kind of 'third literacy' to develop a new media fluency. More than information literacy, this fluency asks patrons to become media authors, producers and participants in new modes of idea exchange.

Media support staff in the Learning Studio are available to coach students and faculty to not only learn to 'read' media, understanding how it works and assessing its effective use, but also begin to 'write' media, producing messages that contribute a point of view through strong audio, video and imagery. Academic libraries have long offered this type of support in writing and speaking centres. If, as Shirky (2011) suggests, media authoring is no longer the province of specialists, then 21st-century libraries need spaces where students and educators from all disciplines can explore these new models.

For us, the transition from media consumers to producers or authors begins with photography. Image sharing is the cornerstone of social media – from Facebook to Instagram – and provides an easy starting place for anyone new to digital creation. Since 2010, the Learning Studio at ACU has found beginning and intermediate instruction in digital photography, introducing basic composition and exposure with shooting sessions and peer critiques, an effective first step in building not only skills but also confidence in working with media. Our media labs also provide patrons access to advanced media editing software as well as checkout cameras, tripods and lighting kits to enable self-directed learning.

As students and faculty become more comfortable working with images, they can move on to training in digital storytelling. Media authoring or storytelling introduces technical training – how to record audio narration, scan images and edit video – within the context of first-person narrative to increase investment in the process. Digital storytelling builds on the core skills of writing and speaking by beginning with a strong script and voice-over narration before adding the cinematic power of image and sound to produce a multimedia message.

Our initial workshops have moved naturally into the curriculum with teachers integrating digital storytelling strategies into a range of student media projects, including literacy narratives for first-year writers, foreign language speaking exercises, research public service announcements in nutrition, and product commercials in introductions to business. Because faculty are first introduced to media production in the studio space, they have been eager to bring students back for initial training in software and storytelling skills as many produce their first media projects. Workshops with dozens of teachers have indirectly impacted over 500 students in the last year.

Libraries and the third literacy

A role of the 21st-century library must be to envision media creation spaces that move beyond information literacy to media fluency. As new generations of readers and authors continue to blur the boundaries of writing, speech and visual representation, the result will require multi-modal tools and rhetorics. Digital storytelling itself has already come to blend first-person narrative, remix videos, photo essays, stop-motion movies, machinima (stories told within video-game environments) and mash-up audio into the broad category. This diversity of meanings is the product of students and faculty increasingly fluent in the building blocks of media culture.

Toward collaborative thinking

A second, and complementary, skill identified as essential to 21st-century learning and innovation is 'working creatively with others'. Collaboration appears across the P21 framework, challenging students to contribute regularly to diverse teams and 'assume shared responsibility for collaborative work and value the individual contributions made by each team member'.

Keith Sawyer emphasizes the power of collaboration in his book *Group Genius* (2008):

> We're drawn to the image of the lone genius whose mystical moment of insight changes the world. But the lone genius is a myth; instead, it's group genius that generates breakthrough innovation. When we collaborate, creativity unfolds across people; the sparks fly faster, and the whole is greater than the sum of its parts.

The lone genius, like the lone researcher, is increasingly an artefact of analogue culture while the power of digital spaces is in connecting us into productive networks.

The learning studio model leverages the power of group genius. First, dynamic collaboration means that tools for idea formation and sharing have to be widely accessible. After looking at dozens of interactive technologies, we ended up covering every available surface with old-fashioned whiteboard: no training, no tech support, just lots of markers. Given access to over 1400 square feet of whiteboard surface, students have developed new approaches to learning. The study of disciplines like biology, chemistry, Spanish and Greek, which previously focused on individual memorization, now bring groups together to study in collaborative teams.

Mobile devices have also changed the way we think about computing. We began by asking how library spaces could be more hospitable to laptops and tablets and simplify the process of sharing content with groups. Our collaboration rooms feature media:scape tables from Steelcase, which enable instantaneous screen sharing and idea exchange. Each table allows up to six students to connect laptops or tablets and mirror their screen on large liquid-crystal display (LCD) displays at the table as the conversation takes an unexpected turn. In other collaborative rooms where we installed computers behind the LCD screen, the only technology on the table is a Bluetooth keyboard and mouse allowing participants to hand off control of discussion mid-stream quickly.

As new wireless projection tools come online, the age of cables and adapters is coming to an end. Future collaborative spaces will move beyond these choices between analogue and digital tools, allowing groups to move ideas from physical spaces into digital research portfolios where they can continue to be refined. Digital media produced by patrons should just as easily be shared on a convenient display or surface. Work created by patrons should also flow into institutional repositories, becoming a part of not simply the collection but conversations that reach across disciplinary and institutional boundaries.

Support for advanced users

The P21 project has focused most of its attention on kick-starting a national conversation around K-12 (primary and secondary) education, so it is not surprising that many of its outcomes involve basic literacies, not only writing and speaking but civic, economic, environmental and health literacies as well.

There is no question that students working in the future will need these foundational literacies in working with an abundance of information, technology and communication tools, and digital media. A growing number of new students and faculty come to us with these foundations already in place and need a place to develop advanced skills and explore more complex tools.

The Learning Studio at ACU has continued to watch emerging trends in the media landscape with implications for the next generation of authors and producers. Mobile devices have brought improved optics and high-definition quality video to the general consumer and every day our students are leveraging tools once available only to professionals. However, we also provide workshops in advanced lighting, sound and digital single-lens reflex (DSLR) cameras in our checkout pool to push those users who want to do more with advanced editing software in our labs. The explosion of mobile media has sparked a growing interest in professional tools globally as well; in 2012 Google announced its first two physical studios for YouTube creators in London and Los Angeles.

Providing advanced media training may require strategic partnerships across the campus or community. We have worked with campus film and photography competitions that challenge students to create work beyond the bounds of a class or assignment. If media production is no longer the work of a single department or major, student projects under way in the learning studio are no longer confined to the curriculum. Where possible, we have also brought experts to campus to lead training workshops and facilitator training to continue to build expertise within the library for the future.

Serving advanced and beginning users requires access to specialized tools housed in flexible spaces. We designed studio rooms with acoustic treatments for recording basic podcasts and interviews but extended them by 6 feet on one end to allow them to serve students wanting to film practice speeches and presentations. When we designed the main HD studio space for advanced projects, we avoided investing in fixed lighting grids or equipment that could only be used in one room in the library. Curtains and green screens were also hung to be quickly used or stored based on the needs of the project. The flexibility of the main studio allows media production specialists to work with students on photographic lighting training then with faculty developing open educational resources in the same afternoon.

Building a coral reef

Legitimate objections can be raised against the total transformation of library spaces into specialized zones that serve niche uses. With efficient scheduling, the physical recording and editing spaces that now occupy 8800 square feet upstairs in the ACU library might have been cobbled together from storage rooms in the basement. However, the Learning Studio facility embodies broader institutional commitments to the role of creativity, innovation and collaboration in 21st-century learning.

In *Where Good Ideas Come From*, Steven Johnson (2011) argues that the explosion of life and creativity reflected in the city, coffee house and coral reef are directly tied to their unique traits:

> What kind of environment creates good ideas? The simplest way to answer it is this: innovative environments are better at helping their inhabitants explore the adjacent possible, because they expose a wide and diverse sample of spare parts – mechanical or conceptual – and they encourage novel ways of recombining those parts.

For Johnson the 'adjacent possible' is a moment of serendipity when someone sees a new connection between two previously known ideas. As we replace the operating metaphors of repository, storehouse or cultural ark, we must take care not to repackage analogue associations in a digital form. The heart of the learning studio metaphor is supporting physical spaces where users produce messages for the world. We need vision to help students and educators see the emerging possible that sparks new ways of teaching and learning. Designing spaces that increase the opportunities for collisions of the 'adjacent possible' is the business of the library of the 21st century.

References

Johnson, S.(2011) *Where Good Ideas Come From: the seven patterns of innovation,* Penguin.

Partnership for 21st Century Skills (2002) www.p21.org (accessed 1 July 2013).

Sawyer, K. (2008) *Group Genius: the creative power of collaboration,* Basic Books.

Shirky, C. (2011) *Cognitive Surplus: creativity and generosity in a connected age,* Penguin.

CHAPTER 20

3D libraries for 3D smarting

Jef Staes

Unintended consequences; book-based learning creates sheep

During one of my meanders around the internet, I stumbled on the idea of unintended consequences. It made me realize how we've transformed so many talented people into passionless sheep. I'm convinced this transformation was not a conscious choice. Teachers, entrepreneurs and policy makers are eager to encourage others to do their work with passion and creativity, but these attributes seem scarce. Maybe this is an unintended consequence of trying too hard to achieve this. I think the lack of passion is a side effect of one of the biggest inventions in history, the printing press, and the resulting education system based on it. Book printing indirectly smothered our children's talents and passions like the wind blowing out a candle. The total absence of passion in our education system is the unintended consequence of the printing press.

In my book *My Organisation is a Jungle* (Staes, 2008), I recall history lessons in which I was fascinated by the timeline hanging above the blackboard. Each period was indicated on it with a name that identified that period. The Stone Age, the Bronze Age and the Iron Age. Time and again people were faced with new ideas and saw them as either a threat or an opportunity. What is happening today is no different, except that it's not the processing of iron or bronze but the processing of an overabundance of information sources. Companies and organizations that are most efficient and effective information processors come out on top and can respond rapidly to the emerging needs of a changing society. New and inspiring information is an important source of learning driving creative entrepreneurship and

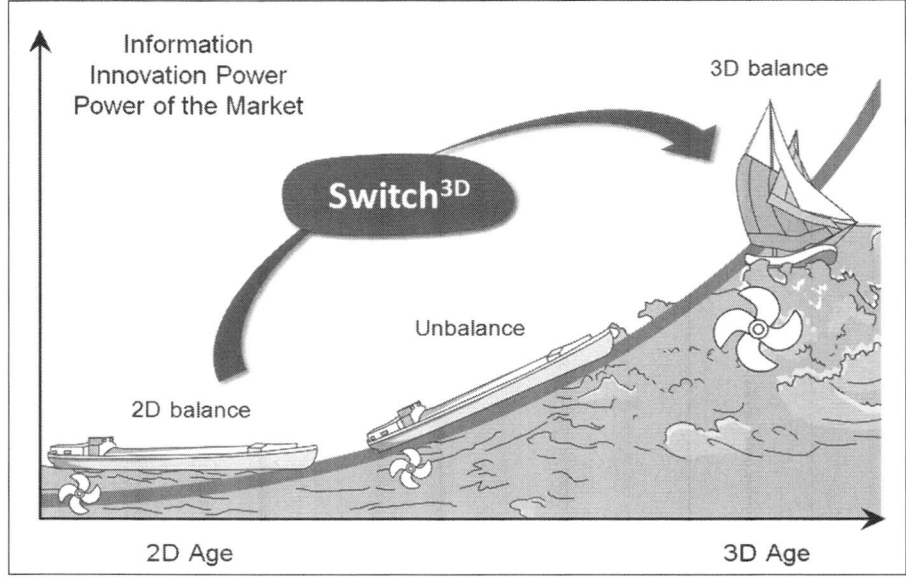

Figure 20.1 *Switch3D, from the 2D Age to the 3D Age (copyright Jef Staes)*

innovation. I see this chaotic period in which we now live and work as the fascinating but dramatic transformation from the 2D Age to the 3D Age (Figure 20.1). The flat, two-dimensional 2D Age, characterized by classroom learning, predictability and continuous improvement, is laboriously making way for the three-dimensional 3D Age. In the 3D Age more and more passionate talents will produce and exploit new information to drive innovation. The greatest barrier to entering the new 3D Age, however, are the invisible walls that 2D teachers and 2D managers have unconsciously erected around our passions and talents.

Switch3D is a chaotic time. A time of crisis. We are moving from a 2D era to an era in 3D. In the two-dimensional era learning was mostly flat. It happened in classrooms, was predictable and came from the urge constantly to improve what was already there. Book wisdom was key. But since the turn of this century, we are moving faster and faster in the three-dimensional direction. What we need now is a total turnaround. We must move from 2D to 3D learning; from 2D to 3D libraries.

2D teachers

You could say that in our current 2D education system not the teacher, but the text book stands at the centre point. The role of the 2D teacher is limited to passing on what is in the book. Even the way he passes on that knowledge is completely outlined in textbooks, manuals and teaching folders. In addition, the government provides him with various guidelines and curricula to ensure that the correct knowledge finds its way to the learner. Colouring outside the lines isn't a real option, partly because of the lack of time. Creativity of teacher and pupil is thus curtailed.

One of the main negative effects of the printing press is the dispassionate knowledge power that we face today: too many 2D teachers, although they have a lot of book knowledge, are often not able to use that knowledge to convey or rekindle passion within their pupils or students.

Smarting

2D textbook education delivered mainly by 2D teachers produces 2D students. They might all have talent, but 2D education doesn't really help to grow that talent. 2D education is like a giant human copier without passion. It creates knowledge clones by the thousands. In the 2D era this was enough to keep a company, organization or society going. We need 'smarting': 'Smarting is the process where Smarts inspire each other. Smarting is an active "learn-from-each-other"-process. Through this, Smarts (all of them) become even "smarter".'(Staes, 2011)

In the 3D era, we must have the courage to rethink the tradition of 2D printing. We must dare to opt for the use of new media and the internet. 2D printing in the 2D era should become 3D book growth for the 3D era. But this is only possible if 'smarting' takes place between 3D teachers and 3D pupils. Without 'smarting', the introduction of new media in education is a waste of time and resources.

Smarts, the new students, teachers and employees in the 3D Age

A 'Smart' is a passionate talent with access to information. Passion, talent and information are the three cornerstones of her learning behaviour. Lifelong learning is not a burden, but a part of her life. A 'sheep' is the reverse of a Smart. Because of the total lack of passion for the new, her talents are not put to use and the vast amount of information has no value. For a sheep there is always too much information. A sheep drowns in the information because she does not know in which direction to swim.

The concept 'Smart' can apply to everyone, regardless of a specific talent, as long as she has passion for her talent and access to information to fulfil her learning hunger.

Learning is a process whereby information provides raw material for the brain. Our brains are never finished. They continually make new connections. Knowledge is stored in association with other knowledge. Acquired skills disappear when we stop using them and will be replaced with better skills. Behaviour evolves. Unused neural connections are broken, new ones are built. In short, our brain is a gigantic construction yard.

In the 3D era the role of Smarts should not be underestimated. They lay the foundation for creative entrepreneurship, prosperity and sustainable development. Companies and businesses are looking for this. For education to become 3D it has to be able to recognize what Smarts are:

- Smarts are selective in finding and processing information. For them information overload does not exist.
- Smarts are generous in sharing knowledge and information. They are open and communicative. Smarts want no more than to be able to transfer knowledge.
- Smarts are quick. They are often one step further than the mainstream. Their talent enables them to home in on the information that they need.
- Smarts keep learning. Their hunger for learning is never over and only stops when they stop breathing.

In the 3D era with its huge array of information Smarts feel like a fish in water. The result of their ability to learn is that they are always smarter and more competent than others. The only way to get them to conform to a 2D group is to kill their passion by restricting their access to information. This is exactly what happens in 2D education. You probably know stories of passionate fellow students who were crippled because they did not fit into the 2D subject-based, drip-feed system of education. Maybe you were such a student yourself? The same goes for teachers – there are stories of teachers who are held back by their colleagues.

The gap between Smarts and sheep is opening up dramatically. In the 3D era, people have the chance to reach their full potential. The more Smarts we have the more sheep will lose their sheep's clothing. You can't force a sheep to become a Smart. They need to see that it's possible to change. Smarts are exemplars of the 3D era.

Based on 2D printing, we developed a 2D education that robs students and their teachers of their passion and talents. To turn the tide in the 3D Age we must urgently move from 2D printing to 3D book growth.

3D Book growth art; the art of making books grow

Smarts have attributes that sheep lack. They are always eager to learn and from that willingness to learn they add information to what already exists. This is an imitation of our brains. The brains are always making new associations by playing with new information. The 2D printing and 2D education prevent this 'brain work' actually happening. This view of learning could bring a revolution in education. The brain does not learn naturally when fenced in.

Now suppose that we say goodbye to 2D education, based on 2D printing. Now suppose we see the textbook or course not as an end, but as a beginning of an information explosion. But what is 'book growth'? The story that follows, illustrates what I mean by the term.

A vision

A passionate, talented teacher looks for an author of a respected book. They come to an agreement. The book is introduced in the classroom of the teacher, not as a textbook, but as a growth book. Internet and new media are then used as tools. The 2D author will initially be somewhat suspicious. It's his book. Can he let his book be used by an unknown – albeit enthusiastic – teacher, so that it starts to live its own life? For both teacher and author, there is an aspect of adventure to it. Fortunately, there is no question of a 2D editor claiming his 2D copyrights.

The textbook is online, not as a static e-book, but as a multimedia, editable document. The book can grow. Together with his students, the teacher interviews the author and expands the online growth book with video footage of that interview. Pupils track other printed and digital information sources. And that information is also added. The book is enriched. It is overflowing with new information.

Some students become so passionate that they add their own chapter to the book. On forums, students discuss with the author, but also with other interested parties. Not only from their own country, or even their own continent, but from all over the world. Other authors join and contribute as well. The author feels new inspiration building and writes his own new chapters. He informs, explains, asks questions and suggests new ideas. For him, the experiment is also a learning experience. He never thought that his static book would suddenly develop into a living dynamic web of knowledge. He is still the proud father of his work but blogs, tweets, posts on social media, podcasts, vlogs, forums and many other new communication channels help ensure that the book is permanently evolving. This is the 3D toolkit of 3D Smarts. Webinars and online meetings ensure that the momentum continues. They are all part of a growing book. 3D teachers and 3D students from different schools join together online in a passionate quest for more information.

The book is no longer the sole property of the author or the teacher. The course is no longer the subject of one teacher. The 'class' is no longer 20 or 30 young people who are physically located in the same room. All these elements together – the collaboration of people from different schools and environments – are a new trend in education: smarting.

'Smarting' is a verb. It indicates the interaction between passion and talent to become smarter. 3D teachers, 3D authors and 3D students: all are passionate about this work. Thanks to 3D interaction, they are smarter and even more passionate – enthusiasm is infectious. 3D book growth makes the book evolve and also stimulates the development of pupils and teachers into 3D Smarts.

Incidentally 2D printing in this story is not finished it's just no longer an endpoint. 2D books are the seeds from which new 3D learning germinates.

3D libraries

Like the wheel, once the printed book was a formidable step forward in the development of mankind. The wheel and the book remain indispensable parts of our lives. Without the wheel, there is no mobility – even airplanes use wheels to land. Without the book 90% or more of the world would be illiterate. In a technological society without 3D book growth future society may be illiterate. So we'd better make our students passionate 3D Smarts and bring new life and purpose to 2D books, ensuring they also have a future.

These are some 3D library ideas to consider:

- Every book of participating authors has a quick response (QR) code to the online growth version of the book.
- Different versions of growth books of the same printed book can co-exist. For example different 3D schools or 3D organizations have different versions.

- Every book has a Twitter account that sends tweets whenever a book grows (book tweets).
- Authors deliver online sessions where they react on the growth of their book.
- 3D libraries represent 3D authors to their clients.
- 3D libraries are real life and virtual places where people go to learn. Maybe 3D libraries with 3D growth books are the real future of education . . . ☺

These future libraries have an important role as a 'home' for 3D growth books and the journeys that these books have made. We will need libraries that are places not just for books but also places with authors. Places where people meet, virtual and live, with authors who write books. To tend the books and make them grow. These living libraries will honour the authors and the users (Smarts) and the process of smarting. Today there is no place where people can meet the authors behind the books – other than to buy a signed copy! For me the opportunity is to create 3D living libraries with a mission of interaction between authors and other readers – a 3D mission.

References

Staes, J. (2008) *My Organisation is a Jungle*, LannooCampus.
Staes J. (2011) IK WAS EEN SHAAP, LannooCampus.

CHAPTER 21

Learning landscapes, the library and the University of Lincoln: efficiency, effectiveness, expression and experimentation

Mike Neary and Sam Williams

The library exists *ab aeterno*. This truth, whose immediate corollary is the future eternity of the world, cannot be placed in doubt by any reasonable mind.

Borges (1964, 79)

E-learning landscapes

The concept of learning landscapes has become ubiquitous in higher education, encouraging universities to create networks of 'discovery, and discourse between students, faculty, staff, and the wider community', with a clear recognition that 'campuses need to use academic space more effectively as well as efficiently', built around 'overlapping networks of compelling places' (Dugdale, 2009).

The University of Lincoln, UK, is applying the concept of learning landscapes to its built estate. Following Dugdale (2009), the focus has been on effectiveness (pedagogical activities) as well as efficiency (space utilization) and the production of compelling spaces. However, beyond Dugdale's definition, these compelling spaces are being designed to express the meaning and purpose of higher education, or 'the idea of the university' (Neary and Saunders, 2011). The idea of the university is much more than its functionally defined subject specificities or technocratic networked spaces; it is derived from a university's 'intimate connection with science and truth' (Habermas and Blazek, 1987, 3). At the University of Lincoln 'the idea of the university' is created through the dynamic of the research process when students collaborate with academics to produce critical practical knowledge. At Lincoln this dynamic between student and academic is defined as student as producer; in other words the 'idea of the university' includes 'the idea of the student'. In order to achieve this connection between the metaphysical idea of the university with the everyday life of its academics, students and professional services, the University of Lincoln has developed its own e-concept: experimentation. Experiment means rigorous empirical methodology informed by appropriate conceptual framework. In this way the University is returned to the essence of its own foundational principles, valuing the principles of academic research around which the concept of student as producer is based (Neary, 2012; Neary, Williams et al., 2010).

Academics already contribute to the design of teaching and learning spaces as clients and customers of the project management process. However, academic involvement can be further enhanced by challenging and inviting academics to intellectualize the debate about teaching and learning spaces by reference to the custom and tradition of their own subject areas, and by creating spaces for dialogue between academics, estates and others outside the time and commercial constraints of the project process. This debate can be generalized to cut across all academic areas by discussing the nature of academic values and culture as part of a wider debate, or 'collective intellectuality' (Bourdieu and Wacquant, 1992). It is this intellectual sensibility which promotes the willingness to apply experimentality to the design of teaching and learning spaces (Neary and Thody, 2009).

This 'collective intellectuality' extends to estates professionals by challenging them to shift their focus from spaces to places. This requires a greater degree of holism in planning estates interventions, stressing that the goals and considerations of place creation are primarily social and pedagogical as well as material and financial. This leads to subverting existing mechanisms of space evaluation, and increasing the scope for greater academic engagement through research methods. This involves inventing outputs and measures of relevance to the academic community, alongside traditional cost-based measures. These can include activity-based metrics of teaching space performance linked to the most effective use of teaching and learning places (Neary, Williams et al., 2010).

Universities can develop processes that promote strategic experimentation which remains connected to the central decision-making structures to encourage imagineering, interactive and free thinking, as a collective intellectual project with staff and academics and support staff. The most innovative spaces emerge from institutions with devolved leadership structures and high levels of staff autonomy, inside and outside the university (Neary, Williams et al., 2010).

At the University of Lincoln all of this is enshrined in the Learning Spaces Group (LSG). A focus of its current work is a new library extension on the Brayford campus.

The Learning Spaces Group

Covey (1989) suggests that all physical things are created twice: first, mental creation, and second, physical creation. Jamieson (2003) emphasizes the importance of a first, intellectual or conceptual creation of learning spaces, which must be undertaken before a second, design creation, and a third, physical creation. Building projects, libraries included, are always faced with all three creations, and must complete these with limited time and other resources, within an inherently constraining structure and a prevailing project management paradigm, which tends to instrumentalize and linearize discussions to align them with a defined delivery programme and budget. The project process is inherently commercial and contractual, and rapidly takes on a life and momentum of its own (Jamieson, 2003). The client's ability to influence change diminishes rapidly and the cost of change increases exponentially (CABE, 2011). Project clients are often surprised by just how early this happens. The die is cast months, sometimes years, in advance of the 'start' of the project process, before anyone even knows they are working on the project. Institutions need mechanisms through which academics, students and support staff can actively, consciously, participate in this casting, by continuously preparing for future projects and learning from completed projects. The creation of a coherent, optimized learning landscape requires the creation of a coherent intellectual network of academics, students and professionals continuously engaged with issues of library and learning space design, outside the constraints of the project paradigm but able to target and trigger projects as needed.

The LSG at the University of Lincoln is a venue of continuous preparation and evaluation. The group brings together academics from across the University with student representatives and key support staff from estates, IT, library and timetabling departments. The group itself is a learning space, with members returning to their communities of practice as advocates and listeners, testing the group's ideas with outside stakeholders. This learning is brought into the development of future library and teaching space projects through critical reflection on past projects. The outcome of these reflections is used to inform a critical debate about how and whether to integrate emerging technologies and trends in learning space design. It is important to prepare the people who will be contributing to project briefs, procuring designers and reviewing designs for new places and spaces by continually developing and challenging their thinking through dialogue with the academics and students who will use those places. Members of the LSG sit on many of the University's key committees (including the Education Committee, the Student Experience Committee and the Student as Producer project management group) and keep them continuously engaged with the LSG's work.

As a University-wide group with academics from all three of the University's colleges (Arts, Sciences and Social Sciences), the group is well placed to discover ecological validity across projects and disciplines: a science laboratory or an architecture studio may contain design elements or concepts which are of great use in the planning of a library space, or a seminar space for humanities subjects, for example.

The group's terms of reference (see below) reflect its chameleonic form and its place within the organizational structure of the University: it is a venue for unconstrained speculation and dreaming, without commitment to execute; but it also governs the more prosaic daily maintenance of the rooms under its stewardship; and it is also capable of shifting into a focused and productive executive mode in which briefs and business cases are written, physical spaces are delivered, and projects rigorously evaluated. One meeting could take the form of a design workshop where new seminar layouts and furniture are imagined; the next might be a rigorous review of a draft business case for a new suite of learning spaces. The group is connected with project steering groups through members of this group being part of other groups, as clients or key stakeholders or as part of the delivery teams. This group formally reports to the University's Teaching and Learning Committee.

These are the terms of reference of the LSG, University of Lincoln:

- to act as joint owners and stewards of the University's centrally managed learning spaces on behalf of students, educators and administrators
- to develop and agree comprehensive specifications for these spaces to embed the University's student as producer and learning landscapes principles
- to review all such spaces against the agreed specifications and prioritize spaces for creation, improvement or replacement

- to produce business cases for projects to create, improve or replace these spaces
- to review and comment on all proposals for university learning spaces, whether centrally or locally managed
- to critically evaluate the results of university learning space projects, capture lessons learned, and ensure their dissemination and transfer to those involved in future projects
- to monitor all sources of feedback relating to learning spaces; receive, share and review such feedback; and respond appropriately
- to oversee regular inspection of centrally managed learning spaces and correction of any defects.

Crucially, the LSG's membership includes the University Librarian, and this has led directly to the development of a new model for library and teaching space at the University.

The Library

One of the lessons learned at Lincoln is that for academic and spatial reasons, institutions should collocate library space with formal teaching spaces. The new library extension at Lincoln is being designed on just this model. The organizing principle for co-locating teaching and library spaces is student as producer, linking University of Lincoln's e-learning landscapes concepts: efficiency, effectiveness, expression and experimentation, within an academic frame of reference encapsulated by 'the idea of the University'.

Efficiency

Co-locating teaching spaces with library spaces offers tremendous space *efficiency*. This is a product of the difference between the core teaching year and the calendar year. Many university librarians run 24/7 or near 24/7 operations for most of the calendar year. By contrast, university timetablers and teaching staff tend to think in terms of a core teaching week and core teaching year. Even the best-used teaching spaces tend to be very lightly used outside their host institution's core teaching week and core teaching year.

Given the pressure for 24/7 or near 24/7 opening, tremendous space efficiency gains are available through collocation of seminar spaces in the library, since they can be easily used as study and groupwork spaces when not in use for teaching.

Library provision at Lincoln should contain as many of the University's central pool teaching spaces as possible, and those spaces should be designed and advertised for dual use – as formal seminar rooms per the timetable, and as social and individual learning spaces for the rest of the day, week and year.

Effectiveness

There is a well established body of research on what constitutes effective teaching and learning in higher education (McLean, 2006; Healey and Jenkins, 2009; Jenkins, Healey and Zetter, 2007; Kuh et al., 2010), with a growing literature on how these practices can be made into compelling spaces (Jamieson, 2003; Boys, 2011). Staff at Lincoln have put these literatures together to construct a briefing tool, 'Teaching with Space in Mind', providing case studies and other relevant materials to inform consultation events between architects and academics (Neary, Williams et al., 2010).

Design of the library extension at Lincoln is ongoing, but the key features of the seminar spaces within the extension will include:

- advertising the availability of rooms in real time and explicitly encouraging use (in the form of digital displays inside and outside the rooms, which clearly state how long remains until the start of the next timetabled event in the room)
- excellent acoustic separation and appropriate visual separation from the adjacent library spaces, while retaining some sightlines (for example, in the form of frosted bands on internal glazed screens)
- generous writing surfaces (in the form of groupwork tables, which also support discursive, group-centred seminars)
- great support for bring your own devices (in the form of fast, robust wi-fi and desktop power sockets for every student)
- providing spaces immediately adjacent to the seminar venue; students will choose to arrive earlier making use of the premium spatiotemporal real estate to prepare for seminars, talk to classmates, reflect and write up notes and so on, as well as linger on campus when teaching is over.

Expression

As the expression of student as producer, the design of the Library is about more than the sum of its functions, and becomes the embodiment of the academic values, moral and ethical framework that form the substance for the 'idea of the university' and 'the idea of the student'. Writing at the start of the 20th century, Walter Benjamin, the German social theorist, considered issues that underpinned 'the idea of the student' (Benjamin, 1996). For Benjamin, universities were not simply buildings but metaphysical structures, which should express the 'conscious unity of student life'. Benjamin explains this unity as 'the will to submit to a principle, to identify completely with an idea' (38), based, in this case, on a notion of generalized scholarship and 'community of learning', culminating in the more expansive and non-empirical 'unity in the idea of knowledge'.

Benjamin argues that 'this idea of knowledge' should not operate by reference to any specific scientific principle, but provide the basis for 'the community of the university' (43), which for him is, 'a life more deeply conceived' (43). For Benjamin this meant that study was much more than 'heaping up of information' but a sort of:

> unceasing spiritual revolution – a point from which new questions would be incubated, in a more ambitious, less clear, less precise way, but perhaps with greater profundity than the traditional scientific questions. The creativity of students might then enable us to regard them as the great transformers whose task is to seize upon new ideas, which spring up sooner in art and society than in the university, and mould them into scientific shape under the guidance of their philosophical approach (43).

Clearly, this approach to the unity of student life is at odds with the current instrumentalist, consumerist, employability-focused model within which the contemporary student is being constructed. For the student to pursue 'a life more deeply conceived' requires a learning environment more akin to the labyrinthine spaces of the library that exists as a central character in Umberto Eco's *The Name of the Rose* (Haft, White and White, 1987), rather than the functionalist information commons that dominate contemporary university library designs.

With this anti-functionalist sensibility in mind students (and staff) are encouraged to 'occupy' library spaces and other learning spaces for their own purposes. Empty spaces are offered without restrictions on use; users are simply encouraged to book in advance, and to leave rooms as they would wish to find them. This use of space is recognized through inclusion in the University's annual occupancy surveys.

Experimentation

The LSG grounds the metaphysical concepts of idea of the university and the idea of student in the empirical world of planning and implementation. It has adopted and adapted the methodology of the plan–do–study–act cycle popularized by William Edwards Deming in the 1950s:

- *Plan*: LSG projects are conceived and planned in and between group meetings, with one or more members agreeing to act as 'clients' to develop the design with the project delivery team. The planning process is as inclusive and public as possible, making use of the Learning Landscapes blog as an interactive place for discussion of proposals, and of the University's committee structure, to critique draft business cases and design proposals more formally, leading up to a final approval by the University's Senior Management Team. Potential projects are required to pass tests of efficiency, effectiveness and expression.
- *Do*: LSG projects are executed by a team led by a project manager within Estates & Commercial Facilities, with the LSG remaining as 'client' throughout to ensure that the detailed design of the new places or spaces is aligned with the purpose of the project. The LSG also works to communicate the projects while in progress, and to inform potential users about the new places and how to exploit them.
- *Study*: The LSG leads academically credible evaluation of the new places or spaces by academics, students and other stakeholders. Study methods may include observation, photography and videography; discussions and focus groups with users; one-to-one interviews; quantitative analysis of space use; and solicitation of comments through the Learning Landscapes blog and other social media.
- *Act*: The LSG guides adjustment of the new places or spaces based on feedback, and revises any documentation produced during the process – for example, standard specifications for furniture, audiovisual equipment, acoustic performance and lighting. Other activities at this stage include further communication to potential and current users of the spaces to ensure the spaces are adopted, and reflection on the project process itself to identify opportunities for more effective project planning and execution in future.

The second phase of the Library at the University of Lincoln is about to become more than an idea. Watch this space!

References

Benjamin, W. (1996) The Life of Students. In Bullock, M. and Jennings, M. W. (eds), *Walter Benjamin – Selected Writings*, Vol. 1, 1936–1926, Belknap Press of Harvard University Press, 37–47.

Borges, J. L. (1964) The Library of Babel. In *Labyrinths*, 78–86.

Bourdieu, P. and Wacquant, L. J. D. (1992) *An Invitation to Reflexive Sociology*, Chicago University Press.

Boys, J. (2011) *Towards Creative Learning Spaces: rethinking the architecture of post-compulsory*, Routledge.

CABE (2011) *Creating Excellent Buildings*, Commission for Architecture and the Built Environment, http://webarchive.nationalarchives.gov.uk/20110118095356/ http://www.cabe.org.uk/publications/creating-excellent-buildings (accessed 20 August 2013).

Covey, S. R. (1989) *The Seven Habits of Highly Effective People: restoring the character ethic*, Free Press.

Dugdale, S. (2009) Space Strategies for the New Learning Landscape, *Educause Review*, **44** (2), March/April, www.educause.edu/ero/article/space-strategies-new-learning-landscape (accessed 19 August 2013).

Habermas, J. and Blazek, J. R. (1987) The Idea of the University: learning processes, *New German Critique*, **41**, 3–22.

Haft, A., White, J. and White R. (1987) *The Key to 'The Name of the Rose'*, Michigan University Press.

Healey, M. and Jenkins, A. (2009) *Developing Undergraduate Research and Enquiry*, Higher Education Academy.

Jamieson, P. (2003) Designing More Effective On-Campus Teaching and Learning Spaces: a role for academic developers, *International Journal for Academic Development*, **8** (1–2), 119–33.

Jenkins, A., Healey, M. and Zetter R. (2007) *Linking Teaching and Research in Disciplines and Departments*, Higher Education Academy.

Kuh, G. D., Kinzie, J., Schuh, J. and Whitt, E. (2010) *Student Success in College: creating conditions that matter*, Jossey-Bass.

McLean, M. (2006) *Pedagogy and the University: critical theory and practice*, Continuum.

Neary, M. (2012) Student as Producer: an institution of the common [or, how to recover communist/revolutionary science], Higher Education Academy, ISSN 1756-848X.

Neary, M. and Saunders, G. (2011) Leadership and Learning Landscapes: the struggle for the idea of the university, *Higher Education Quarterly*, **65** (4), 333–52.

Neary, M. and Thody, A. (2009) Learning Landscapes: designing a classroom of the future. In Bell, L., Stevenson, H. and Neary, M. (eds) *The Future of Higher Education: policy, pedagogy and the student experience*, Continuum.

Neary, M., Williams, S., Harrison, A., Crellin, G., Parekh, N., Saunders, G., Duggan, F. and Austin, S. (2010) *Learning Landscapes in Higher Education, University of Lincoln and DEGW*, sponsored by the Higher Education Funding Council for England, the Higher Education Funding Council for Wales and the Scottish Funding Council.

CHAPTER 22

Viral design: learners building better learning environments together

Stephen Heppell

The way it was

As we look back, the 1950–2000 era of education already seems like an aberration. A rapid population growth post Second World War in Britain and elsewhere led to a panic move into industrial scale learning. At one point in the 1970s England alone was opening a school every weekday to keep pace with the post-war baby boom and a design plague of galvanized windows and revolting toilets were just some of the sad consequences. The design of learning space was something that was done for children or, perhaps more accurately, something that was done to them. Children were subjects (Rosenthal and Jacobson, 1968), but rarely collaborators. The libraries in these factory schools, with racking, stacking and rules, were often uninspiring too. Children would have done it differently. When eventually we asked them, they did.

Co-construction

Happily, as the panic baby-boom building, and the shock of the inequalities revealed by conscription, all calmed a little, the rhetoric of education began to see the learners themselves as helpful co-constructors. With time to do it better, for some it made sense to do it together. In the 1980s and 1990s this rhetoric of co-construction grew, propelled in part by the impact of educational technology. From the 1980s, with BBC and Research Machines computers in UK schools, it was clear that children, with their Spectrums and Commodores at home, had a capability that we would ignore at our peril. Smart schools embraced the geeks within the student body and a feverish two decades of programming, robotics, art installations and more saw children very much as co-creators of a digital curriculum in classrooms and clubs. Libraries then were at serious risk of being left behind – an analogue backwater in a digital world.

However, for perhaps the first time since the 1944 Education Act, many were comfortable to acknowledge that children might, in some 'modern tech' areas, know as much or more than their teachers. The confident, creative, empowered children who emerged from this collaborative era today form the backbone of the colossal and lucrative UK creative industry of games, SFX, animation, advertising, fashion and more. That creative industry is second only to banks' scale in our economy (NESTA, 2011). Of course, in time that parity of esteem of learners and teachers was reeled in with a host of dull and formulaic ICT capabilities, with even duller examinations – the unpredictable and exciting robots retreated to the cupboards; spreadsheets and 'word processing' were made safe to examine, and were simple to teach. The quiet of the new computer lab trumped even the quiet of the traditional library. Shoulders drooped a little.

Listening to learners

An incoming Blair Labour Government in the UK in 1997 proclaimed education, education, education as a central policy tenet, which allowed the Government to focus, among other things, on the building stock of the nation's schools; it was found to be wanting. What should replace it?

Mukund Patel and Chris Bissell at the Department for Education and Skills led an initiative called Classrooms of the Future (DfES, 2002). David Miliband, the then 'Ministerial design champion', wrote in the introduction to the report:

> We are going to make sure that our school buildings provide us with a better
> environment for teaching and learning, we need to ensure that all of the
> capital going into modernizing and renewing buildings is being effectively
> invested to deliver excellent facilities for today and tomorrow. We need to try
> out new ideas now.

Often the large learning space at the heart of the school, the library, became the focus for these spirited makeovers. There was no doubt about the importance of the learners' voice in this. To confirm it, Miliband added:

We are learning from the exciting ideas emerging from the 30 pilot projects, and will continue to do so once teachers and pupils start using them. They were involved in developing design concepts and ideas, and they will tell us which ideas are the best and should be replicated as we modernize our school buildings.

By 2003 many of these radical Classrooms of the Future designs were nearing completion. Patel and Bissell had prefaced their project brochure with children's designs and often project prototypes relied heavily on a close dialogue with learners about designs, many of which proved to be spectacularly effective. Among them, some astonishing libraries began to emerge: timetable free, full of collaborative endeavour, family tables, natural light, soft furnishings, beanbags and laughter.

With the evidence of the effectiveness of these single large room, agile prototypes, a plan was developed to replace substantial numbers of entire secondary schools. If one new library space, or an atrium, could be impactful, a whole school would surely be transformative? The Government embarked on Building Schools for the Future from 2005. A scheme as ambitious as Building Schools for the Future was bound to attract complex bureaucracy with everything from procurement to noise and energy compliance carefully prescribed. Ironically, although the framework for Building Schools for the Future was rather fierce about many tiny details, it didn't really lay down any design advice about learning. Children involved in the design process were horrified to find that their carefully researched and tested suggestions to make learning demonstrably better flew in the face of these prescriptions. Effective learning needed natural light – but energy efficiency imposed small windows; celebration and exhibition were central to any model of engaged learners, but the private finance initiative (PFI) contracts stopped many schools from developing wall displays; large super-classes with multiple teachers were fun to be in and moved at a jaw-dropping pace, but for some unimaginative architects the Building Schools for the Future prescriptions put walls and corridors between learners, limiting class size. Often, even after the battle for learning had been fought and won, value engineering decision makers lobotomized the to-be-built environment without asking the children or the teachers. But the best schools built were still as seductive as the best libraries had been. The genie was out of the bottle – with our students we really make learning better by design.

And something remarkable happened at the end of this era of co-

construction. Many schools reported significantly varied solutions, but these were nevertheless often similarly effective; curiously, many hopelessly compromised buildings also worked, despite some hideously foolish design impositions, and many disengaged students became miraculously re-engaged even before their new buildings were completed. It was starting to look as if the dialogue about better learning was as effective as the designs intended to engender it. This shouldn't have been a surprise. A vast literature had developed in educational journals about the impact of reflective practice in teachers. Projects like the EU i3 éTui project (1997) indicated that children as young as four could, given the relevant focus of a learning construction task (in that case an intelligent 'learning' robotic toy), elicit meta-cognitive reflection and a resultant heightened engagement. Brave schools like Thomas Mitchell School in east London had children sitting at the back of classrooms observing lessons before unpacking reflective observations with their teachers ('Have you thought about this, miss?'). Reflective practice was effective practice. As the children became more and more involved in the design process, the stark insight was that it was the act of engaging children in the design of their learning spaces that produced engaged, reflective, better learners. The mutuality and collegiality was there for all to see in the discourse analysis as engaged children spoke of 'our' and 'we', where before they had spoken truculently of 'me' and 'mine', or 'them' and 'theirs'. Better than that, because learning is something that children do day in and day out, they had genuine insights and wisdoms to offer, and they had the technology to do rapid and effective research into others' exemplary design details. This was a win–win for education: asking children to design better learning engaged them, but it also produced better learning designs too! What was not to like!

This was rather good news in a post-global economic collapse world where the largesse of Building Schools for the Future, and indeed substantial amounts of public funding, were gone. In answer to the question 'How might we build better learning now?' the rather stunning answer turned out to be simply 'ask the children to research it, and then trust them'. Thus we find ourselves having lived through the two eras of children as subjects and then of children as co-constructors, to be now in an era where, rather seductively, children-led design is burning brightly. When money is tight, effective and affordable solutions are noticed and thus the user-led design of learning now finds itself centre stage.

There are masses of caveats, inevitably. The methodology of 'just asking the children' is not to ask naively 'What would you like?', but requires children themselves to actively research, through Skype and visits and reading and searching the world wide web, the many ingredients found to be working elsewhere before proposing a local 'recipe' for better learning. Not 'What would you like?', but 'What would work here?'. With the new technology at their disposal these children have the social tools to seek, question, critique, observe and conclude – and then to share. That sharing is beginning an era of viral exchange. So it is no surprise that around the world this new viral era of learner-led design turned out to flourish strongest in the libraries. School libraries have always been places where small trusted communities thrived, where the act of scholarship and research was mainstream, where the librarian was the one teacher who didn't 'deliver' knowledge, would never teach by 'stand and deliver', had no whiteboard. In Australia when an enlightened government sought to bottom out the first signs of recession by offering each school a Building the Educational Revolution building it was libraries and sports halls that were chosen so often as the focus for these new developments. Without changing the whole school it turned out that the newly seductive library was often enough of a catalyst to produce significant and enduring institutional change.

Conclusion

So what characterizes the best of these new user-led designed library spaces as they infect their institutions with a new vigour? They enjoy a huge diversity of furniture, and not too much of it. Very often they are shoeless places. Children rightly pointed out that nowhere in the world would a child voluntarily read on the hard high backed chairs that fill our schools. Observing their own leisure reading they saw the need for relaxed comfort, bean bags and sofas, clean carpets and a lot less furniture. They relished the immersion of heads down and focused work in great light, for longer blocks of time; they relished the collegiality and mutuality of 'family' conversations around big tables. They saw the motivation of celebration and exhibition, but their wall displays narrate process, with storyboards and drafts framing finished work. Walls, ceilings and windows celebrate text, letters and typography; they are spectacularly connected to the rest of the planet with their Skype bars and screens. Most obvious of all, they are full of children and you can't get them to leave! They speak of their space, their learning, their innovation, their future.

Two quotes close this chapter rather neatly. This is not about policy at the national level, it is not about ministers or departmental prescription. Sarah

Teather (2011), then English Minister for Children and Families, commented, ironically at the annual Learning Without Frontiers conference in London, that 'it's right for children to have a voice, but not to have decision making power; they are children after all'.

She could not have been more wrong, or more last century. But she could not have been less relevant either. This is a transformation led from the bottom up. Not quite a pedagogic Egypt, but something quite precipitate nonetheless. In London's Lampton School (Heppell, 2013) a group of children made over their own classroom with a tight budget. As the project progressed a parent e-mailed in to reflect on her daughter, commenting that

> it got to the point that she was in school all the time. Instead of having a row with her in the mornings, we stopped arguing about her being late in, but argued about her being late home, because she wanted to be working on the project in school.

What is on offer here as we pass the reigns over to the children is learning so good that the children don't want to go home; learning that lifts standards even as it lifts spirits. Best of all, doing it cheaply, led by children, means that we might also impact on the learning needs of many other parts of the world where money is very tight, but interested children are abundant.

Teachers retain a role, of course: tasking children with building better learning; supporting and resourcing their investigations and research. Holding them to a tough budget. Developing their scholarship. Then trusting their judgement unequivocally. Fighting for and implementing their designs. And taking joy in the remarkable, stellar progress that results. Oh yes!

References

DfES (2002) *Classrooms of the Future*, Department for Education and Skills, http://rubble.heppell.net/places/media/classrooms_of_the_future.pdf (accessed 24 May 2013).

éTui project (1997) *éTui: an i3 experimental school environments project*, http://rubble.heppell.net/archive/etui/default.html (accessed 14 May 2013).

Heppell, J. (2013) *Designing a Learning Space: when students dream of learning*, iTunes Store.

NESTA (2011) *Next Gen: transforming the UK into the world's leading talent hub for the video games and visual effects industries*, www.nesta.org.uk/library/documents/NextGenv32.pdf (accessed 14 May 2013).

Rosenthal, R. and Jacobson, L. (1968) *Pygmalion in the Classroom: teacher expectation and pupils' intellectual development*, Holt, Rinehart and Winston, 240.

Teather S. (2011) Learning without Frontiers conference, London, UK.

CHAPTER 23

The interior designer's view

Val Clugston

Introduction

In *Interior Design of the 20th Century*, Anne Massey (1990) states that 'Interior design is a phenomenon born of the 20th century, to be precise the latter half of the 20th century'.

The profession of interior design is a young, evolving discipline that was first formalized in the UK as recently as the late 1960s when a number of tertiary level education courses were inaugurated. One of the most recent environments to employ interior design is the education sector and in particular libraries and learning commons. In the last ten years there has been a surge of interest in the design of 'learning environments', which has stimulated widespread refurbishment and building programmes in higher and further education institutions. This interest has been influenced by a complex number of cultural, pedagogic and technological developments and influences. In addition, widening access to higher education has led to greater diversity in student populations.

Oblinger (2003) provides a useful overview of the new student:

The 'new' student may be a seventeen-year-old high school student (a 'Millennial') who uses instant messaging to contact peers and teachers. The 'new' students may be a twenty-six-year old college student (a 'Gen-X' whose expectations of customer service are radically different from those of previous generations. Or the 'new' student may be a forty-year-old working mother (a 'Baby-Boomer') who is completing a degree via e learning so that she can balance work and family responsibility.

The most significant factor driving these changes is the explosion of new technology, particularly social media that enables students to participate in and debate information while sharing this with friends and colleagues often entirely online. Despite this many educators believe that there is a greater need than ever for new spaces to provide opportunities for face-to-face interaction and collaboration. The introduction of technologies to support learners has significantly changed the way that libraries, in particular, look. Evolution from banks of desktop computers to hand held or mobile devices has driven demand for new types of furniture, lighting and accessible power and data outlets. Presentation equipment supporting face-to-face collaboration has further changed the landscape of spaces, emphasizing flexible semi-private spaces with many libraries using pods or booths to facilitate this activity.

The degree of interest in new learning spaces coupled with increased competition among UK universities and colleges for students has created an environment of innovation at both large architectural scale and especially at the smaller every day human scale. Human scale is the level at which interior design specialists operate and can add significant value through technical and creative thinking and intimate knowledge of how people use and move about space.

People-centred design

People-centred design is a methodology that places the end users of a space at the heart of the design process combining field research methods with participatory design approaches. Associated with product design people-centred design uses field methods for exploring and understanding spaces and their use adapted from a number of disciplines such as anthropology, architectural psychology, environmental psychology and city planning. These methods include mapping, observation, interviews and photo-journals. A combination of some or all of these methods reveals a great deal about the use of space and how it can be improved. The understanding of softer aspects of a place, such as history, culture and identity, requires a participatory or collaborative approach.

Methodology

Over the course of the last six years Nomad Research Design Consultation Ltd has worked with many higher education institutions in the UK designing and installing people-centred projects. During this time we have interviewed 600+ students, designed and held 75+ creative workshops, mapped 200+ student or staff journeys, generated eight blogs and social media platforms, and carried out countless days of observation. This extensive body of work has enabled us to refine our people-centred approach and highlighted some of the basic design principles and processes behind a positive user-centred space.

Some basic principles

Developments over the last decade have produced a set of principles to guide the design of new libraries and learning commons. They identify the types of spaces that support different types of learners, the relationship of these spaces to one another and the means to make these spaces as flexible as possible. The most frequently recurring principles are the need for:

- flexible or multi-functional space that can be reconfigured daily, weekly or monthly to suit a number of functions ensuring the space is fully used
- creation of choice with a variety of spaces to suit different learning styles and needs
- provision of sufficient volume of space to ensure that learners are comfortable
- removal of barriers between formal and informal spaces
- inclusion of collaborative and social spaces
- clear, direct information and communication.

Our work with universities, colleges, their staff and students across the UK has reinforced the importance of these principles and these ideas will remain a significant feature of new libraries and learning commons in the future. In addition, clients often highlight the importance of spaces that will actively encourage cross-disciplinary discourse, a sense of community, a feeling of belonging and a sense of place. These ideas are often described as soft targets and there is little information or guidance on how these goals might be achieved; yet it is these notions that are often most persistently referred to when engaging in discussions with our clients and their users. The following is a brief description of some of the main processes and principles being developed to give our clients the best opportunity of achieving innovative, lasting and individual solutions for their future spaces.

Other spatial models

Our first recommended process is to look beyond education and libraries to other spatial models. For example, futurist Don Norris (Bleed, 2001) suggested that the 'great and good' buildings in the public realm, science centres, museums and libraries may be useful models for new learning spaces:

> Despite people retreating, in some ways, to their homes and their computers, at the same time they are being drawn to great and good public places that satisfy and nurture their need for community and human interaction and the excitement of city spaces.

What types of every day spaces provide opportunities for human interaction and community? Commercial and leisure spaces work hard to win customers and retain them. Is there a language in these spaces that we can borrow for a new model of library space? New workplaces share many of the requirements of libraries. Global companies such as Google or Facebook reflect their company ethos and culture through the design or their highly creative and fun spaces. It is worth exploring and experimenting with the spatial concepts expressed by these companies when seeking a spatial model for the future of the library.

A collaborative approach

Library learning spaces are undoubtedly a focus of institutional differentiation and are complex places populated by a wide variety of people with varying degrees of expertise, knowledge and talent. At Nomad Research Design Consultation Ltd we believe the best opportunity to innovate future space is by collaborating with existing users, leveraging the wealth of technical, creative and cultural knowledge that they bring to a project. Involving multiple stakeholders with the project also has the added benefit of helping to build empathy and understanding between competing groups and encourage a sense of ownership of the project for everyone. Our second recommended process is therefore to employ a collaborative approach from the outset. As Jamieson (2008) observed:

> The design process should involve a multi-disciplinary team drawing on the mix of expertise and perspectives of key institutional stakeholders, including 'facilities management' information technology, audio-visual systems, design,

academic development and teaching and learning: In addition, each participant should be encouraged to contribute equally regardless of rank or professional role

In 'Space Strategies for the New Learning Landscape', learning environment strategist Shirley Dugdale (2009) also advocates a collaborative approach with a focus on students:

> In a period of such rapid change, it is more important than ever to understand users' needs through a planning process that engages constituent groups from the beginning. Although surveys provide useful campus-wide data, facilitated interactive workshops can become energizing and creative with activities that draw out information about student culture and perceptions and that engage students in co-creating their vision for the future of the campus.

Designers can gather a wealth of important information about the space and users simply by spending some time observing and interacting with people in the space. This interaction provides insights into the real, rather than perceived, use of the space including planning issues, ergonomics, learning styles and desirable types of spaces, popular spaces, the reasons behind this popularity, and the overall culture and identity of that place and people.

Interviews, creative workshops and online platforms are excellent means to reach out and engage with stakeholders while mapping and observing the way in which a space operates reveals much about the operation of the services and how they can be improved. A multi-disciplinary approach using the skills and expertise of staff, students and design professionals helps establish pedagogic goals and principles to inform the design of teaching and learning spaces.

Community identity and communication

The concept of community and the idea of belonging to a community recur across all of our research and is one of the 'soft' targets of primary importance. Belonging to and participating in a community provides students with a powerful sense of identity. Freeman (2005) discusses the concept of community in relation to the academic library:

> It is a place where people come together on levels and in ways that they might not in the residence hall, classroom, or off-campus location. Upon entering the

library, the student becomes part of a larger community – a community that endows one with a greater sense of self and higher purpose.

Providing students with a sense of self and purpose is not the only benefit of a community model. Students are highly social, and generating spaces where they can meet other students, academics and staff in a social setting improves the collegiate experience and provides increased opportunities for improved learning. Bickford and Wright (2006) observed:

All aspects of education – including the planning of space design – should acknowledge community. Just as a learning paradigm focuses on the importance of learning, we argue for a community paradigm that emphasizes the role social interactions play in facilitating learning and improving student engagement: through community, learning can grow.

Understanding how the concept of community works spatially in everyday surroundings shows that being part of a community is not influenced by active spaces alone; passive spaces such as bus stops, park benches and information nodes encourage people to interact and communicate. These passive spaces are often located on the edges of space at thresholds, such as entrances or exits. People intuitively recognize the values of these spaces to deliver information and signs; posters and notices will inevitably start to appear. In our research we have found that places that communicate information well have a greater sense of community. In the best examples the edges or thresholds of space are richly detailed with information. Clear sightlines and circulation routes communicate the best method to navigate the place. The type of information available is also important. Providing basic information about the building and the services on offer is vital. Community information about social, cultural and even political events is equally important. Edges if properly detailed can be used to create a window onto a space where people will naturally gather building a sense of place and nurturing a sense of community.

The physical design and layout of space can encourage community by providing opportunities to connect. The identity of space and how this relates to the users is equally important and is the focus of our final recommendation. Graetz (2006) commented on the importance of environments that elicit positive emotional responses:

Environments that elicit positive emotional responses may lead not only to enhanced learning but also to a powerful, emotional attachment to that space. It may become a place where students love to learn, a place they seek out when they wish to learn, and a place they remember fondly when they reflect on their learning experiences.

Generally the public is becoming increasingly design and style conscious and care should be taken to ensure the identity a space projects is relevant to them and reflects or embodies the identity of the institution and the students therein.

Physical environments are increasingly recognized as the 'container' that gives context to group interactions, and thus the physical design of these spaces and the furnishings within them need to be explicitly considered, along with any technology system interface, as a component of the user's overall experience (Milne, 2006).

Identity is part of everyday modern life. It is where the idea of brand begins. This language of brands or identities is well established in the commercial world as a means to communicate important information to customers about the vision and values of a place. It would therefore seem logical that public spaces including libraries might also use a brand or identity to communicate with their customers.

Our role as designers is to uncover the identity of each space and reflect this in the best way we can. We have found that each public space or institution has its own identity, a kind of community identity within which individual identities exist. This is usually a mixture of the formal identity that the institution or place projects and the 'real' identity and culture created by the inhabitants of the space. When the right identity is projected then users will want to be in the space; they will feel a sense of pride; some may even feel like they are at home.

Conclusion

I am confident that the library will remain the academic centre of the campus or community and believe that despite technology people will continue to want to meet face to face to share, collaborate or simply feel part of a community. However, the types of spaces contained within the library and how they look will embrace collaborative and social activities, encourage debate and express the identity of the community they serve. As these spaces develop we should also take care to maintain or even improve traditional silent spaces, which continue to be popular, particularly with postgraduate students and researchers or during the exam season.

The big change that will distinguish libraries and other public or institutional buildings from each other and the past will be the people themselves. Not only how they inhabit and use the space but how they choose to become involved with the design of these places and how their real rather than perceived needs, desires and identities are expressed.

Both the types of spaces I have outlined and the role of the interior designer are changing and evolving. We are now at a point where a people-centred approach to the design of spaces and collaboration is becoming increasingly popular. This type of approach, coupled with interior designers' established tools of culture and intuition, suggests exciting possibilities for future spaces. Global design firm Ideo sums this up: 'Radical innovation requires both evidence and intuition: evidence to become informed, and intuition to inspire us in imagining and creating new and better possibilities' (quoted in Fulton, 2008).

We often quote architect Berthold Lubetkin who is reputed to have said, 'Nothing is too good for ordinary people.' We think that this statement sets a benchmark as we explore the future of libraries and learning spaces with our changing understanding of learning and of the habits and practices of people.

References

Bickford, D. J. and Wright, D. J. (2006) Community: the hidden context for learning. In Oblinger, D. G. (ed.) *Learning Spaces*, 4.1–4.22, Educause.

Bleed, R. (2001) A Hybrid Campus for the New Millenium, *Educause Review*, Jan/Feb, 16–24, http://net.educause.edu/ir/library/pdf/erm0110.pdf (accessed 14 May 2013).

Dugdale, S. (2009) Space Strategies for the New Learning Landscape, *Educause Review*, March/April, 51–63.

Freeman, G. T. (2005) The Library as Place: changes in learning patterns, collections, technology and use. In CLIR, *Library as Place: rethinking roles, rethinking space*, Council on Library and Information Resources.

Fulton, S. J. (2008) Informing our Intuition Design Research for Radical Innovation, *Rotman Magazine*, **53**.

Graetz, K. A. (2006) The Psychology of Learning Environments. In Oblinger, D. G. (ed.) *Learning Spaces*, 6.1–6.14, Educause.

Jamieson, P. (2008) Creating New Generation Learning Environments on the University Campus, Woods Bagot, www.woodsbagot.com (accessed 19 August 2013).

Massey, A. (1990) *Interior Design of the 20th Century*, Thames and Hudson.

Milne, A. J. (2006) Designing Blended Learning Space to the Student Experience. In Oblinger, D. G. (ed.) *Learning Spaces*, 11.1–11.15, Educause.

Oblinger, D. (2003) Understanding the New Students, *Educause Review*, July–August, 37–47.

CHAPTER 24

Furniture fit for the future – a brief exploration of library and learning furniture today and for the coming generation

Paul White

What is furniture for?

In this article I endeavour to investigate the trends driving library and learning spaces forward from a furniture designer's perspective and explore how furniture may evolve to facilitate this journey.

The advance of technology has led us all a merry dance over the last 30 years. In 1983 I rang people on my telephone – it is now 2013 and my smart phone sits on the desk beside me. On last count this clever, potent machine has replaced no fewer than 45 products and services in my life. Irrefutably, technology's rapid rate of change promises to influence the furniture used in library and learning spaces dramatically.

Let us focus on the furniture we currently use and consider where this may lead in the coming generation. To put our investigation in context let us underpin it with three simple ideas:

- Furniture is for people. For the most part people need somewhere to put themselves (typically a seat) and somewhere to put things (shelves) and do things (worktops). Good furniture is about 'people fit'.
- Change is certain, and great flexibility in library and learning furniture is absolutely key to future-proofing.
- People will always seek social context in community hubs and they will always need to learn. The future of libraries and learning facilities is assured, though their forms will continue to transform.

Staff versus the machine

Recent surveys indicate that for many library users interaction with staff remains an important component of their library visit.[1] Apart from offering practical assistance librarians are people helping people and providing important social context – there is no replacement for a welcoming smile. Though libraries will undergo continuing automation staff–user interaction will remain an important part of library life and furniture will continue to be needed to support this.

Front of house minimized

We are in the midst of a general trend to break down the barriers in search of enhanced customer experience. This has been supported by the move to customer self-service models, including issues, returns and reservations, which make the old-style circulation counter (I call them fortresses) increasingly redundant. The replacement is the standalone help point positioned at the entrance and key locations throughout the library and used in tandem with staff roaming models; preferably these staff stations are

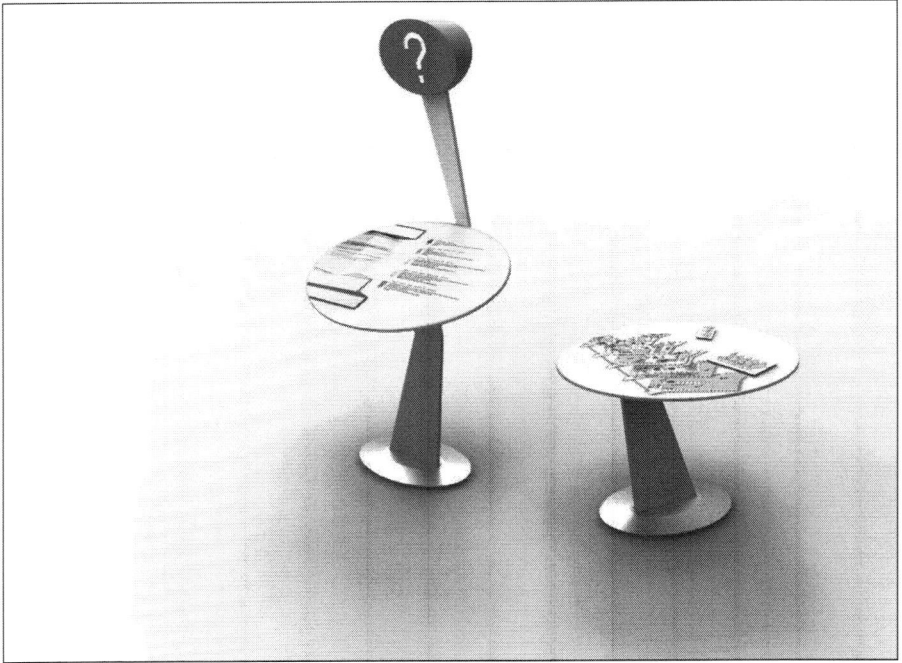

Figure 24.1 *Stations equipped with powerful interactive digital worktops (copyright Cie Ltd, 2013)*

mobile and height adjustable, enabling use while seated or standing. Though some argue that roaming models require no furniture at all it is our observation that people need a 'place' to return to and therefore the staff station in some form will remain. Future front of house staff will use staff stations equipped with powerful interactive digital worktops (Figure 24.1).

In Figure 24.1 we envisage a front of house 30 years from now, featuring help points where the tablets of the future are still carried by staff and customers, and thanks to the potential of rock star materials like graphene[2] the whole staff station desktop is now a powerful interactive screen. Couple this with voice activation and emerging gesture control technologies (like Leap Motion[3] or Samsung's promised eye activated scrolling) and our voices, eye movements and gestures have become the interface, making the mouse, keyboard and even touch screens obsolete. Design of the help point is still centred on the 'people fit'; seated to standing adjustment continues to be essential, and because the need to respond to change remains critical the workstation is still mobile. Today we need power points to recharge dead devices; in our scenario there is now a wireless power pad incorporated in the desktop.[4] Elsewhere in our future front of house, we suggest customer book-processing kiosks have now disappeared, made redundant by automated management systems, though books, and therefore the returns slot, still remain.

Managing your total library experience

While for some library members interaction with staff remains important, recent surveys also show that people are becoming increasingly happy and able to manage their own library experience.[5] Future customers will self-manage their activities via interactive digital portals like these kiosks deployed throughout the space (Figure 24.2).

In Figure 24.2 we focus on this self-help aspect in a generation's time whereby the same help points shown in Figure 24.1 are also available for direct use by the library user. This will offer via its 'magic pool' tabletop a powerful interactive portal to library activities, resources and the customer's personal account. Such help points will be deployed throughout the library and could also be integrated into library tables or other pieces of furniture. A step further and interactive holographic technology may allow us to say goodbye to the screen forever.

Figure 24.2 *Interactive digital portals like these kiosks deployed throughout the space (copyright Cie Ltd, 2013)*

Flexibility

Furniture deployed in library spaces must be highly flexible. As libraries offer increasingly more diverse programmes a theatre analogy fits very well, as spaces become stages and furniture the props responding to each production and change of scene. The highly successful Norfolk and Norwich Millennium Library in the UK demonstrates the need to be light on one's feet by providing versatile furniture, which is able to support diverse activities, including craft sessions for kids, knit and natter circles and board game afternoons. Worcester's Hive (see case study in Chapter 1) takes this priority for flexible furniture one step further, combining the diverse needs of public and university libraries under one roof. For some years now the question 'how else might this item be used?' has been at the forefront of library designers' creative thinking.

Tables and chairs

Tables and chairs have been present in libraries since libraries began. They will always be there because the 'people fit' encompasses the fundamental need for people to sit down and put things they wish to interact with in front of them at a comfortable height. In today's library, tables have adapted to a

Figure 24.3 *Library tables as e-readers of the future (copyright Cie Ltd, 2013)*

variety of purposes other than reading and writing, notably supporting devices like computers and audiovisual equipment. Tables are now often mounted on castors and incorporate tilt tops for ease of moving and storing. The traditional rectangular tabletop is now complemented by a myriad of shapes, including round, oval and teardrop, to ensure the best functional fit for the space. Library tables themselves may become the e-readers of the future. Mobile space dividers may also act as data shows, providing information access and ambiance.

We suggest in Figure 24.3 that in the library of the future, devices mounted on tables will diminish (for example, we are already seeing PC numbers in libraries drop), and we may find ourselves sitting down reading the table itself as interactive screen technologies take over the whole tabletop. Newspaper and magazine resources are a deployment challenge for librarians. Already we are seeing libraries providing access to some titles only via iPads.[6] Predictably the digital trend will continue and with tabletop-sized screens the cyber newspaper may be opened fully and comfortably perused – perhaps with pages turned at the blink of an eye.

Love to lounge

Providing welcome havens in a busy world, lounge areas are quite rightly expected in today's library-scape; they are our community living rooms. Typically such areas are populated by various soft seating options such as tub chairs, sofas and ottomans, which are usually augmented by coffee tables. In recent years, customers have started to bring their own devices to the library; consequently new elements have appeared like portable laptop tables. Lounge areas encourage connective social experience and, particularly in tertiary libraries, support informal learning interaction. The fact that many lounge chairs in use today are derivatives of designs from as far back as the 1930s suggests that lounge areas are unlikely to change significantly in the next 30 years; we will however see more integrated technology. In today's library we find chairs with power outlets and chairs designed for gaming or as listening posts. In the future such chairs may support 3D holographic interactions and experiences.

My space your space

Space division is an important component in encouraging personal or group activities and achieving efficient space utilization. Spontaneous space division is typically achieved using sound absorbing mobile screens, which often double as pin boards or white boards. In larger spaces, human nature being what it is, people will first populate the corners of the room, then line the walls and only when these spaces are full spread into the centre of the room. By deploying mobile screens to create spontaneous zones spaces are better used; people are more comfortable when their space is defined, a human attribute unlikely to change in the future. Figure 24.3 (on the previous page) shows a mobile space divider of the future also acting as a data show for providing information access and even ambiance; convert your reading room into a tropical paradise.

Display

Good display gets products noticed and makes them easily accessible. With the move to digital, many physical library products will disappear including CDs, DVDs and potentially a large percentage of books, newspapers and magazines. Regardless of whether a product is physical or digital the principles of good display will remain valid and relevant for libraries. Theme displays, focus displays and face display will continue to 'dress' library spaces, enriching the user experience. Thus the familiar display stands will remain useful but products and services will increasingly be promoted via digital media, such as promotions on 'billboards' mounted throughout the library.

Kids are the future

In our travels we have seen much creative work in children and youth zones. Story time areas where the adults can comfortably fit too, hidey holes, imaginatively themed kiddy furniture and increasingly the introduction of iPad and touch-screen-based activities. Appropriately New Zealand's new 'super city' of Auckland, created from the amalgamation of several councils, now has 55 libraries and cites their commitment to children and young people as the top priority of their ten-year plan.[7] Kids love knowing this is their special place; they love to roll around on the floor, to reach things and do things for themselves. Libraries can play a key role in developing children's knowledge and creativity. Exploring furniture designs that 'understand' kids will greatly assist libraries to make the most of this opportunity. Life is a serious game; keep creative – they are worth it.

Learning spaces

As technology revolutionizes the way we learn exciting new ideas like massively open online courses (MOOCs) are being trialled and models around lifelong learning pursued.[8] Whatever the outcomes it remains likely that getting together in groups will remain an important component of learning, and the spaces and furniture used will need to be highly adaptive. Worktables are now designed around the optimum learning group size (typically comprising three people). Ideally they are easy to store and deploy, with the ability to link to other tables and enable teachers to work naturally with individuals, groups or multiple groups. Technology is focused on access, capture and sharing, currently using whiteboards, data shows and projectors, all of which will eventually give way to interactive digital walls and surfaces. In Figure 24.4 we take a glimpse at learning space furniture a generation from now, where furniture will support information access, capture and sharing in future learning spaces.

Focus space

When work needs to be done focus space for individuals and small groups is important. Of late, high-back chairs, mobile screens and 'diner booths'

Figure 24.4 *Furniture to support information access, capture and sharing in future learning spaces (copyright Cie Ltd 2013)*

have arrived to complement the traditional study carrel and meeting room. We will see much more experimentation with furniture design in this area as learning theory evolves. For example the 'birdnests' in use at Coventry University's Hub in the UK – round, low-walled enclosures, complete with bean bags and plenty of power outlets – provide popular hang outs for students to gather.

Outside – the unexplored asset

The weather does not always co-operate, but library and learning facilities often include wonderful outdoor areas. These are inevitably populated with traditional park benching and often supported by reasonable wi-fi cover. There is great potential to make better use of these spaces with well designed outdoor furniture, which creatively addresses comfort, community and cover; watch this space.

So where to from here?

For library and learning institutions in the coming generation the challenge is not just to survive in a continually changing world, but to use new technology and ideas to maximize their relevance to the communities they serve. Furniture design is responding to provide the 'objects for living' that staff and visitors will require, and we are seeing many fresh ideas arriving on the scene. Inevitably we can look forward to a highly automated technology-rich future; nevertheless, successful furniture for library and learning spaces will continue to focus on the 'people fit'.

Notes

1 Pew Research Centre, *Importance of Staff Interaction*, http://libraries.pewinternet. org/2013/01/22/library-services/ (accessed 19 August 2013).
2 Learn more about graphene at http://en.wikipedia.org/wiki/Graphene (accessed 19 August 2013).
3 Explore Leap Motion, https://www.leapmotion.com/ (accessed 19 August 2013).
4 Learn more about wireless power at http://news.nationalgeographic.com/news/energy/2012/12/121228-wireless-power/ (accessed 19 August 2013).
5 Pew Research Centre, *Importance of Staff Interaction*.
6 Access via iPads, www.onlinecollege.org/2011/09/05/20-coolest-ipad-ideas-for-your-library/item, 14 (accessed 19 August 2013).
7 Report on the creation of Auckland Libraries, www.questia.com/library/1G1-315068865/towards-the-world-s-most-liveable-city-the-creation (accessed 19 August 2013).
8 Lifelong Learning, www.enotes.com/continuing-education-lifelong-learning-trends-reference/continuing-education-lifelong-learning-trends (accessed 19 August 2013).

CHAPTER 25

Conclusions

Les Watson

The agenda for libraries back in the final decade of the last century was focused on technology and how it was affecting their key resource of information. The debate was concerned primarily with digitization and the format of materials – but also with the early signs of the potential disappearance of library space (Crawford and Gorman, 1995). Almost 20 years later, following significant progress with digital and virtual libraries, the emphasis has shifted from the potential disappearance of physical libraries to a real threat as technology has permeated not just the resources and materials that we use but has become essential to our lives as readers and learners. The threat now to library space is not that the digital resources will replace physical collections but that universal access from personal devices will remove the appetite and necessity of users to visit. Add to this the eagerness of politicians and educational managers to save money and the library as place is under more pressure to prove its worth than ever before. The argument in this book is that the library as a place of learning is its most fundamental attribute and if developed as such libraries as places will have an assured future.

That libraries and their spaces have an essential role in personal, societal and community learning is illustrated by the worldwide case studies described in the first part of this book. Part 1 has examples of many learning spaces in education and elsewhere that closely fit their community's needs. That many of these case studies describe the 'look and feel' of the libraries and their spaces indicates that the most important aspects of an effective library learning space are intangible 'soft' factors, which have emotional and psychological effects defying categorization. The hope of a systematic scientific recipe for the design of successful library learning spaces is currently elusive – as I mentioned in the introduction to this book the process of space development is more art than science. But this does not mean that we cannot shift the balance to remove some of the uncertainty about the potential success of a new space. Part of this activity has to be based on the experiments of small-scale trials preceding large-scale projects where feasible, experiments with pop-up spaces and furniture, and mash-ups of activities that create new ideas for space. Modelling user(s) to capture their variety of need, and the detail of that need, is also an essential activity if we are to match expectations and create great experiences.

In Part 2 there are many ideas about technology, learning, spaces themselves, and possible approaches to inform the development of new spaces. These ingredients and methods will help the creation of new spaces if used wisely, for example using a cut, edit and paste approach to creative swiping of ideas rather than simply cutting and pasting ideas that don't quite work for the culture of a new space. The emphasis placed on imagination and professional 'expert' intuition in this book is vital to ensure that ideas and inspiration are at the heart of new space and to redress the balance with the rationality of project implementation, achieving a 'both and' approach. Technology should be deeply embedded in the 'idea' for the space and be future focused. In Kelly's (2010) view this should 'always act to increase choice'. The idea of library as a technology system and of developing the library as a system that works to increase choice provides a powerful perspective, which ensures we focus firmly on the members of the library.

In Chapter 6 Roland Sussex, commenting on the importance of a close fit between library and community, notes that libraries 'are now increasingly planned in consultation with the communities that they serve' and the result is libraries 'which are welcoming, open, attractive and responsive to community needs'. Consultation and engagement in idea generation should be as wide as possible, and ideally start well before there is even a project on the horizon and continue after it is completed, so that there is sound knowledge of the needs, wants, feelings and ideas of users, enabling an evidence base with local context to be built to ensure that future spaces will be more certain of success. This metamorphosis of consultation into evaluation is vitally important for developing our understanding of what works.

A recent investigation, mentioned in Chapter 10 (Painter et al., 2013), into learning space design for all types of learning spaces in higher education concluded that 'the field of learning space research lacks systematic, longitudinal research' and noted a failure of new space projects to evaluate the space in the context of learning outcomes and that the tendency is to 'present data on frequency of use; faculty evaluation of the efficacy of a space, its arrangements, or its technology; students opinions about the space or its furnishings; or an appraisal of building systems such as lighting and thermal comfort'. And commenting on informal learning spaces, mostly found in libraries, Painter et al. state, 'Whatever lack of rigour we have found in the body of work on classroom design, we find that it is even more challenging to apply rigorous research designs and data collection methodologies to informal learning spaces.' There is clearly a job to be done here that requires a longitudinal approach, uses tools such as the experience sampling method and others mentioned in Part 2, and exploits the knowledge and expertise of behavioural scientists and ethnographers; to date the research in this area lacks significant review or meta-analysis. An evidence base is needed to guide future library learning space development, which also acknowledges the importance of locality and community; and an action research programme that addresses the agenda of the role of space in creating innovative learning futures is required.

As I wrote in the final paragraph of Chapter 10:

> The discussion also demonstrates the need to start to apply a more rigorous approach to data and information collection, the range of data and information collected and its analysis and synthesis so we can identify what works. What makes a great library or learning space is not just the architecture or interior design, it is the ideas that are realized in the building. Most importantly the ideas that make libraries and learning spaces work best come from the insights of educators, learning specialists and librarians.

Throughout this book the emphasis has been on the 'soft' aspects of space. While improved evaluation techniques are needed it would be inappropriate to adopt a reductionist approach. What is needed is a rich descriptive approach to evaluation that captures the effects of excellent informal learning space and shows that better space enables better learning.

Part 3 of this book has provided an ideas bank for future thinking that is firmly rooted in the present. Throughout these chapters there is reference to generic aspects of people-centred design, activity-led analysis and people-fit furniture as ways of approaching design projects and a focus on diversity and equality of people as participants in the process of planning: for example, children as designers and a methodology for university-wide engagement in the design and planning process. The challenges of the networked society, super-convergence and competing priorities – for learners, researchers and specialist facilities of media labs and research commons – all feature in these chapters. More than one essay suggests that libraries might not be needed as places; if library as place is still needed, will it become populated not with books but with authors working with others to 'grow' their books? What this broad set of ideas does is to illustrate diversity of possibility for the library and highlight the need for each one to carefully consider the subtleties and nuances of what it offers and how it is both special and adapted to its locality and community.

Creating the 21st-century library learning space currently remains a risky but rewarding activity. It requires a mindset that sees users as producers of new knowledge and understanding rather than consumers of information; takes an approach to planning and development that is both rational and intuitive focusing on innovation; has a view of learning that puts construction before instruction; runs excellent operations to achieve great experiences for users; manages both processes and resources; sees technologies in the context of the technium; recognizes that environments impact emotions; rejects feedback in favour of real-time data; sees the underlying feelings that drive opinions; and values learning above all else. Or in short . . . the 21st-century library is a technology system, which through the activities of its staff and the environments that it creates provides access to knowledge and understanding and engages its community in the processes of learning so that new knowledge and understanding can be created in that community and beyond.

References

Crawford, W. and Gorman, M. (1995) *Future Libraries, Dreams Madness and Reality*, American Library Association.

Kelly, K. (2010) *What Technology Wants*, Penguin.

Painter, S. et al. (2013) *Research on Learning Space Design: present state, future directions*, Society for College and University Planning, www.scup.org/page/pubs/books/rolsd (accessed 14 August 2013).

Index